Protecting Your Business in a Pandemic

Plans, Tools, and Advice for Maintaining Business Continuity

GEARY W. SIKICH

Foreword by Charles P. Carey
Chairman, Chicago Board of Trade

Westport, Connecticut
London

Library of Congress Cataloging-in-Publication Data

Sikich, Geary W.

Protecting your business in a pandemic : plans, tools, and advice for maintaining business continuity / Geary W. Sikich ; foreword by Charles P. Carey.

p. cm.

Includes bibliographical references and index.

ISBN: 978-0-313-34602-6 (alk. paper)

1. Emergency management. 2. Crisis management. 3. Business planning. I. Title.

HD49.S563 2008

658.4'77—dc22   2008009952

British Library Cataloguing in Publication Data is available.

Library of Congress Catalog Card Number: 2008009952
ISBN: 978-0-313-34602-6

First published in 2008

Praeger Publishers, 88 Post Road West, Westport, CT 06881
An imprint of Greenwood Publishing Group, Inc.
www.praeger.com

Printed in the United States of America

The paper used in this book complies with the Permanent Paper Standard issued by the National Information Standards Organization (Z39.48–1984).

10 9 8 7 6 5 4 3 2 1

This book is dedicated to the visionaries, those unique individuals who are not afraid to speak out and let their voices be heard. These are the individuals who embrace change and see it as a challenge; an opportunity, not a disruption of the status quo. To those who, when they are told "it can't be done," find a way to get it done, I offer you this text. You are willing to see things from a different perspective and often take the unpopular path, because it is the right thing to do. To those who have taken the chance and learned not to repeat their mistakes, I hope that this text stirs your interest and pushes you to look anew.

To these individuals, these creative thinkers, who tinker and are inspired by their restlessness to get out, seek, explore, and find new challenges, I wish you speed on your journey. To all of us who look at life as an adventure and a journey without end, I dedicate this book.

Initiating a New Order of Things

It must be considered that there is nothing more difficult to carry out, nor more doubtful of success, nor more dangerous to handle, than to initiate a new order of things. For the reformer has enemies in all those who would profit by the old order and only lukewarm defenders in all those who would profit by the new order. This lukewarmness arises partly from the fear of their adversaries, who have laws in their favor, and partly from the incredulity of mankind, who do not truly believe in anything new until they have actually experienced it.

—Niccolo Machiavelli, *The Prince*

Contents

Foreword

Three influenza pandemics occurred in the twentieth century, with a combined loss of life in excess of 55 million people. Today we are faced with the threat of another influenza pandemic that could result from a mutation of the H5N1 virus, commonly known as bird flu.

There is a very strong possibility that the global marketplace would be severely impacted by the loss of life and by the tremendous economic damage that a pandemic could create.

During my tenure as a member of the Chicago Board of Trade and Chairman of the Board of Trade since 2003 (Vice Chairman of the CME Group since July 2007), the world has seen many catastrophic events occur. There was September 11, Hurricane Katrina, the Tsunami of 2004, numerous regional conflicts, and market fluctuations. The emerging risks of our modern world can threaten any organization, yet with proper preparation and guidance from business continuity professionals, I know that you can lessen the impact that certain catastrophic events can have on your organization.

This is not to say that we will no longer be affected by sudden disruptive events. None of us will ever be totally prepared for the unforeseeable catastrophic event, but I can personally attest to the business continuity system presented in this book. With it, companies have managed to work through disruptions caused by the spectrum of threats posed by natural and manmade events on the day of occurrence and during the subsequent challenges that your organization will face in the areas of strategy, competitive intelligence, and event management.

Although no one can predict when the next pandemic event will occur, all of us can—and must—prepare for the reality that a pandemic will affect all of us in some way.

By its nature, a virus mutates, targeting vulnerable populations. In its continually evolving forms, a virus has become one more risk that all companies must acknowledge and prepare to face. We should also note that terrorism, along with workplace violence, industrial accidents, product tampering, natural disasters, and other disruptive events, will not cease to happen just because we are dealing with a pandemic. We must be prepared if we are to ensure the survival, growth, and resilience of our enterprises.

Having served as Chairman of the Chicago Board of Trade, one of the largest commodities exchanges in the world, I appreciate the importance of addressing the needs of our business, its value chain, and its many stakeholders. We can address those needs only by making a sincere and concerted effort to attend to our people, the most valued asset of any organization.

Geary Sikich has distilled his knowledge and expertise into this book to create a powerful and compelling argument for redefining business continuity planning as we know and currently practice it. Business continuity must become a way of doing business, not an adjunct to the business that we do. This book will help you lead your organization through the creation of resiliency through the systematic assessment and evaluation of the complex touch points within and external to your organization. It facilitates the blending of strategy, competitive intelligence, and event management into a business continuity system that saves time, money, and energy, leaving your organization better prepared to face disruptive events that could possibly destroy it.

The goal of business continuity is for your organization to be resilient, to survive, and to grow. You may never get back to exactly where you were before, but a well-managed event can actually leave your organization stronger, more resilient, and better tuned to the world than it was before.

The need to prepare your organization for disruptive events has never been so clear. The guidance you need is in this book.

Charles P. Carey
Chairman, Chicago Board of Trade

Charles P. Carey served as Chairman of the Board of Trade from 2003 until its merger with the Chicago Mercantile Exchange in 2007. He currently holds the position of Vice Chairman of CME Group. A partner in the firm Henning and Carey, Carey is chairman of the Finance Committee and a member of the Human Resources Committee. As a member of the Chicago Board of Trade, he served as First Vice Chairman of the Executive Committee, Chairman of the Finance Committee, and on numerous other committees, special committees, and task forces.

Preface

History is not necessarily indicative of future results. Strategy involves risk of loss. But history tends to repeat itself if we choose not to learn from it.

It started with a cough, headache, and a feeling of general tiredness. Was it the travel? Was it the late night entertaining clients? Perhaps it was just a twenty-four-hour bug? You go to your next scheduled client meeting, or conference, or board a plane and fly to another destination or back home. You are feeling better; must have just been the late night with the clients. However, that dry cough still persists. You shrug it off and go on with life. You are not exhibiting any symptoms. You are, however, already a vector spreading a lethal cocktail with each cough and each placement of your hand on a surface after coughing. Soon, you have spread the virus that you are hosting to others around you. Still, no symptoms show. It is just a cough and a few aches that will soon, you are sure, go away.

Could this be a scene from the opening chapter of a Michael Crichton thriller? No, this is what we may experience at the beginning of a pandemic, a flu virus that could affect up to 30 percent of the population.

The threat of a pandemic, whether it is an influenza pandemic or a plague in the making, such as the infamous "Black Death" (*Yersinia pestis*) of the 1300s, has the World Health Organization (WHO) concerned. The numbers being tossed about are almost beyond comprehension. An influenza pandemic resulting from the H5N1, or avian influenza, could tally anywhere from 100 million to 1 billion victims, many of whom will die.

How should business leaders react to this forecast? Should companies begin to develop pandemic plans? Should they begin stockpiling personal protective equipment, such as gloves, masks, antiviral medication, and decontamination equipment? What are the ethical obligations that a company has to its employees, to their families, and to expatriates? That is what this book is all about.

It suggests possible options that businesses can use to respond to a pandemic, manage its effects, recover from it, and restore operations. Through the use of scenarios, historical reference, recognized continuity planning "best practices," and analysis of current data, this book provides a roadmap business executives can use as they face the potential threat of a pandemic. It will also provide a template that can be modified for use in addressing other area-wide events (such as natural disasters) that, although not as devastating to life, may pose a threat to survival of the enterprise. Not that we can plan for everything.

Most doctors in this and other countries around the world see influenza annually. However, I think that it is safe to say that not one doctor practicing today was alive during the 1918–1919 influenza pandemic. Furthermore, it is again safe to say that the post–World War II generations have never experienced an economic downturn as severe as the Great Depression of the late 1920s. A pandemic could combine rarely seen health challenges with rarely seen economic devastation.

In fact, the consequences of an influenza pandemic go far beyond the medical aspects that are, as we will see, mind boggling. An influenza pandemic brings with it economic and geopolitical consequences that could reshape the balance of power as we currently know it. A "Great Reckoning" could be on us should a global pandemic occur and follow historical patterns.

The prospect of a worldwide flu pandemic is one example of a large-scale threat that would have far-reaching consequences for governments and businesses worldwide. The WHO, Centers for Disease Control (CDC), and other experts warn that it is not a question of "if" but "when" the next influenza pandemic will occur. Considering the world's reliance on trade, economies could suffer staggering losses, and the restoration to pre-pandemic socioeconomic activity levels could take decades to accomplish. Am I too pessimistic? Consider this fact: if crossings at the Canada–United States border were restricted—not closed, just restricted—it could cost Canada as much as $60 billion or more.

Because pandemics come in waves and historically last 500–800 days, the loss of staff for business will be not sudden. It will be a grinding process over the course of the pandemic. Each day will require some realignment of the business operations to deal with the absence of someone's skill set. Human capital will experience attrition, stress, fatigue, and failure. Many businesses will cease to exist because of a lack of demand for their products or services or because they do not have the skill sets to function and cannot find the skill sets to replenish their workforce.

When a pandemic strikes, the biggest initial impact will be on people. For business, that means that, although some employees could be ill, others might be too frightened to come to work, and many might have to stay home to care for affected family members. Experts suggest that businesses should anticipate absences of up to 50 percent of their staff for about two weeks at the height of a severe pandemic and lower levels of absences for a few weeks on either side of the outbreak's peak. However, the experts also predict that pandemics run their course in a series of waves, meaning that there will be ups and downs in staffing patterns.

There is much you can do for yourself and your business to avoid worst-case scenarios. Businesses can take steps to maintain continuity of operations in the face of a catastrophe of global proportions.

In this book, I will offer my thoughts on the possible scenarios that could unfold if an influenza pandemic were to occur. I will offer some tools that I have found useful in planning for uncertain, random events that you can adapt to your current situation. I also do some "what if" speculation and some historical review as I attempt to explain the possible consequences of a global pandemic from a socioeconomic standpoint.

The materials here are applicable not only to a pandemic situation but to any situation that carries with it a broad impact, be it a natural disaster, technological disaster, or manmade calamity.

ROADMAP FOR THE BOOK

Considering that many experts view a pandemic event as something overdue, you cannot afford to view business continuity as an adjunct to the business. Businesses must view business continuity as a way of doing business. Development and implementation from the top down and the bottom up of an integrated business continuity process, something you will learn about in the coming pages, is essential for businesses to survive, grow, and ensure resilience in these uncertain times.

This book is all about agility and flexibility. Recognize that most disruptive events that occur in business will not trigger the activation of an organization's business continuity plan, regardless of the severity of the event, unless the business continuity plan is integrated into the way the organization does its business. A pandemic requires that your organization has the ability to perform the following:

- anticipate change (forward thinking)
- recognize information that is of value (intelligence)
- be innovative and responsive in the face of rapidly changing business circumstances

- recognize complexity impacts, which often lead to "activity traps" (doing a process for the sake of the process instead of focusing on what the process should accomplish)

- recognize and change processes that no longer accomplish what they were initially designed to do as a result of changing business circumstances

Protecting Your Business in a Pandemic offers you a practical guide for assessing the threat of pandemics and for developing business continuity plans to deal with the economic and medical consequences of a pandemic. Step-by-step guidance in the form of assessment tools, exercises, and detailed examples are provided in a user-friendly format. This book thus constitutes a ready reference guide, designed to help readers focus on making their enterprises operationally resilient. The book also offers a practical "hands on" approach to designing, developing, and implementing responsive business continuity plans.

Each chapter is designed to build on the principles and lessons learned from the previous chapter. At the end of each chapter is a summary that ties key points together and introduces the next chapter topic and a list of chapter references.

Chapter 1 provides an overview of the current situation (at time of writing) with the H5N1 virus. It is a call to action, outlining the current and projected impacts of a pandemic. In this chapter, I also provide recommendations highlighting precautions that are applicable to pandemics and other disruptive events. It further provides an overview of pandemics from a historical perspective and projects potential consequences associated with a pandemic occurring now. This chapter presents an assessment of not only the medical consequences but, just as important, the economic consequences of a pandemic for government and business.

Chapter 2 investigates global interdependencies. This chapter defines and explains systemic and asymmetric threats, establishes the context for risk assessment modeling, and defines and discusses conflation and confluence scenarios. An assessment of World Health Organization Pandemic Classification criteria is presented, along with a discussion of global medical initiatives. The chapter concludes with a discussion of a hypothetical scenario based on projections by WHO, the United Nations, CDC, and other public- and private-sector entities watching for the signs of a potential pandemic. It provides a global sector analysis for the following:

- information and communications sector
- banking and finance sector
- energy (exploration, production, distribution, oil, gas, and fuels) sector
- physical distribution (utilities, such as electric, gas, and water) sector
- vital human services (medical, insurance, agricultural, and housing) sector

- hospitality and entertainment (hotels, leisure, and gaming) sector
- transportation (air, sea, and land) sector
- manufacturing (heavy or light manufacturing) sector
- outsourcing sector
- distribution (Retail and wholesale networks)
- governmental and nongovernmental agencies

I revisit these sectors throughout the book as we view the potential impact of a pandemic as time progresses.

Chapter 3 investigates three scenarios, a mild pandemic, a moderate pandemic, and a severe pandemic, and their potential impact on the sectors identified in Chapter 2. Possible outcomes for each of the scenarios and how each sector could be affected are also discussed. I also introduce new tools for analyzing risk and preparing for uncertain outcomes.

Chapter 4 continues the investigation of the three scenarios in a progressive manner, comparing them with the timeframes of previous pandemics and projection of a timeframe for the pending pandemic. This chapter introduces readers to the process of identifying the stress indicators induced by a pandemic and how these stress factors (stress, surge, and reactivity) can affect their enterprises. I offer suggestions for developing strategies for how to manage them and to prevent them from becoming a crisis for the business. Tools for developing an operationally resilient organization are introduced in Part 2. Readers will learn that, through the ability to organize, connect, adapt, and keep pace with change induced by a pandemic, they can create a resilient organization.

Chapter 5 introduces the reader to the resources they will need for identifying and responding to the long-term and/or possibly permanent changes to the operating cycles for each of the sectors presented in Chapter 2. Events that can affect the business, if they are not addressed quickly, are presented in each of the three scenarios. The chapter concludes with a discussion about how to organize research and analysis for success.

Chapter 6 discusses possible outcomes for the global economy as the world emerges from the pandemic. It also covers important aspects of how business operations could be altered by the pandemic. It asks many questions, but the answers cannot yet be known. As we become more removed from contact with other people as a result of the pandemic, will the virtual work world of the office in the home, Internet shopping, and changes in the nature of work resulting from market alterations become a permanent element of the global economy? Will the global economy be altered to an extent that global finance, trade, and markets reflect a new balance of power? This chapter concludes by assessing and identifying time-dependent issues that could become essential elements for survival in the post-pandemic global economy.

Chapter 7 discusses some of the possible geopolitical ramifications of a pandemic. What paradigm shifts will occur? What nations will emerge as global economic powerhouses, and what nations will fare poorly, potentially emerging into economic chaos? The chapter concludes with guidance on business continuity plan modeling and the value of geopolitical modeling.

Chapter 8 provides a look at the geopolitical impact a severe pandemic might have. It summarizes the potential impacts of the three pandemic scenarios (mild, moderate, and severe). This final chapter offers the reader perspectives on possible socioeconomic situations in the post-pandemic timeframe and ties together the creative approaches for blending strategy, competitive intelligence, and business continuity management into a comprehensive and useful plan that have been presented in the previous chapters.

My suggestion as to how to read this book is to take the scenario material presented at the beginning of the chapters and use these scenarios in conjunction with the worksheets and forms to develop "what if" assessment guides for your organization. In this way, you can build planning for a pandemic into the organizational fabric, increasing the chances that your business survives.

ACKNOWLEDGMENTS

There are many who assisted me with the refinement of the thoughts that I have turned into the pages of this book. I wish to express my thanks. Specifically, I want to thank my colleagues and dear friends, Jay and Cathy Pierce, Charles P. Carey, John Stagl, John P. Williams, Michael Huggins, and Brian Meyers, for their contributions and encouragement in pushing me to complete this text. A special thanks to my editor, Jeff Olson, who took the time to ensure that the right words fell into the right places. I also want to thank my sons, Aaron and Drake, for being who they are. To all of you, thanks and good reading.

1

A Call to Action: The Danger of H5N1

From time to time, we invest time and resources not just to learn about a new set of uncertainties but to expand our ability to learn about them.
—David Apgar, Risk Intelligent Organization

The objective of this book is to help business and government leaders cut through the complexities posed by the emerging pandemic and make well-informed decisions before you are thrown into the chaos of a pandemic crisis. You will soon be exposed, no pun intended, to a variety of terms that may be quite new to you. At the end of the book, I have provided definitions to aid you in reading this material. The influenza virus and the potential for a global pandemic is but one of the many viruses that could threaten us in the near future. There are many, many more viruses that pose significant threats to humanity, and, lest we forget, there is the threat of a manmade catastrophe that could be chemical, nuclear, or biological. Being prepared will be a key to surviving as individuals, communities, businesses, and countries.

WHAT IF...?

At the time of this writing, H5N1, known as avian flu, has occurred in Asia, Europe, and the Middle East. Currently, it has manifested itself in more than sixty countries. Recent outbreaks have occurred in England, Poland, Romania, India, Germany, France, and the Czech Republic. As the virus is currently structured, it has one of the highest mortality rates of any flu virus of the previous century. Even the Great Influenza (Spanish Flu) of 1918 did not have as high a morbidity and mortality rate as H5N1. On a near-daily basis, the World Health Organization (WHO), Centers for Disease Control (CDC), or the popular media give us some revelation regarding H5N1. Because a deadly influenza pandemic appears all but inevitable, health authorities are preparing for the worst. Governmental entities at the federal, state, and local levels worldwide are developing plans and holding summit meetings to discuss what can be done. Medical experts fear that the virus will eventually develop into a virus transmissible from human to human, spawning a pandemic that could take a devastating toll across the globe.

What can be done to prevent this potential cataclysm? The simple answer is nothing. That is correct—nothing. Viruses mutate to adapt. It is the nature of a virus to survive, and mutating is a virus's defense mechanism against manmade antibiotics. When H5N1 mutates to allow human-to-human transmission, the stage will be set for a global pandemic. All the planning, stockpiling, training, and drills will potentially be for naught. I say potentially, because, from what I have observed, we seem to be addressing the wrong problem precisely. We are applying conventional planning—response, mitigation, and recovery techniques—to a problem that is asymmetrical, not systemic. Applying standard triage strategies to attempt to stop the pandemic from occurring will be a vain attempt at best. As stated previously, viruses mutate to adapt. Dr. David Nabarro, chief avian flu coordinator for the United Nations and former chief of crisis response for the World Health Organization, is quoted in a recent *New York Times* article: "That rampant, explosive spread, and the dramatic way it's killing poultry so rapidly suggests that we've got a very beastly virus in our midst."[1]

Do you think that the high mortality rate associated with the H5N1 virus, almost 50 percent, is bad? One would think it is very bad. However, if you were a virologist, the high mortality rate would be good. Why? Because the high mortality rate actually keeps the virus from being able to spread rapidly. The host does not stay alive long enough to infect others. Should the mortality rate drop to say, 2 to 4 percent (the Spanish Influenza had a mortality rate of approximately 2.5 percent), virologists would be very worried, as should you and everyone else be. What this means is that the virus is more readily able to sustain transmission as it passes from person to person. More people will get ill, but the death rate will be less (a good thing). However, this does not mean that the overall death toll will be diminished from the numbers currently projected. When the mortality rate drops, the infected person stays alive longer and therefore passes the virus to others more easily. Of course, this is a simplified example and not meant to more than illustrative of how little we, the general public, actually knows about viruses, influenza, and the common cold.

Developing strategies and plans for dealing with the effects and consequences of the pandemic will be a far more useful exercise. If we consider a pandemic as a massive "dirty bomb" or a series of dirty bombs, we may be able to understand better what kind of planning and response is required. I am not attempting to downplay the significance of initial response planning, which is going to be significant, but all of the prevention planning in the world cannot stop the pandemic from materializing if the virus mutates to a human-to-human transmissible form.

In the aftermath of Hurricanes Katrina and Rita, the Gulf Coast of the United States has been reeling from the devastation. In spite of significant warnings, New Orleans, the State of Louisiana, and the Federal Government were overwhelmed by the impact of Katrina and the cascade effect of the rains from Hurricane Rita. Katrina, a category 4 hurricane, rendered effective allocation of resources and rapid response totally ineffective. Hurricane Rita's rains reflooded an already devastated New Orleans. If we look historically at great pandemics of the past, the Black Plague and the Spanish Flu, parallels immediately come to mind. Why? These pandemics came in waves. They did not occur as a single point event. They occurred as rolling events. The Great Influenza lasted from 1918 to 1919 and came in four distinct waves. There was an initial wave that pretty much went unnoticed, then came the second wave that produced the most devastating death tolls in September through December 1918, then the third and fourth waves with lesser death tolls.

The consequences of a rapid spread of H5N1 in a human-to-human transmissible form from a continuity planning perspective cannot be overlooked. If Hurricanes Katrina and Rita put the people of New Orleans and the Gulf Coast in a fight for their very survival, what will a pandemic do?

WHY IS SO MUCH ATTENTION BEING PAID TO H5N1?

According to Dr. Michael T. Osterholm, Director of the Center for Infectious Disease Research and Policy (CIDRAP) and a professor in the School of Public Health, University of Minnesota, infectious diseases remain the number one killer of humans worldwide. Most infectious-disease experts believe that the world stands on the verge of an influenza pandemic, yet, according to the WHO, "Considerably more attention has been focused on protecting the public from terrorist attacks than from the far more likely and pervasive threat of pandemic influenza."

Human influenza is caused primarily by one of three types of influenza viruses, type A. Within type A, there are many distinct subtypes that keep mutating. This is why new influenza vaccines must be produced each year. Influenza viruses are some of the most infectious agents known to man. Although there are other viruses that are more deadly (that is, they kill a higher percentage of those infected), such as

the Ebola and Marburg viruses, influenza viruses are far more contagious. According to the CDC in Atlanta, Georgia, every year in the
United States, on average 5–20 percent of the population gets the flu.
More than 200,000 people are hospitalized from flu complications, and
about 36,000 people die from the flu. This is the annual influenza with
which we are all familiar. Annual influenza is responsible for $1–3 bil-
lion in direct costs for medical care in the United States.

At present, the transmission of H5N1 has been limited to animal-to-
human transmission. This has limited the number of people who have
become infected by the virus. That could easily change.

In 2005, Mortimer B. Zuckerman wrote the following in the *New York
Daily News*:

> Should we sound the alarm for a worldwide epidemic that might not
> occur? There is no choice with the avian flu emerging from Asia. Should it
> adapt to be able to be transmitted from human to human, international
> health experts warn, bird flu could spark a global pandemic, infecting as
> much of a quarter of the world's population and killing as many as 180
> million to 360 million people—at least seven times the number of acquired
> immune deficiency syndrome (AIDS) deaths, all within a matter of weeks.
> This is utterly different from ordinary flu, which kills between 1 million
> and 2 million people worldwide in a typical year.[2]

To better understand some of the attention that is being paid to
H5N1, we need to comprehend just how difficult the virus is to detect
and measure. The table below depicts the sizes of various viruses and
compares them with known entities, such as dust mites, pollen grains,
and human cells. Viruses are very, very small; are difficult to protect
against; and mutate almost constantly. Figure 1.1 provides a comparison of viral sizes.

Virus Measurement

1 millimeter = 0.001 meter
1 micron = 0.000001 meter
1 nanometer = 0.000000001 meter

Viruses are nearly invisible without magnification. The table below shows virus
sizes. The abbreviation nm means nanometer, which is one billionth of a meter.

Virus Size	
BacteriophageMS-2	20nm
Hepatitis 24nm	30nm
HIV (AIDS)	80nm
Cytomegalovirus	100nm
Untested H5N1 virus	**100 nm**
Orthomyxovirus	120nm
Coronavirus(SARS)	80nm–160nm

Figure 1.1. Virus Measurement and Size.

Source: Adapted from information at www.cellsalive.com.

A good explanation regarding H5N1 was published by the U.S. Department of Agriculture (release number 0296.06):

AVIAN INFLUENZA LOW PATHOGENIC H5N1 VS HIGHLY PATHOGENIC H5N1

There are two types of avian influenza (AI) that are identified as H5N1. A difference exists in the virus classification; one is low pathogenic (LPAI) and the other is highly pathogenic (HPAI). Pathogenicity refers to the ability of the virus to produce disease. HPAI H5N1, often referred to as the "Asian" H5N1, is the type causing worldwide concern. LPAI H5N1, often referred to as the "North American" H5N1, is of less concern. Following is an explanation of the differences between them.

LPAI H5N1 ("North American" H5N1)

LPAI, or "low path" AI, commonly occurs in wild birds. In most cases, it causes minor sickness or no noticeable signs of disease. It is rarely fatal in birds. LPAI strains are not a human health concern. This includes LPAI H5N1. Evidence of LPAI H5N1 has been found in wild birds in the United States in recent years and is not closely related to the more severe HPAI H5N1 circulating overseas....

HPAI H5N1 ("Asian" H5N1)

HPAI, or "high path" AI, spreads rapidly and is often fatal to chickens and turkeys. This includes HPAI H5N1. Millions of birds have died in countries where HPAI H5N1 has been detected. This virus has also infected people, most of whom have had direct contact with infected birds.

HPAI H5N1 has not been detected in the United States. However, other strains of HPAI have been detected and eradicated three times in the United States: in 1924, 1983 and 2004. No significant human illness resulted from these outbreaks.

The 1924 HPAI H7 outbreak was contained and eradicated in East Coast live bird markets.

The 1983-84 HPAI H5N2 outbreak resulted in humanely euthanizing approximately 17 million chickens, turkeys and guinea fowl in Pennsylvania and Virginia to contain and eradicate the disease.

In 2004, USDA confirmed an HPAI H5N2 outbreak in chickens in Texas. The disease was quickly eradicated thanks to close coordination and cooperation between USDA and State, local, and industry leaders.

For a pandemic to occur, three requisites must be present. First, a novel strain of virus emerges for which humans have no natural immunity. Second, the virus causes serious illness and/or death. Third, the virus is easily transmitted from human to human.

The current strain of avian flu meets the first two requirements, and there is speculation that it has already been transmitted from human to human. The good news is that, if you are inclined to take it this way, well over half the people who have contracted this virus have died, a mortality of +50 percent. Why is this good news? It actually prevents the virus from spreading rapidly because those who become infected die before they can spread it easily to others. If the mortality were to drop significantly, the third condition, mutating so that it can spread rapidly from human to human, could be achieved. If that happens, be very afraid.

The WHO provides a running account of H5N1 statistics on its website (http://www.who.int/csr/disease/avian_influenza/en/). The WHO also has downloadable historical documentation that will facilitate the development of educational materials for your employees. I will not get into the current statistics because they change almost weekly.

If you look carefully at what is presented in the weekly WHO Cumulative Statistics (http://www.who.int/csr/disease/avian_influenza/country/en/), you will see that the death toll continues to rise as the virus spreads. Another point is that the WHO reports only on laboratory-confirmed cases. This may be significant; there could be underreporting of cases because of a lack of knowledge about the symptoms of H5N1 versus the annual flu and the common cold. Could it also be that cases are going unreported because they are occurring in remote areas where medical assistance is not readily available? One has to wonder how bad the situation really is based on the statistics that are provided.

The types of antiviral drugs that may be effective against H5N1 may have been diminished since 2006 as the result of giving Tamiflu, one of the antiviral drugs, to infected birds in Asia. Stockpiles are slowly being replenished at the time of this writing. This should be of concern, because Tamiflu is being stockpiled by many countries as their first line of defense against H5N1. Additionally, it should be noted that antiviral drugs are essentially only effective as long as you take them. What this means is that your body does not develop immunity to the virus from taking antiviral drugs. Unlike a vaccine, antiviral drugs only minimize the impact of infection.

It should also be noted that, of those who have become ill with H5N1, approximately half have died. The eventual mutation of H5N1 virus into a form that can be transmitted easily from human to human has experts around the world worried because of the high mortality rate. When this mutation occurs, the current worst-case forecast is for a worldwide pandemic even worse than the Spanish Flu (estimated global deaths at 40–50 million). Recent worst-case scenario figures for an H5N1 are in the range of 180–360 million, whereas best-case scenarios give a figure of 2–7 million deaths worldwide. Deaths aside, an H5N1 pandemic could affect between 20 and 50 percent of the total world population.

If H5N1 has a mortality rate even half of its current rate, estimates of the deaths worldwide will range from 40 to 100 million. Even more important, experts are predicting that the morbidity rate will be around 33 percent of the population. In the United States, current medical facilities would be overwhelmed trying to manage more than 80 million sick individuals.

Why should we as business continuity planners be concerned? The WHO issues many warnings. For example, a recent WHO advisory stated the following:

> The World Health Organization has warned of the rapid spread of an atypical strain of pneumonia which appears to be resistant to conventional treatments. Reports of the illness have been received from Canada, China, Hong Kong Special Administrative Region of China, Indonesia, Philippines, Singapore, Thailand, and Viet Nam. Businesses should be aware of the risk to staff, especially those that have recently traveled to any of the affected countries. The new disease could be the cause of a global pandemic.

However, in this case, the warnings are echoed by many others. A recent Reuters story reveals that H5N1 is showing resistance to Tamiflu, whereas *The Lancet* carried an article that said the following:

> The current epidemic of the highly pathogenic H5N1 strain of avian influenza, with a mortality of 58 percent, appears relentless in Asia, particularly in Vietnam and Thailand. Although inefficient, there is some evidence of human-to-human transmission for the H5N1 virus. A possible catastrophic pandemic could, therefore, emerge should re-assortment of viral antigens occur resulting in a highly infectious strain of H5N1.[3]

Gardener Harris of the *New York Times* wrote this:

> A plan developed by the Bush administration to deal with any possible outbreak of pandemic flu shows that the United States is woefully unprepared for what could become the worst disaster in the nation's history.
>
> If such an outbreak occurred, hospitals would become overwhelmed, riots would engulf vaccination clinics, and even power and food would be in short supply, according to the plan, which was obtained by The New York Times.[4]

Clearly, people at the highest levels of the medical establishment, and the government, are concerned, and, if it is not bird flu, it may be something else: severe acute respiratory syndrome (SARS), Ebola, or some as yet named or identified virus with pandemic potential. Moreover, it is not just the naturally occurring viruses; it could be genetically engineered/altered viruses developed by a terrorist organization or an unfriendly government. We still see outbreaks of plague in the U.S.

Southwest, and, although these have not been epidemic or pandemic creators, the fact is that they do exist and have a potential to become widespread (e.g., MRSA [methicillin-resistant *Staphylococcus aureus*], the recent super-staph bug that has emerged as a threat).

PANDEMIC PLANNING: WHAT ARE YOU DOING?

Many in the business community and especially those who develop business continuity plans seem to be wary of addressing the issue of a pandemic as a viable scenario for planning. It seems that those who are addressing it are doing so at a very tactical level, developing laundry lists of things to procure such as latex gloves, face masks, and other personal protective equipment.

I recently did a tabletop simulation for a corporate client, another for a government client, and a presentation on pandemics at a business continuity summit. The corporate tabletop participants reflected on the experience and uniformly expressed to me that the tabletop was one of the most stressful and frustrating experiences in which they had participated. The governmental participants were vocal in their response that they would be overwhelmed by the events that were presented to them. Both corporate- and government-sector clients expressed concern that, if the pandemic were to last 500–800 days, their organizations might not survive as currently configured. The business continuity summit attendees, and many of the speakers who followed me, continued to comment on the material presented, stressing that they needed to rethink their plans. Participants in the three events expressed the hope that a pandemic would not materialize. Hope is a straw for which too many seem to be grasping.

Pandemics cause major economic losses as a result of absenteeism. Experts predict that, during a pandemic, up to 30 percent of the global workforce could either be off work because of sickness or stay away because of fear. Absence levels at the expected rates would cause severe problems.

The economic impact of H5N1 will be felt around the world. The impact will initially appear in two primary aspects of business. The first will be the availability of the workforce, and the second and more unique impact will be in the marketplace. Helen Branswell of the *Canadian Press* wrote the following:

> A major Canadian brokerage firm has added its voice to those warning of the potential global impact of an influenza pandemic, suggesting it could trigger a crisis similar to that of the Great Depression.
>
> Real estate values would be slashed, bankruptcies would soar and the insurance industry would be decimated, a newly released investor guide on avian influenza warns clients of BMO Nesbitt Burns.[5]

Lack of buying as a result of illness and psychological reactions to a pandemic will present a new form of business impact that is often not addressed in business continuity, disaster, crisis management, or recovery plans. Traditional plans start with an assumption that the marketplace is still viable; this could be an inaccurate assumption. Traditional plans are designed to get an organization back into the market as quickly as possible. In many plans, you will see the acronyms RTO, RPO, and MTO, in which RTO is recovery time objective, RPO is recovery point objective, and MTO is maximum tolerable outage. In the case of a pandemic, markets may no longer be viable. A consequence is that the revenue that is derived from that market may be restricted and/or completely gone.

A study called *Thinking Ahead: The Business Significance of an Avian Influenza Pandemic* by James Newcomb (June 2005), released by Bio Economic Research Associates, finds the following:

- Over the past decade, major livestock disease outbreaks have caused more than $60 billion in economic damages worldwide.
- Concern about a possible influenza pandemic has led to more research and development of a wide spectrum of items from diagnostic testing devices to antiviral drugs.
- Governments around the world are purchasing antiviral drugs and stockpiling them for their populations.
- Flu vaccine manufacturers are accelerating research for an effective vaccine against H5N1.
- New technologies are being developed to supplement and/or replace current production technologies.

We have not experienced this type of business problem in our lifetime. The last generation to have to address economic devastation was that of our grandparents and parents during the Great Depression. We do not have any leaders in business or government who lived through the 1918 Spanish Flu Pandemic or the Great Depression; that experience base is lost to us. Our best option, therefore, is to start to think about the possible problems we may have to confront and take steps to avoid or deal with them in our businesses. If we wait until the pandemic starts, it will be too late.

Even if a pandemic were mild, it is estimated that about one-third of the world's population would fall sick over a period of months and millions would die. If the strain is virulent, the death toll could mount to several million over a relatively short period. If we look at previous pandemics (Spanish Flu in 1918–1919, Asian Flu in 1957–1958, and Hong Kong Flu in 1968–1969), we see that they generally run their course in eighteen to twenty-four months. The economic consequences could be staggering. SARS wreaked economic devastation on affected cities and countries in a relatively short period. SARS is a viral

respiratory illness caused by a coronavirus, called SARS-associated coronavirus. SARS was first reported in Asia in February 2003. Over the
next few months, the illness spread to more than two dozen countries
in North America, South America, Europe, and Asia before the SARS
global outbreak of 2003 was contained.

The U.S. Department of Health and Human Services (DHHS) plan
outlines a worst-case scenario for an influenza pandemic in which more
than 1.9 million Americans would die and 8.5 million would be hospitalized, with costs exceeding $450 billion U.S. The World Bank has
recently upped its estimate of the cost of an influenza pandemic to more
than $1 trillion U.S.

PLAN NOW OR PAY

Current forecasts predict that the H5N1 pandemic will spread around
the world in a historically short period of time. One expert believes that
the pandemic will spread from the West Coast to the East Coast in a
week. When SARS spread from China just a couple of years ago, it was
in five countries in three days and in twenty-four countries in three
months. Time to react will be virtually nonexistent. If we are to add
value as business continuity planners, we need to react now! The companies that survive this extraordinary disaster when it occurs will have
heeded the words of Sun Tzu centuries ago: "Victorious warriors win
first and then go to war, while defeated warriors go to war first and
then seek to win." Planning today will prove to be the only viable strategy to ensure a company's "victory."

AND IF IT'S FOR NAUGHT...

What if the pandemic does not materialize? Do we have the proverbial
"egg on our face" situation? In the event that this pandemic does not materialize, your planning will not be lost. Most of it will be transferable.
There will be future pandemics (and they occur approximately every
thirty to forty years), not to mention the ever-present threat of terrorist
attacks using chemical/biological/nerve agents. Business survivability in
the face of disaster is imperative to maintain the economic strength of the
world community. We have an obligation to be forward thinking and to
see what others choose not to recognize until it is upon them.

In November 2005, the DHHS recently published the revised national
plan for influenza pandemic. Among other things, it said the following:

Pandemic planning is based on the following assumptions about pandemic
disease:

- Susceptibility to the pandemic influenza subtype will be universal.
- The clinical disease attack rate will be 30 percent in the overall population.
  Illness rates will be highest among school-aged children (about 40 percent)

and decline with age. Among working adults, an average of 20 percent will become ill during a community outbreak. Of those who become ill with influenza, 50 percent will seek outpatient medical care.

- The number of hospitalizations and deaths will depend on the virulence of the pandemic virus. Estimates differ about 10-fold between more and less severe scenarios. Because the virulence of the influenza virus that causes the next pandemic cannot be predicted, two scenarios are presented based on extrapolation of past pandemic experience.

- Risk groups for severe and fatal infections cannot be predicted with certainty. During annual fall and winter influenza season, infants and the elderly, persons with chronic illnesses and pregnant women are usually at higher risk of complications from influenza infections. In contrast, in the 1918 pandemic, most deaths occurred among young, previously healthy adults.

- The typical incubation period (the time between acquiring the infection until becoming ill), for influenza averages 2 days. We assume this would be the same for a novel strain that is transmitted between people by respiratory secretions.

- Persons who become ill may shed virus and can transmit infection for one-half to one day before the onset of illness. Viral shedding and the risk for transmission will be greatest during the first 2 days of illness. Children will shed the greatest amount of virus and, therefore are likely to pose the greatest risk for transmission.

- On average about 2 secondary infections will occur as a result of transmission from someone who is ill.

- Some estimates from past pandemics have been higher, with up to about 3 secondary infections per primary case.

- In an affected community, a pandemic outbreak will last about 6 to 8 weeks. At least two pandemic disease waves are likely. Following the pandemic, the new viral subtype is likely to continue circulating and to contribute to seasonal influenza.

- The seasonality of a pandemic cannot be predicted with certainty. The largest waves in the U.S. during 20th century pandemics occurred in the fall and winter. Experience from the 1957 pandemic may be instructive in that the first U.S. cases occurred in June but no community outbreaks occurred until August and the first wave of illness peaked in October.

WHEN THE PANDEMIC IS DECLARED

How long will the pandemic be underway before it is declared a pandemic? Experts at the WHO and elsewhere believe that the world is now closer to another influenza pandemic than at any time since 1968, when the last of the twentieth century's three pandemics occurred. Currently it takes four to five days for the symptoms of H5N1 to manifest such that the patient would go to the hospital. In that time, the virus is highly contagious and can spread rapidly. Sampling, testing, and diagnosis also take time. Currently, a window of ten to fourteen days exists for intervention. A spokesperson for WHO said, "We're not going to know how lethal the next pandemic is going to be until the pandemic begins." How do you plan for the pandemic? The answer involves more than planning to respond to the medical aspects of the pandemic; having a methodology matters as much as the question itself. It will be important to choose the proper methodology and the correct focus of the planning effort. Indeed, methodology will matter more than anything else. Understanding the current WHO, CDC, and other government entities' planning methodologies will facilitate your organization's development of a pandemic preparedness materials that will supplement current contingency plans.

The WHO uses a six-phase pandemic alert system (Table 1.1) (you can download the most up-to-date version from the WHO website, http://www.who.int) to inform the world of the seriousness of the threat and actions that should be undertaken. The designation of phases, including decisions on when to move from one phase to another, is made by the Director-General of the WHO. Each phase of alert coincides with a series of recommended activities to be undertaken by the WHO, the international community, governments, and industry.

The world is presently in phase 3: a new influenza virus subtype is causing disease in humans but is not yet spreading efficiently and in a sustainable manner among humans.

There are three elements to a pandemic. First, a virus emerges from the pool of animal life that has never infected human beings, meaning no person has antibodies to fight it. Second, the virus has to make us seriously ill. Third, the virus must be capable of moving swiftly from human to human through coughing, sneezing, or just a handshake.

For avian flu, the first two elements are already with us. Well over half the people who have contracted it have died. The question now is whether the virus will meet the third condition: mutating so that it can spread rapidly from human to human.

RECOMMENDATIONS FOR PREPARING FOR A PANDEMIC

All companies, large and small, should include the possibility of an avian flu pandemic in their business planning and as a supplement to the existing emergency-response, business continuity, disaster-recovery, and crisis-management plans (hereafter collectively referred to as contingency planning). Although the format for the influenza plan will vary from company to company based on industry sector and degree of commitment to pursuing such things as providing personal protective equipment, I have generally found that the following process works well.

Table 1.1. WHO's Pandemic Phases

Phase	Description
Interpandemic Period	
Phase 1	No new influenza virus subtypes have been detected in humans. An influenza virus subtype that has caused human infection may be present in animals. If present in animals, the risk[a] of human infection or disease is considered to be low.
Phase 2	No new influenza virus subtypes have been detected in humans. However, a circulating animal influenza virus subtype poses a substantial risk[a] of human disease.
Pandemic Alert Period	
Phase 3	Human infection(s) with a new subtype, but no human-to-human spread, or at most rate instances of spread to a close contact.[b]
Phase 4	Small clusters of human-to-human transmission but spread is highly localized, suggesting that the virus is not well adapted to humans.[b]
Phase 5	Larger cluster(s) but human-to-human spread still localized, suggesting that the virus is becoming increasingly better adapted to humans, but may not yet be fully transmissible (substantial pandemic risk).
Pandemic Period	
Phase 6	Pandemic increased and sustained transmission in general population.[b]

[a] The distinction between phase 1 and phase 2 is based on the risk of human infection from circulating strains in animals. The distinction is based on various factors and their relative importance according to current scientific knowledge. Factors may include pathogenicity in animals and humans, occurrence in domesticated animals and livestock or only in wildlife, whether the virus is enzootic or epizootic, geographically localized or widespread, and/or other scientific parameters.

[b] The distinction between phase 3, phase 4 and phase 5 is based on an assessment of the risk of a pandemic. Various factors and their relative importance according to current scientific knowledge may be considered. Factors may include rate of transmission, geographic location and spread, severity of illness, presence of genes from human strains (if derived from an animal strain), and/or other scientific parameters.

First, conduct a business impact assessment (BIA) to determine the internal and external impacts that would arise from a pandemic. This is, however, not the traditional business impact assessment that we see performed by most firms. You need to focus on degradation of human capital, depth of staff (bench strength, to use a sports term), critical skill sets, client base, stakeholders, demand for your product/service and how it might change, financial reserves (amount, liquidity, and accessibility), supply chain, and outsource providers.

Second, develop a plan that coincides with the strategic plan for the organization. The pandemic plan should describe how your organization will achieve its strategic goals and objectives in the event of a pandemic. Six key elements of the plan that should be described in detail are as follows: strategy, what you are committed to doing in your plan; concept of operations, how you will fulfill these commitments and implement the plan; structure, how your organizational structure will best serve your needs should a pandemic occur; resource management, how you will manage your human capital and other assets (buildings, hardware, and capital); core competencies, what skill sets are necessary to continue operations and what degree of succession planning is needed to ensure stability and continued operation; and pragmatic leadership, what levels of authority will exist and what decision rights can be exercised during a pandemic.

Third, develop and execute a regular training, drill, and exercise regimen for your organization.

Fourth, develop a robust maintenance program to ensure that your plan is kept up to date and that the information in it reflects the current operational focus of your organization.

Fifth, develop an outreach program to facilitate the integration of your plan into that of the community and your value chain (suppliers, customers, and stakeholders).

These five elements will be discussed in the subsequent chapters of this book in more detail. Many of these may already be present in your current contingency plans. However, the key for successful execution of your pandemic plan will rest with your people, and this may be the most difficult part of pandemic planning. Because of the random nature of illness that will occur in a pandemic, you will not be able to make assumptions with any degree of certainty as to whom will be available to implement the plan. It is therefore incumbent that your organization is fully engaged in the planning process, training, and exercising, and in the depth of succession planning that must take place.

Some considerations that are unique to pandemic planning include the following.

Duration: You must plan for the long term, 500–800 days minimum, for the pandemic period. You also need to plan for the post-pandemic recovery and restoration period (perhaps decades). You need to develop pre-pandemic plans that allow you to be flexible in acquiring necessary supplies that your organization consumes on a regular basis and that will quickly become difficult to acquire during the early stages of a pandemic.

International travel: Depending on the severity of the outbreak, quarantines may result in travel bans or travel delays. Health checks for travelers would likely be commonplace. Many trips could be cancelled. Would this materially affect your organization? Even if the bulk of travel is domestic, prudent planning measures include an assessment of employee travel plans for conferences or vacations.

Local travel: In cities or countries where an outbreak occurs, travel may be severely restricted or even impossible for periods of time. This should be a prime focus because travel for company business within domestic borders could be significantly affected by any travel restrictions.

School closures: Schools in affected cities would likely close and thereby force many parents to stay home and care for their families. Recent CDC guidance on nonpharmaceutical interventions recommends the closure of school and restricting of gathering at places such as shopping malls. Your planning should consider a survey of employees to determine which employees would be affected and to prepare plans for them to work from remote locations and/or for the disbursement of their duties to employees who would not be affected by school closures.

Health systems: Medical facilities could be overwhelmed depending on the size, virulence, and locations of the outbreak. Your planning should consider an assessment of healthcare providers in your company's operating area (or operating areas if you have multiple locations) to determine which are highly likely to be significantly affected by a surge in patients.

Economic impact: Experience with SARS demonstrated that industry sectors such as travel and hospitality would be rapidly affected, with follow-on effects occurring in other parts of the economy. Some sectors, however, would benefit, such as technology companies that provide solutions for remote workplaces. An assessment of operations to determine which of your organization's normal business operations would be most prone to economic impact should be undertaken. The assessment should also consider your "value chain" vulnerability exposure. I define value chain as every touch point that your organization has, from vendors to customers. Plans should be developed to counter and/or offset the effect on business operations that would be affected by a prolonged degradation, in either personnel and/or demand for products and services.

Supply chains: Supply chains (part of the value chain) would likely be affected because of inspections and logistics disruptions, especially where countries with high infection rates are involved. An assessment of critical supply chain links for the company should be considered to determine if stockpiling of supplies necessary for the functioning of the business is necessary.

Human capital (personnel): Widespread illness could result in staff shortages. An assessment of staffing needs, to include skills, training, staff demographics, and ease of replacement, should be conducted to determine susceptible populations and to develop succession plans, altered work schedules, and staff repopulation plans.

Overall business slowdown: With travel limited and spending reduced in many areas, sales and marketing campaigns could be affected. Merger and acquisition deals and other transactions could be delayed or suspended. Servicing clients will present a challenge. You should consider an assessment of potential situations that would cause business operations to be affected by a slowdown. This will be discussed when we take a look at customer vulnerability/exposure indexing.

Fear, uncertainty, and doubt: Even if only a few people are infected, the threat of disease could greatly affect the behavior and normal business activities of others. Discussion and speculation about the situation would further reduce workforce productivity. Your organization should consider developing an aggressive education program for your staff and their immediate families.

Your organization needs to develop a clear picture of the current state of its business system network. My company, Logical Management Systems (LMS), calls this "Constructing a Mosaic" or "Active Analysis." It is a process of getting enough bits and pieces of information in place to be in a position to transform seeming chaos into recognizable patterns on which decisions can be made. Using this process allows you to assess the collective consequences of seemingly insignificant or single-point events that have limited impact on your organization. We will discuss this in more detail when I present *LMSCARVER*™, a tool for business impact assessment.

Second, your organization and its value chain must develop as comprehensive a plan as possible for dealing with the business consequences of a pandemic on its own. Recognize that you cannot depend on public authorities to provide support for the company during a pandemic or perhaps any large-scale disruption. Public-sector entities will have too many issues to deal with and they will also be affected by the pandemic. Employees of civil organizations are just as susceptible to contracting the disease.

Rethink the basis on which your current crisis-management, business continuity, disaster recovery, and emergency plans were developed. Perhaps a consolidated contingency plan that combines them all is needed. Survey the risk management and strategic planning personnel in your organization to find out what they are looking at currently with regard to business expansion, business contraction, or risk mitigation.

They should be aware of potential problems as a result of the recent hurricanes, earthquakes, tsunamis, and general competitive forces in the economy. Your organization should develop the ability to ensure that its business systems and its network (value chain) can maintain a level of functionality if forced to operate at reduced capability.

Your goal is to develop and implement an effective surveillance system. Once complete, "detectors and indicators of change" metrics can be used to facilitate the constant analysis of the state of operations and value chain. These metrics can provide the early warning basis for event classification at the lowest (least severe) levels. I term this "Graceful Degradation and Agile Restoration." We will discuss the concept in subsequent chapters.

Third, your organization should train, drill, and exercise its staff on pandemic preparedness, dealing with the business disruptions associated with an outbreak. All the planning in the world is never going to be effective unless it can be implemented. One key to implementation of any contingency type of plan is having a trained crew that can step in to implement plans. That means that your organization should consider training not only the identified primary position holders in the organization but also those at a secondary or tertiary level within the company. Remember, you cannot predict who will get sick or who will refuse to come to work.

Many experts are offering their recommendations on how to deal with the pandemic threat. The CDC provides pandemic checklists for business and individuals. Your organization should consider using the CDC checklists as a guide for developing more detailed and company/business operation-specific checklists. Below are some questionnaire considerations that you should evaluate for applicability to your company and its operations. (To obtain additional information, I recommend www.pandemicflu.gov and www.cdc.gov/business.)

The following tables (Tables 1.2 through 1.7), created by the U.S. Department of Health and Human Services, provide points for consideration that can be used to assess the level of preparation in your organization. These tables are not meant to be comprehensive; rather, they should provoke thought and idea generation regarding the focus of preparedness for your organization. You do not have to focus specifically on a pandemic; these tables can be generalized to reflect preparation for any type of contingency that your organization may face. The tables are subdivided into the following categories: planning for the impact on your business, planning for the impact on your employees and customers, identifying policies and procedures that may require modification, allocating resources, communicating information, and coordination with external organizations.

Table 1.2. Plan for the Impact of a Pandemic on Your Business

Points for Consideration	Response
Identify a pandemic coordinator and/or team with defined roles and responsibilities for preparedness and response planning. The planning process should include input from labor representatives.	
Identify essential employees and other critical inputs (e.g., raw materials, suppliers, etc.) required to maintain business operations by location and function during a pandemic.	
Determine potential impact of a pandemic on company business financials using multiple possible scenarios that affect different product lines and/or production sites.	
Determine potential impact of a pandemic on business-related domestic and international travel (e.g., quarantines, border closures).	
Find up-to-date, reliable pandemic information from community public health, emergency management, and other sources and make sustainable links.	
Train and prepare ancillary workforce (e.g., contractors, employees in other job titles/descriptions, retirees).	
Develop and plan for scenarios likely to result in an increase or decrease in demand for your products and/or services during a pandemic (e.g., effect of restriction on mass gatherings, need for hygiene supplies).	
Establish an emergency communications plan and revise periodically. This plan includes identification of key contacts (with backups), chain of communications (including suppliers and customers), and processes for tracking and communicating business and employee status.	
Implement exercises/drills to validate your plan, and revise periodically.	

Source: Adapted from U.S. Department of Health and Human Services information.

Table 1.3. Plan for the Impact of a Pandemic on Your Employees and Customers

Points for Consideration	Response
Forecast and allow for employee absences during a pandemic due to factors such as personal illness, family member illness, community containment measures and quarantines, school and/or business closures, and public transportation closures.	

(Continued)

Table 1.3. (*continued*)

Points for Consideration	Response
Implement guidelines to modify the frequency and type of face-to-face contact (e.g., hand shaking, seating in meetings, office layout, shared workstations) among employees and between employees and customers (refer to CDC recommendations).	
Encourage and track annual influenza vaccination for employees.	
Evaluate employee access to and availability of healthcare services during a pandemic, and improve services as needed.	
Evaluate employee access to and availability of mental health and social services during a pandemic, including corporate, community, and faith-based resources, and improve services as needed.	
Identify employees and key customers with special needs, and incorporate the requirements of such persons into your preparedness plan.	

Source: Adapted from U.S. Department of Health and Human Services information.

Table 1.4. Establish Policies to Implement in a Pandemic

Points for Consideration	Response
Establish policies for employee compensation and sick leave absences unique to a pandemic (e.g., non-punitive, liberal leave), including policies on when a previously ill person is no longer infectious and can return to work after illness.	
Establish policies for flexible worksite (e.g., telecommuting) and flexible work hours (e.g., staggered shifts).	
Establish policies for preventing influenza spread at the worksite (e.g., promoting respiratory hygiene/cough etiquette and prompt exclusion of people with influenza symptoms).	
Establish policies for employees who are exposed to pandemic influenza, are suspected to be ill, or become ill at the worksite (e.g., infection control response, immediate mandatory sick leave).	
Establish policies for restricting travel to affected geographic areas (consider both domestic and international sites), evacuating employees working in or near an affected area when an outbreak begins, and guidance for employees returning from affected areas (refer to CDC travel recommendations).	

(*Continued*)

Table 1.4. (*continued*)

Points for Consideration	Response
Set up authorities, triggers, and procedures for activating and terminating the company's response plan, altering business operations (e.g., shutting down operations in affected areas), and transferring business knowledge to key employees.	

Source: Adapted from U.S. Department of Health and Human Services information.

Table 1.5. Allocate Resources to Protect Your Employees and Customers During a Pandemic

Points for Consideration	Response
Provide sufficient and accessible infection control supplies (e.g., hand-hygiene products, tissues, etc.) in all business locations.	
Enhance communications and information technology infrastructures as needed to support employee telecommuting and remote customer access.	
Ensure availability of medical consultation and advice for emergency response.	

Source: Adapted from U.S. Department of Health and Human Services information.

Table 1.6. Communicate with and Educate Your Employees

Points for Consideration	Response
Develop and disseminate programs and materials covering pandemic fundamentals (e.g., signs and symptoms of influenza, modes of transmission), personal and family protection, and response strategies (e.g., hand hygiene, coughing/sneezing etiquette, contingency plans).	
Anticipate employee fear and anxiety, rumors, and misinformation, and plan communications accordingly.	
Ensure that communications are culturally and linguistically appropriate.	
Disseminate information to employees about your pandemic preparedness and response plan.	
Provide information for the at-home care of ill employees and family members.	

(*Continued*)

Table 1.6. (*continued*)

Points for Consideration	Response
Develop platforms (e.g., hotlines, dedicated websites) for communicating pandemic status and actions to employees, vendors, suppliers, and customers inside and outside the worksite in a consistent and timely way, including redundancies in the emergency contact system.	
Identify community sources for timely and accurate pandemic information (domestic and international) and resources for obtaining counter-measures (e.g., vaccines and antivirals).	

Source: Adapted from U.S. Department of Health and Human Services information.

Table 1.7. Coordinate with External Organizations and Help Your Community

Points for Consideration	Response
Collaborate with insurers, health plans, and major local healthcare facilities to share your pandemic plans and understand their capabilities and plans.	
Collaborate with federal, state, and local public health agencies and/or emergency responders to participate in their planning processes, share your pandemic plans, and understand their capabilities and plans.	
Communicate with local and/or state public health agencies and/or emergency responders about the assets and/or services your business could contribute to the community.	
Share best practices with other businesses in your communities, chambers of commerce, and associations to improve community response efforts.	

Source: Adapted from U.S. Department of Health and Human Services information.

POSSIBLE PANDEMIC ECONOMIC SCENARIOS

Will your organization and its employees emerge from a pandemic or other large-scale, long-term event as an ongoing concern? The likelihood is that your company will be able to continue its operations and to continue to provide its products and/or services to its customers. A greater question is, "How will the markets that your enterprise currently operates in change?" There are other equally important questions:

- Will your organization emerge as a financially sustainable and efficient business?

- Will your organization's relationships with its value chain, from vendors and suppliers to customers, remain intact?
- Will your organization continue to be able to perform its mission?
- Will your organization be able to repopulate its workforce with people who have the requisite skills that ensure that the company can continue to provide the high level of services that the value chain expects?
- Will your organization be able to maintain its strong local presence in the communities that it serves?
- Will your organization have enough demand for the same services/products after a pandemic as there is now, or will the value chain demand new or significantly altered products and/or services?

These are questions that your organization needs to answer now, before a pandemic, as part of its pandemic planning efforts.

To assess the potential impact of a pandemic and/or other long-lasting event, first you need to understand three terms: "time critical," "time sensitive," and "time dependent." Table 1.10 is a graphic depiction of these terms as they would be applied to an assessment of potential impacts to your organization as a result of a loss or disruption of one of the areas listed in the three columns that comprise the table.

Time critical is the loss of any business function, related value chain component, and internal and/or external infrastructures that poses an imminent threat to the survival of the enterprise. Time-critical issues are things that, if disrupted, can cause an immediate "crisis" for your enterprise. They are also the issues that have the most immediate impact on your enterprise.

Time sensitive is the loss of any business function, related value chain component, and internal and/or external infrastructures that poses a near-term threat to the survival of the enterprise. Time-sensitive issues are the issues that, if left to smolder, will sneak up and cause a crisis for your enterprise. They are also the issues that have both long-term and short-term impacts on your enterprise.

Time dependent is the loss or degradation of any business function, related value chain component, and internal and/or external infrastructures that poses a long-term threat to the survival of the enterprise. Time-dependent issues are often overlooked during a crisis situation. Time-dependent issues, nonetheless, can cause a crisis for your enterprise. They are also the issues that have the most long-term impacts on your enterprise.

In Table 1.8, I used a timeframe that is stated in months. Your organization may have circumstances in which the timeframe could be measured in hours. In some cases, a timeframe may actually be measured in minutes. This table is provided as a sample of the items that you will have to consider as you develop your plan. Please note that planning for

Table 1.8. Time Critical—Time Sensitive—Time Dependent

Time Critical	Time Sensitive	Time Dependent
Critical Infrastructure Loss	Finance	Government Relations
Telecommunications, Data and Other Information Systems	Vendor/Supplier Business Applications Human Resources and Staffing	Corporate Relations Corporate Image Banking and Finance Assigned Relocation Sites
Transportation (air, land, water)	Legal Oversight/ Documentation	Communication Systems Requirements
Utilities (gas, electric, water)	Transition to Recovery Organization	Operations Systems Requirements
Energy Supply	Recovery Operations	Personnel Requirements
Critical Services	Humanitarian Assistance	Documentation of Facilities Recovery
Access Denial	Infrastructure Restoration	Assessment of Operations Requirements
Degradation/Loss of Critical Operations	Information and Operations Recovery and Synchronization	Building Documents/ Records Required in an Emergency
Loss/Degradation of Operational Capability	Resumption of Critical Business Functions	Public Sector Contacts
Loss of Electrical Supply Sources	Full Function Restoration	Forms and Supplies
Loss of Telecommunication Data, Other Information Sources	Permanent Restoration	Associated Plans and Information
Loss/Degradation of Buildings/Occupancy		Insurance and Risk Management Plan
Disruption of Transportation		Treasury Contingency Cash Plan
Disruption of Water Supply		Controller's System for Tracking Recovery Expenses
Disruption of Emergency Services		Vendor/Supplier/Consultant List
		Floor Space Alternatives Outside Main Office
		Records Planning, Storage and Retrieval

disruption of these areas is applicable to situations that are not pandemic related. Any type of disruptive event could have a serious impact over time on these areas. The issue with a pandemic is that the disruption could be so widespread that you will not have alternate locations to go to reestablish operations. For example, I was consulting to a hospital group that sought to determine its needs for a backup facility, referred to as a "hot site," for their data center. We interviewed the data center personnel and were fairly comfortable with the progress of the assessment. As we began the user-group interviews, we were stopped in our tracks when the laboratory group announced that fifteen minutes of downtime equated to approximately four hours of recovery time for them. After hearing what one hour of downtime would require in recovery time, we immediately rethought the time-critical, time-sensitive, and time-dependent equations.

The following three graphs present hypothetical scenarios developed by LMS that highlight at a high level some of the potential economic consequences associated with a pandemic. The three graphs are also illustrative of the need for cooperation between public- and private-sector entities, not to mention cooperation between and among private-sector entities. This cooperation is not relegated to responding to a pandemic (the tactical level) but to addressing the economic conse-quences of the pandemic (the grand tactical level) and its aftermath (the strategic level). Each of the three scenarios unfold over a period of 500–800 days, the relative time that previous pandemics have been seen to run their course. Time, as with all else associated with H5N1, will be an unknown that will have to be addressed as the pandemic begins to ex-hibit its characteristics and courses throughout the global population.

The "Mild" Pandemic Event

As depicted in Figure 1.2, a mild pandemic event could be similar to those experienced during the Asian Flu (1957–1958) and Hong Kong Flu (1968–1969). These were the two relatively mild pandemics of the twentieth century.

This graph represents what could be the outcome of a mild pandemic event. One must realize that a pandemic will not have a set timeframe. My estimates are based on historical information and projections that I am making based on assumptions that we will experience a pandemic of similar duration as previous ones in the twentieth century. We really have no idea how long a pandemic cycle could run.

In this event, the time-critical phase would be the first 180 days with regard to the probability of the greatest number of cases being reported. As life returns to normal during the 180–320-day timeframe, we would see less medical concern regarding the number of cases seeking hospital treatment, but there would be a reactive shock to the economic system worldwide, resulting in a potential short-term downturn. Recovery and restoration would most likely occur with some robustness returning to the worldwide economy during the latter part of the time-sensitive phase and full robustness returning during the time-dependent phase (321–800 days). Although the exact cycles cannot be determined with any finiteness, this is one possible outcome associated with a relatively mild pandemic event scenario.

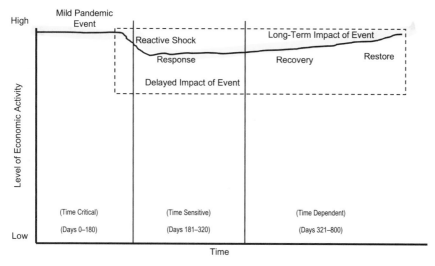

Mild Pandemic Event Scenario

Figure 1.2. Plan—Respond—Manage—Recover—Restore
Source: Scenario produced by Logical Management Systems, Corp.

Would your organization experience an initial downturn in its ability to meet its customer obligations? Or would a surge in demand for your product/service create a crisis for your organization as a result of a portion of your staff requiring treatment for influenza? Several influencing factors would need to be considered that would have to be identified on an individual basis and are beyond the scope of these examples. Under this scenario, it is not envisioned that organizations would suffer any substantial degradation of their operations or cash reserves.

The "Moderate" Pandemic Event

Again, one must realize that a pandemic will not have a set time-frame. Figure 1.3 includes estimates based on historical information and projections that I have made. The graph represents the outcome of a moderate pandemic event. In this scenario, the event's time-critical phase would be the first 180 days, with the first sixty days likely to be the most disruptive. This is when the greatest number of cases would be reported. In days 180–320, fewer people would seek hospital treatment. The reactive shock to the economic system worldwide would last longer and perhaps result in a potential medium-term economic downturn. Recovery and restoration would most likely occur with less robustness returning to the worldwide economy during the latter part of the time-sensitive phase and the long-term effect of the pandemic

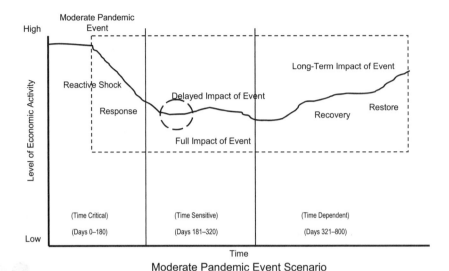

Moderate Pandemic Event Scenario

Figure 1.3. Plan—Respond—Manage—Recover—Restore
Source: Scenario produced by Logical Management Systems, Corp.

being a slower recovery during the time-dependent phase (321–800 days). Recovery could also see weaker economic activity because of an increased number of deaths, resulting in more economic dislocation. Although the exact cycles cannot be determined, this is one possible outcome associated with a moderate pandemic event scenario.

How would your organization deal with a sustained downturn in its ability to meet customer demand or lack thereof? A larger portion of your staff would most likely require treatment for influenza. Other influencing factors include value-chain disruption from both suppliers and customers. Under this scenario, an organization would likely suffer some degradation of its operations and cash reserves for a period of time beyond the 800 day cycle represented in the graphic. For publicly held organizations, this might trigger some of the reporting requirements under legislation such as the Sarbanes-Oxley Act. Regulatory requirements will play a role in whether or not your company meets its obligations to its employees and its shareholders during the pandemic period.

The "Severe" Pandemic Event

Figure 1.4 represents what could be the outcome of a severe pandemic event. In this event, the time-critical phase would be the first 180 days, and, within that timeframe, the first sixty days would again most likely be the most disruptive. Most cases would be reported during the first 180 days. In the second phase (181–320 days), second and even

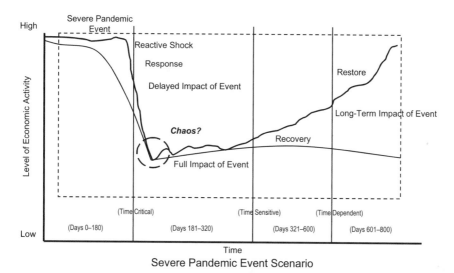

Figure 1.4. Plan—Respond—Manage—Recover—Restore
Source: Scenario produced by Logical Management Systems, Corp.

third waves of infection and influenza could occur. Days 180–320 could see a continuing strain on the medical capabilities as people continue to seek hospital treatment. The reactive shock to the economic system worldwide would potentially be deeper and more severe, lasting longer and perhaps resulting in a potential for a significant downturn in economic activity. Recovery and restoration would most likely occur with significantly less robustness returning to the worldwide economy during the latter part of the time-dependent phase (days 600–800 and beyond). The long-term effect of this pandemic scenario could be a significantly slower recovery, altered workforce structures, and a time-dependent phase (321–800 days) that could extend past the 800-day timeframe. Recovery could also see significantly weaker economic activity because of the large number of deaths estimated and the resulting economic dislocation. Although the exact cycles cannot be determined, this is one possible outcome associated with a severe pandemic event scenario.

What would your organization most likely experience during a sustained downturn in its ability to meet its customer obligations? What if the reverse was instead the case, and, because of a surge in demand coupled with permanent staff dislocation (attributable to death or long-term illness), your organization was not able to meet its obligations? A larger portion of your staff may require treatment for influenza over a longer timeframe. This could cause significant disruption to the continuity of operations. Other influencing factors (much as in the moderate pandemic scenario) would include the value chain being affected negatively. Under this scenario, it is envisioned that organizations could suffer significant degradation of their operations and depletion of cash reserves for a period of time beyond the 800-day cycle represented in the graph.

INDICATORS: LACK OF PREPAREDNESS OR LACK OF KNOWLEDGE?

Current research indicates that a small portion (5 percent) of businesses today have continuity plans, but virtually all realize they are at risk to the effects of a pandemic. The Center for Resilience at the Ohio State University defines a resilient enterprise as one that "has the capacity to overcome disruptions and continually transform itself to meet the changing needs and expectations of its customers, shareholders and other stakeholders."

The University of Minnesota's CIDRAP recently concluded a two-day national summit called "Business Planning for Pandemic Influenza." The conference was hosted by CIDRAP in collaboration with the Minnesota and U.S. Chambers of Commerce. Participants came from more than 200 companies, including 40 percent of the Fortune 50, that together employ more than 7.5 million people. The healthcare sector was the most heavily represented, supplying 22 percent of the attendees. The retail and wholesale trade, manufacturing, professional services, financial, and insurance sectors each accounted for about 15 percent. Below are summary results of a conference poll and discussions by businesses, most of which believe a pandemic will occur in the next ten years (and a bare majority within two years):

- A majority of those polled believe that an influenza pandemic would significantly affect their business, but only 18 percent of the companies have completed a preparedness plan.
- Fifty-nine percent indicated that their companies had started working on pandemic preparedness but did not yet have a plan in place.
- Twenty-one percent said they had not started planning.
- Two percent said they would rely on their existing crisis management plan.

PLANNING CONSIDERATIONS

Of primary importance to your organization will be the ability to draw on an adequate workforce given predictions that a large percentage of workers may be unable to fulfill their responsibilities over the span of a pandemic. Given this forewarning, your organization can do a number of things to ensure staff availability and productivity. First, your organization should consider assessing the feasibility of being able to support working from home or other remote sites. Even with the potential lack of infrastructure support, you have to consider this as a remedy. Second, your organization should consider developing staff training programs that emphasize cross-training, replacement training, and recalling and training retirees. Third, your organization should assess its product and/or service offerings to determine whether there will be demand for them or not. Fourth, your organization should assess customer and supplier (value chain) vulnerability/exposure to determine whether their product and/or service will be in demand during a pandemic.

Along with a critical focus on staff, several other areas of primary importance for your organization to consider in pre-pandemic planning including the following:

- The need to liaise with government leaders at the highest levels in developing planning strategies.
- The need to reconsider the consequences of the current "just-in-time" model for obtaining materials, supplies, and goods.
- The need to address global considerations that include staffing issues, cultural differences, and government regulations and restrictions.
- Surplus operating capital, ensuring that you have sufficient resources to manage operations.
- Bond and stock ratings: effect of potential downgrading of investment vehicles.
- Worker shortages, including immediate workforce and extended workforce.
- Business continuity, which is the ability to maintain operations at sustainable levels.
- Community obligations, identifying resources that could be forwarded to the community.
- Financial impairment of customers, including market share degradation/disintegration.
- Deterioration of asset value, which is the fixed asset value versus costs of maintaining.
- Investment in subsidiaries, which is the ability to maintain subsidiaries with surplus operation capital.
- Facilities plans: if your organization owns its facilities, your facilities management staff should develop and implement plans and policies for isolation areas, transition areas for workers returning to work after illness, and space allocation studies for space allocation in accordance with the current federal influenza plan for employees.
- Medical surge capacity, identifying location-specific medical capabilities and capacities.

Specific strategies or "best-practice" approaches to planning include development of systematic and proactive procedures to shut down and restart operations. These actions would include assessing cash reserves and developing modeling of time periods for shutting down. In addition, managing value-chain expectations in advance will be as important as maintaining stability of operations.

CONCLUDING THOUGHTS

Your organization's management has a responsibility to protect the enterprise by facilitating continuity planning and preparedness efforts. Today, we cannot merely think about the plannable or plan for the unthinkable, but we must learn to think about the unplannable.

Humans by their very nature are resilient. We have managed to evolve through the ages and have survived ice ages, volcanic eruptions, wars, pandemics, and other maladies. Although your organization will most likely survive the challenge presented by a pandemic, it may not, however, return to the status quo that existed before the pandemic.

The mortality rate of the pandemic will only be the tip of the iceberg. The speed with which it achieves global contamination and the economic impact over time will be the major issues with which your organization has to contend. Preparing your organization now is one of the key steps to effectively dealing with the disruption that occur. Your organization cannot afford to abdicate personal responsibility for its well-being to entities that may not have the capability to ensure that well-being. By being personally responsible as an organization, you can engender personal accountability, something that we need to instill now, not when the pandemic is on us.

As I was making some final edits to this chapter, I received the following Google alert:

Resistant Bird Flu Alert: March 10, 2007. Fears that the first line of defence against a bird flu pandemic—the anti influenza drug Tamiflu—could become less effective as the virus becomes resistant is voiced today by scientists. Swedish researchers have discovered that the drug oseltamivir (Tamiflu) passes out of the body in urine and is not removed or degraded by sewage treatment. Consequently, in countries where Tamiflu is widely used, there is a risk that its concentration in natural waters can reach levels where influenza viruses will develop resistance.[6]

(Note: The reader can access and receive Google Alerts using keywords such as "H5N1," "pandemic," and the like. The reader will receive e-mails containing notices and articles related to the selected keywords.)

If this is in fact what is happening, then all stockpiles of the drug would be less effective and could require dosages that could prove toxic to the individuals taking them. As we consider planning options for personal protection, it is extremely important that we get the best information available and that we continue to monitor the information that is put forth to ensure that what we are doing is going to be effective.

In the next chapter, we will investigate and present a discussion on approaches to getting started with pandemic preparedness activities. Specific tools that will aid you in your pre-pandemic planning efforts and that can be readily used to address general contingency planning issues will be interspersed throughout the remainder of this book.

2

The First Wave:
Pandemic Surprise

A black swan is a highly improbable event with three principal character-istics: it is unpredictable; it carries a massive impact; and, after the fact, we concoct an explanation that makes it appear less random, and more predictable, than it was.

—Nassim Nicholas Taleb, *The Black Swan: The Impact of the Highly Improbable*

This chapter consists of two parts. In the first part, I will provide an overview of what I think the first 180 days of a pandemic might look like. This is, of course, pure conjecture on my part, backed up with some historical reference on the Great Plague and what we all see soci-ety doing during the onset of a hurricane or severe winter storm (panic). At the conclusion of the scenario portion and sector analysis of this chapter, I will turn to what you can start to do now to prepare for a pandemic. The second half will provide some tools and thoughts on planning for a complex, long-term, and immensely disruptive event. The tools are designed to address the first step in the planning process: assessing business impacts.

PART 1: THE HORROR BEGINS

Humans need to be able to imagine the impossible: to learn to think, not in terms of specifics, but about generalities and to take into consid-eration things that we do not know. How long will the pandemic be underway before it is declared a pandemic? Experts at the WHO and elsewhere believe that the world is now closer to another influenza pandemic than at any time since 1968, when the last of the twentieth century's three pandemics occurred. A Bloomberg article stated the following:

> Insurance claims could increase as much as $47 billion in the event of a bird-flu pandemic killing 609,000 people in the US and Europe, Fitch Ratings said.
>   If a pandemic killed 400,000 people in Europe, insurance claims would increase by £20 billion ($29 billion), the ratings company said today in a news release. A pandemic killing 209,000 in the US could increase claims by $18 billion, said Fitch, which based its estimates on "published expert opinions."[1]

Although the numbers cited in the article are extremely conservative compared with those of WHO, CDC, World Bank, and others, the economic costs reflect potentially staggering shockwaves for the global economy. These shockwaves, should a pandemic occur, will have long-lasting consequences for the global economy. Although tragic events, such as September 11, the Tsunami, the War in Iraq, and Hurricane Katrina, to cite but a few examples, have had significant regional impacts, their effects were not as globally felt as a pandemic will be.

SARS cost the world economy an estimated $58 billion; the pain was mainly felt by the economies of Southeast Asia. SARS was a relatively insignificant event in that only 8,078 cases were diagnosed, and, of those, only 775 people died. SARS was quickly suppressed, yet SARS effectively shut down the City of Toronto for weeks. This ended up costing the Canadian economy more than $1 billion. SARS is not as easily transmissible as influenza.

Dr. Sherry Cooper, an economist,[2] believes that a moderate pandemic could create a $1.1 trillion loss in the first three months, with the United States bearing more than $220 billon of that price tag. She states that a more serious pandemic could cost the world more than $3.2 trillion, with the United States' share being a staggering $670 billion. These figures do not account for the post-pandemic recovery and restoration period.

I have conducted several tabletop exercises designed to introduce the pandemic scenario to the participants. I can state that, in a four-hour tabletop exercise, one cannot replicate what could unfold during the first wave of a pandemic for the participants. The stress and duration of the pandemic timeframe cannot be appreciated in a four-hour exercise. A pandemic will be an event that grinds on for a long time. We will have to get used to being inconvenienced and experiencing disruption to our lifestyles unlike anything that we can imagine. Perhaps the only thing that comes close would be the dislocation from a hurricane, earth-quake, or war that destroys your home and makes it necessary to relo-cate. Even that does not take into account having to deal with the potential sickness that could result from catching influenza. Remember my premise: a pandemic is a 500–800-day event with waves of outbreak lasting up to twelve to fourteen weeks.

I have also designed and implemented for a client a fourteen-day exercise that replicated the initial wave of a pandemic, each day being the equivalent of one week. Each day, the participants received four to five e-mails with scenario information. Although the exercise was designed not to solve problems but to identify issues, the participants all agreed that the stress and fatigue factors by day eight were almost overwhelming. All acknowledged that they anticipate that, in a real pandemic, the workload, stress, fatigue, and other factors would be even greater. The scenario that I present in the next few pages, although based on historical facts, current studies, and estimates, is purely specu-lative, and it would probably be worse in that random, unpredictable events would result from unexpected actions and reactions by nations, businesses, and individuals.

Shock and Awe: The Reactive Phase (the First 180 Days)

As you read these paragraphs, think about what could have been done to prepare your enterprise for the initial shock that would accom-pany a pandemic. WHO declares phase 4 of a pandemic event and a widespread panic, fueled by media stories, has people stockpiling everything that they think they may need. This may be the initial shock to the world economy. WHO declares phase 5 and things really start moving. Media stories are constant; fear is running rampant. People demand answers.

The WHO declares phase 6 and the world sets out to minimize the impact of the pandemic (tactical response). Mobilization of assets by WHO, the international community, governments, and industry begin. This may be too late for effective response because the pandemic has al-ready spread, and now defensive actions are the only and very limited option. In this scenario, a reactive fear-based response is the overriding driver.

Some countries react by closing their borders. This action, although purely defensive, has many implications from an economic perspective. Other countries begin to close their borders, further exacerbating the sit-uation. As borders are closed, international trade is brought to a stand-still or is carried out on a very, very limited basis. If the pandemic in any way parallels the influenza of 1918–1919, it is estimated that approximately 66 percent of the deaths will occur in a period of twenty-four weeks (approximately 168 days), and more than 50 percent will occur in even less time. The potentially staggering death toll and the reactive response to the pandemic will lead to slowdowns of already fragile economies, leading to accelerations of workforce layoffs worldwide as markets react, rapidly shrink, and/or completely cease to exist.

Faced with suddenly idled workers worldwide and the need to provide medical aid to populations that are succumbing to a global pandemic, governments are thrown into chaos. How will they deal with this? Keep in mind that governments are generally funded through the collection of taxes (individual and corporate). Without its revenue base (taxes), a government's ability to assist will be restricted. Government assistance will be further restricted because the government will be faced with the same problem that nongovernmental entities are faced with: a workforce that is stricken with the virus.

Traditional services of government, such as military, police, fire, emergency medical services, administrative, and tax functions, are soon strained to the point of breaking. Governments worldwide begin to organize military forces to keep order internally and to supplement police, fire, and emergency medical services. The situation is soon made worse because many of the government's own are falling victim to the influenza.

Soon, the world economy screeches to a halt as the wheels of commerce grind to a stop, creating a state of stagnant economic inertia. Once this state is reached, the real problems related to the pandemic start to surface. In trying to keep their economies growing, governments worldwide, through organizations such as the Federal Reserve Board, try to steer an economic course between too rapid growth that leads to inflation and too slow growth that leads to recession. Steering an economy in any direction is a very difficult job in any time period. Steering an economy during a pandemic will be almost impossible. First, it will be difficult to determine which sectors are hit hardest by the pandemic. Second, the speed of the pandemic's spread will cause economies to become more reactive. Third, and by far the biggest problem, is that economies are really the sum total of the actions of hundreds of millions of individual decision makers all over the world buying and selling. The pandemic will have an immediate influence on these decision makers' actions. Because the pandemic will be a rapid and uncertain event, no government will have the power to actually control all these decision makers because they will not have the economic strength to revitalize their economies through government spending. Government will not be able to spend its way out of the stagnation created by the pandemic. Business will not be able to spend its way out of the stagnation created by the pandemic, either.

As the pandemic runs its course in the ensuing eighteen to twenty-four months (approximately 600–800 days), the worldwide economy begins to experience severe pains as the population is faced with short-ages, bans on international and domestic travel, and a troubled trans-portation system, among other problems. Commerce moves to a cash basis and becomes localized, meaning that if you cannot get it locally and you cannot pay in cash, you are probably not going to get it. Worldwide society moves to "barter in isolation" as a way of life as the normal flow of goods and services is disrupted.

Sector Analysis (the First 180 Days)

The Department of Homeland Security has identified seventeen criti-cal infrastructures that require planning. I will highlight what could possibly occur to some of these sectors as the pandemic begins to take hold during the first 180 days.

The financial sector, having experienced runs on banks, is faced with solvency issues. Institutions such as the World Bank, International Mon-etary Fund, and Asian Development Bank see donor nations suspend their commitments of funds and see recipient nations petition for restructuring of their loans.

The manufacturing sector is affected as factories are forced to close ei-ther because of quarantine or from a lack of raw materials and curtail-ment of imports and exports attributable to border closures. Firms dependent on outsourcing and parts made overseas are forced to curtail operations.

The service sector, comprising volume-driven firms, sees volume dwindle and the forced layoff of many workers. Severe strains on the fi-nancial health of the service sector begin to appear as credit and debit card firms see defaults on payments due. Fraud becomes an increas-ingly significant issue for this sector.

The telecommunications sector is under intense pressure as workers attempt to telecommute.

The insurance sector sees an upsurge in claims for medical benefits, causing a slowdown because of volume impact. This in turn affects the healthcare providers who depend on insurance payments to continue operations.

The healthcare sector is overwhelmed by patient volume as the pan-demic takes hold and more people fall victim to the influenza. This is complicated by the surge of people who think they have exhibited the symptoms of the influenza and seek medical aid. In addition, this sector is affected by limited supply availability as a result of border closures.

The energy sector sees a decline in demand as well as a spike in prices for raw materials. Demand declines are attributable to a shift in the need for fuel as curtailments of international and national transportation systems beget less demand. The shift from occupied offices in cities to stay-at-home workers also reduces the demand for fuel. However, because of the curtailment of international trade, there is a spike in commodity prices attributable to the lack of raw materials getting into countries.

The utility sector sees a spike in residential demand as more and more workers are forced to stay at home because of quarantine, facility closures, lack of work, and fear of exposure. With its fragile infrastructure that is the result of years of low maintenance, lack of new construction, and aging facilities and equipment, the utility sector begins to experience brownouts and blackouts, in part because of the age of the system, lack of fuel supplies, and distribution issues but also in part because of people defaulting on their payments and illegal connections being made by people who do not have the resources to continue to pay for the services that they require.

The agriculture sector sees a demand for food products that cannot be met as transportation sector assets are idled by quarantine and border closure restrictions. As a major importer of foodstuffs, the United States suffers regional spot outages as grocery stores are forced to close because of lack of inventory. A critical issue for this sector will be the depth of bench strength for agriculture inspectors (how many do we have and how many are sick). Food does not move without the stamp of approval of an agriculture inspector. Government food warehouses are unable to alleviate the shortages because of the impact of fuel distribution problems affecting the transportation sector, shortages of personnel, and transportation system closures attributable to quarantine and border closures. Spoilage becomes a factor in planning for this sector.

The education sector shuts down as students and teachers are furloughed when schools close because of health concerns, quarantine, and transportation system impacts that preclude travel to and from school for health reasons.

The high-technology sector sees demand for access and support related to the Internet grow but is faced with a workforce that has the same exposure, in some instances great exposure, as the other sectors. Because many call center operations are located overseas, the issue of exposure to the flu could become a major issue for companies that are dependent on these call centers for their operations.

By the time that we enter the sixth month of the pandemic, most sectors will have either scaled back operations such that they are operating with minimal staff or they will voluntarily shut down as a result of lack of staff and/or resources, or they may be forced to shut down as a result of quarantine by the government. We may indeed see rationing of critical resources and limited distribution capabilities, creating duress on societies worldwide. For those societies, like the United States, with a population that is used to getting what is needed to sustain day-to-day living, this may be quite a shock. There could be outbreaks of violence (New Orleans after Katrina is an example) that will require force to quell.

Countries with low levels of preparedness may resort to even more repressive actions to control their populations, and there will always be the specter that a country will fear an attack by a neighbor while they are in a weakened state. Speculation and fear could rule the day during this timeframe.

Although this picture of the first phase of the pandemic is pretty bleak, it is not without precedent in recent history. We have experienced violence and looting after hurricanes, earthquakes, and other natural disasters. The world, unfortunately, is still not as civilized as we would like it to be.

Indications: Fitting the Pieces Together to Form a Mosaic

If SARS cost the world economy almost $58 billion, what would a global influenza pandemic cost the world economy? Estimates by the World Bank now state that a pandemic could cost more than $1 trillion U.S. Identifying global threats, risks, hazards, and vulnerabilities and how they might affect the global economy is all about being cognizant of trends and "connecting the dots," creating a mosaic that provides a complete picture from which one can make decisions. This requires the ability to see through the complexity of issues in today's global economy and identify trends before they materialize into threats. Unfortunately, there is a widespread tendency among many governments and businesses to prepare based on the last event that has occurred, not the next one coming around the corner.

The totality of recent news reports is scary: people and banks running out of cash, businesses becoming insolvent, whole industries (think restaurants) dropping by the wayside, and rampant predictions of country-specific economic doom. Would a pandemic really have that effect? The fact is, we live and operate in an entirely different economic model than the world that experienced the Great Influenza of 1918–1919, the 1957 Asian Flu, or the 1968 Hong Kong Flu. Today's global economy is so closely linked that very little, if any, stress and/or surge capacity exists.

How Long

At the present time, it takes approximately four to five days for the symptoms of H5N1 to manifest to the point that a patient has to go to a hospital. In that time, the virus is highly contagious and can spread rapidly. Sampling, testing, and diagnosis also take time. Currently a window of ten to fourteen days exists for intervention. A spokesperson for WHO said, "We're not going to know how lethal the next pandemic is going to be until the pandemic begins." How does one plan for the pandemic? The answer involves more than planning to respond to the medical aspects of the pandemic; one's methodology for handling the crisis matters as much as the question itself. As businesses plan, it will be important to choose the proper methodology and correct focus for the planning effort. Indeed, methodology will matter more than anything else.

Faced with an unprecedented physical disaster that threatens the fiscal viability of governments and corporations worldwide and their ways of doing business, how does an adroit, skillful, and successful manager respond? How are the lives of government and corporate workers and their families affected? What choices do managers have to make as they guide their organizations through a pandemic crisis that may not adhere to any conceptual model that business schools teach or to any experience that today's managers have ever faced? It is a matter of fact that most, if not all, business and government leaders today have never been faced with a situation like a global pandemic. Usually, a single point event with limited area impact occurs and is addressed. A pandemic poses a far greater challenge than any faced to date by government and industry.

PART 2: RISK-ANALYSIS PLANNING TOOLS FOR YOUR ORGANIZATION

Part 2 of this chapter presents some risk-analysis planning tools that you can use to facilitate an assessment of where your organization stands not only in respect to pandemic preparedness but also in terms of general business continuity and contingency preparedness. Treat the scenario presented in Part 1 of this chapter as a baseline for what could possibly happen. That way, you can build an assessment of where your organization is on the preparedness spectrum by applying the tools presented herein.

One of the most important steps that your organization can take is to assess its risks, threats, vulnerabilities, and hazards; additionally, the consequences of an event materializing need to be an integral part of the analysis process. The tools presented here focus on the business aspects of your organization, such as human capital, clients, customers, supply chain, and finances, and not just on the exposure that your organization may have from the loss of technology or facilities.

Planning Horizon for a Complex Emergency

In this section of the chapter, I will discuss the complexity associated with planning for a pandemic. One has to remember that natural disasters and manmade disasters will continue to occur during a pandemic, and we have to include their potential cumulative effects in our impact analysis and planning processes. In the sections that follow, I will introduce concepts and tools that are designed to broaden your understanding of the risks involved. I also give you the tools to conduct business impact assessments that go beyond counting the number of workstations, identifying applications, and determining what is "mission critical."

To understand why we need to rethink business impact assessment in light of pandemic preparedness, we need to understand the complexity of the planning issue and be aware of the possible cascade effects that can be caused by a pandemic. A cascade is created when there is a failure that causes other parts of the organization to also fail. This phenomenon is not limited to a single entity; the cascade effect can create multiple failures that go beyond the organization. The result is a potential increase in the impact of the disruption.

First, let us look at what the U.S. government is doing to prepare. It has created a National Strategy for Pandemic Influenza. This strategy provides a framework that outlines how federal and state government, private-sector organizations, and individual citizens can prepare for such an event. Its three pillars are the following:

Preparedness and communication: Activities that should be undertaken before a pandemic to ensure preparedness and the communication of roles and responsibilities to all levels of government, segments of society, and individuals.

Surveillance and detection: Domestic and international systems that provide continuous "situational awareness" to ensure the earliest warning possible to protect the population.

Response and containment: Actions to limit the spread of the outbreak and to mitigate the health, social, and economic impacts of a pandemic.

Next, the National Infrastructure Advisory Council has taken steps to protect the Nation's Critical Infrastructure with the Prioritization of Critical Infrastructure for a Pandemic Outbreak in the United States. Six specific issues considered key to protecting the U.S. economy and social stability should a pandemic occur are as follows: (1) identifying and defining "critical services" that must be maintained in a pandemic; (2) establishing criteria and principles for critical service prioritization; (3) defining critical services priority (with principles for variation, if needed); (4) identifying critical employee group(s) in each priority critical service; (5) building a structure for communication and dissemination of resources; and (6) identifying principles for effective implementation by the Department of Homeland Security and DHHS.

Although government can mandate its planning through the Department of Homeland Security, Federal Emergency Management Agency (FEMA), and other agencies, the private sector generally follows planning requirements when they are levied by regulation. In the private sector, it is the culture of the enterprise that influences the acceptance and integration of contingency planning (such as emergency, business continuity, disaster recovery, and crisis management) as a way of doing business or as an adjunct to the business of the organization. If an organization adopts contingency planning as a way of doing business, a dynamic and risk-resilient organization can emerge. If contingency planning is treated as an adjunct to the business, there will be little value placed on the process. As a result, the organization may experience many surprises caused by a lack of awareness of threats, hazards, risks, and vulnerabilities.

Anticipating and preparing for future challenges, trends, and opportunities, as the U.S. government is doing right now, are essential components of any organization's strategy. What is your organization's overall planning horizon? Is it one, five years, or even twenty-five years? Most organizations opt for a five-year planning horizon that is usually quickly modified or discarded. Today, business conditions change quickly, requiring a strategy that is flexible. If your organization's strategy has to be nimble, what does that say about your business continuity plans? The business continuity plans that an organization develops have to be even more responsive than the strategy the organization opts to implement. This is attributable to the need to ensure continuity of operations under a myriad of business conditions.

As public relations expert Chris Woodcock recently said, "Every ambitious business wants to know what's coming next and how to handle it. So much so, that the practice of horizon scanning is becoming a major strand in proactive risk management and business continuity."[3]

This intrigued me, so I began to research "horizon scanning" and came up with the following definition from the Office of Science and Technology located in the United Kingdom: "The systematic examination of potential threats, opportunities and likely future developments, including (but not restricted to) those at the margins of current thinking and planning."

Horizon scanning thus explores novel and unexpected issues as well as persistent problems or trends. With this idea in mind, I applied some horizon scanning to the issue of planning for complex emergencies such as a pandemic.

Figure 2.1 illustrates the shaping of business continuity plans in relation to enterprise culture and the reshaping of culture through the development of a business continuity mindset. In the following paragraphs, I will talk us through the flow depicted in the figure. Although the figure is complex, the intent behind it is simple: we need to rethink business continuity as we know it. This requires that we incorporate into the current planning cycle (analysis → planning → training → exercising → maintenance) a new way of looking at business

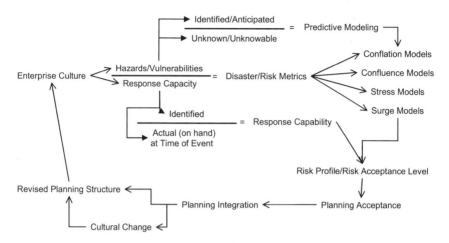

Figure 2.1. Planning Horizons—Complex Emergencies

continuity and business impacts. We need to not merely think about the plannable or plan for the unthinkable, but we need to learn to think about the unplannable. Figure 2.1 expresses this intent. In subsequent sections of this chapter and the remainder of this book, I will provide tools and methodologies designed to encompass a broader array of issues with which we should be concerned as business continuity planners and business managers.

The simple fact is that today, no matter how small or large the business enterprise, you have to assess and plan for disruptions that can occur and, even if they appear removed from your business, will have an influence on your operations. A good example is the current crisis in subprime mortgages. The spillover effect is an effect on credit cards and interest rates. This negative impact could create a cascading failure as defaults on mortgages turn into defaults on credit cards, creating a need by financial institutions to write down more bad loans and push up interest rates to compensate for their losses.

The next section provides an explanation of Figure 2.1 and some theory regarding planning horizons, complexity, reshaping business continuity thinking, and the need to change enterprise culture to gain acceptance of the value-added proposition that business continuity planning can provide.

A Model for Business Continuity Planning

We begin with enterprise culture. Specifically, you should seek to determine your enterprise's risk-acceptance culture. Overall culture is critical to understanding risk acceptance within your organization. Culture is, most of the time, unspoken. It permeates the organization, requiring one to learn quickly or suffer the consequences. For example, does senior management readily accept bad news or have people learned to present only good news? Bad news being glossed over or covered up to make it look less unpleasant is still bad news and eventually has to be addressed. Most organizations address bad news when it erupts as a crisis. It may cost someone, or several individuals, their jobs. Do the top leaders of your organization want to hear about pandemic preparedness? If your organization accepts the possibility of an influenza pandemic as part of the overall risk management process, you are well ahead; if not, then you have a precipitous climb ahead. You will have to do a lot of convincing to get any acceptance of pandemic preparedness as a valuable process for the enterprise. However, it is worth your time, because heads will otherwise roll when a pandemic crisis occurs.

Let us say that you are successful in getting someone to sponsor the development of your pandemic preparedness initiative. The next step in the figure is evaluating hazards and vulnerabilities against your response capacity. Most businesses perform a BIA, either formal or informal. Current BIA methodologies tend to reflect a tactical assessment of what is required if the business is forced to relocate because of a disruption. The typical output of a BIA is a report chock full of tables and lists that detail how much time it would take to get back up and running, how many workstations will be affected, relocation options, information loss potential, and so forth. Terms like RTO and RPO are strewn throughout the report like snowflakes in a blizzard. The assessment is generally internally focused and limited to processes that the organization performs.

This is a good start, but in preparing for a pandemic, one has to rethink hazards and vulnerabilities. Rather than taking a purely tactical perspective, a BIA must include a strategic assessment that focuses on the effects of failure to achieve enterprise goals and objectives. For example, failure to achieve financial goals and objectives as a result of market conditions, competition, client-base erosion, or reputation damage—all possible outcomes of a pandemic—carries a far greater business impact for the enterprise. Why? Because these outcomes can be long lasting.

At this point in my explanation of the figure, all I want you to do is to think about the issues that you may face. Literally expand your current concepts of analysis regarding hazards, vulnerabilities, risks, and threats. I will provide some working tools later in the chapter that you can use to create lists and perform an analysis. Think about the return on effectiveness that you seek from your planning efforts. (Return on effectiveness can be defined as the targeted application of corporate assets to achieve the company's goals and objectives. These may include stock price appreciation, return on investment, market share growth, profitability, retention of clients, or competitive advantage.)

Move up from the Hazard/Vulnerabilities line in the figure and you will see that it divides into Identified/Anticipated over Unknown/Unknowable. Should an influenza pandemic occur, what are the identified/anticipated effects to your organization? Some of these can be readily assessed. For example, loss of human resources (HR) is one of the most apparent. However, has your enterprise anticipated the potential surge in demand for your services or products? Equally important, has your enterprise identified whether your products or services will be in demand during a pandemic or whether they will be considered luxuries?

The unknown/unknowable must be factored into your analysis of identified and anticipated hazards and vulnerabilities, but how do you define what is unknown and/or unknowable? You will have to create some hypothetical situations. The result will be the development of a battery of predictive models.

Before we turn to predictive modeling, let us look at the response capacity element. Response capacity can be subdivided into two categories, identified and actual (on hand) at time of event. Identified response capacity is generally one of the BIA report outputs, and it is based on the assumption that identified assets, such as human resources, information technology, and cash, will be there when you require them. This is perhaps a good assumption under ideal conditions, but conditions will not be ideal in a pandemic and you are not likely to have the needed response capacity. This is why you have to determine what you think will be the most likely or actual response capacity at the time of an event. The result is an estimate of response capability.

Once you have considered potential hazards and vulnerabilities, you will be in a position to establish some disaster/risk benchmarks or metrics. Here is where predictive modeling becomes useful. Predictive modeling is an analytical tool in support of strategy mapping. Using predictive modeling can help you identify and strengthen your organization's distinct capabilities. Predictive modeling can help you go beyond statistics, regression analysis, and data reporting. In one respect, it helps the organization create a mosaic by bringing together various parts of the organization to create a composite derived from vast volumes of information that, although meaningful to each part of the organization individually, collectively may help you form an entirely different perspective.

In Figure 2.1, I have identified some predictive models that I think will be helpful for pandemic preparedness, including conflation models, confluence models, stress models, and surge models.

Now is not the time to create a report or plan or conduct an exercise. Rather, at this point, we should experience a change in our thought processes related to planning. As you expand your planning horizon, you create a need to involve more disciplines in the process. For example, human resources, risk management, and operational management can all become involved in the planning process and have a vested interest in the outcome. If you are feeling a bit frustrated at this point, good. We are beginning to see that the business continuity planning process is not a linear exercise. Business continuity planning is, and should be, nonlinear, especially when we factor in the tremendous complexity of a pandemic and the randomness of reaction to the pandemic event. As such, we should challenge our thought processes regarding how we accomplish planning and rethink how we go about the business of planning for a disaster.

Once the initial modeling results and the response capability figures are available, you can determine the risk profile/risk acceptance level for your organization. This allows you to determine the level of acceptance for contingency planning within the organization. If your organization has a high planning acceptance level, you will find that contingency planning is embraced as a "value-added" component of the business. This naturally leads to planning integration. In other words, you make contingency planning part of the business that your organization performs. You do not treat it as an adjunct to the business of the organization. Once contingency planning is integrated into the business as part of day-to-day operations culture, change generally results, leading to a planning structure that is dynamic and proactive versus static and reactive.

Where does all this refocusing of business impact assessment lead us? Hopefully, it leads us to a better understanding of pandemic risk, resulting in an improved decision-making and enhanced communication model for the organization. The planning process is complex, and adding the high impact that a pandemic has and the randomness of contagion, effect on markets, and effect on product/service demand makes it even more complex. Figure 2.2 reflects the flow for the business impact assessment based on the expanded model. Again, this is important work. As Woodcock stated in the article cited previously, "Anticipating and preparing for future challenges, trends, threats and opportunities is an essential part of any organisation's strategy. The more complex and global your market, the more you are going to benefit from looking beyond the parameters of your one-to-three year business plan."

As shown in Figure 2.2, there are different levels of involvement in the business impact assessment that are brought together by the process to produce an output that can be certified by management. From a pandemic preparedness standpoint, it is critical to develop the proactive posture that will facilitate early recognition and response to unfolding events. Interestingly, the methodologies presented in the figures can

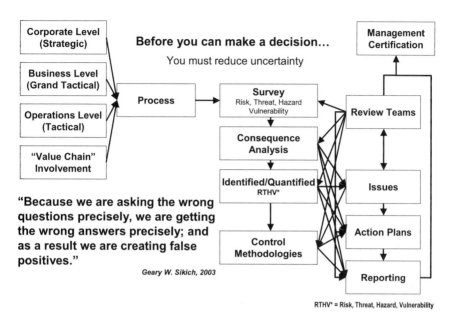

Figure 2.2. Complex Decision Making

readily be applied to most business situations that require an active analysis process. It should be the goal of contingency planners to develop and implement plans that are easily shaped to meet the needs of the organization during an event, regardless of its nature.

The degree of uncertainty and the ability to embrace adaptability may define how your organization addresses and perhaps survives an influenza pandemic. If we apply horizon scanning properly, it becomes part of the way the organization does its business and, as such, creates a value-added component much like contingency planning (acting as an umbrella for the various disciplines described in the table below) can create "value" for the organization.

Table 2.1 is my attempt to organize the various planning disciplines within an organization by categorizing them against criteria that each addresses to some degree during their activity cycles.

Some terms will be unfamiliar and need to be defined and clarified. I have introduced three terms; I feel these terms reflect how business continuity planning should be organized: strategic, grand tactical, and tactical.

The tactical level (down in the trenches) is where most of the current efforts in business continuity take place. Tactical plans are response oriented, are internally focused for the most part, and deal with the specific response to a disruptive event. Most tactical-level plans are very

Table 2.1. Planning Horizons

	ERP*	DRP*	BCP*	CMP*	CMMP*	CP*	SP*	OP*
Duration	Prior	Prior	Prior	Prior	Prior	Near	Semi-Annual	Quarterly
Focus	Response to events	Technology recovery	Business recovery	Stakeholder issues	Media response	Identified contingencies, Near-term Issues	Objectives, Goals	Operational Goals, Business Issues
Basis	Risk Survey—Risk, Threat, Hazard, Vulnerability	Risk Survey—Risk, Threat, Hazard, Vulnerability	Risk Survey—Risk, Threat, Hazard, Vulnerability	Issues, Potential Consequences, Anticipated Consequences, Threats (Changes in Markets, Global Situation, Complexity of Enterprise, Exposure)	Issues, Potential Consequences, Anticipated Consequences, Threats (Changes in Markets, Global Situation, Complexity of Enterprise, Exposure)	Enterprise Goals, Objectives, Issues, Potential Consequences, Anticipated Consequences, Threats (Changes in Markets, Global Situation, Complexity of Enterprise, Exposure)	Enterprise Goals, Objectives, Mission, Vision, Values	Enterprise Goals, Objectives, Near Real-Time, Incident Driven, Availability of Resources

Level	Tactical	Grand Tactical	Strategic	Strategic	Tactical	Strategic	Strategic	Grand Tactical
Integration	Limited—Life Safety, Physical Assets Protection	Narrow—main focus Information Technology Recovery	Marginal—main focus should be on business operations; however, as currently practiced it is an extension of DRP in many instances	Marginal—main focus should be on stakeholders; however, as currently practiced it is an extension of CMMP in many instances	Limited—main focus on media	Marginal—main focus should be on broad-based issues management; however, as currently practiced it is a compilation of ERP and BCP in many instances	Limited—main focus on financial goals, objectives—often not well communicated through the organization	Limited—main focus on near term (quarterly) financial goals, objectives—often not well communicated through the organization

* Definitions: **ERP** = Emergency Response Planning, **DRP** = Disaster Recovery Planning, **BCP** = Business Continuity Planning, **CMP** = Crisis Management Planning, **CMMP** = Crisis Media Management Planning, **CP** = Contingency Planning, **SP** = Strategic Planning, **OP** = Operational Planning.

short term in their orientation, focusing on the mitigation of the event and the displacement of the workforce for a limited period of time. The tactical level actually forms the base for the other two levels (strategic and grand tactical). Three elements, focus, expectations, and agenda, are common to all levels. At the tactical level, the focus is on response operations; expectations are for support from the next higher level (generally grand tactical), and the agenda is to mitigate and get back to normal as rapidly as possible.

At the grand tactical level, generally the business unit or operational element, the plans should focus more on the business operations, preventing cascade effects, and ensuring customer responsiveness and workload shifting. Grand tactical plans are gaining acceptance as more companies assess and understand the complexities of their operations and the effects on the value chain that an incident can have. The focus at the grand tactical level should be on minimizing the effects of disruption and providing support to the tactical-level response. Expectations at this level are that the next higher level (strategic) will facilitate the adjustment of goals and objectives and support any operational realignment that must occur to maintain continuity of operations. The agenda at the grand tactical level should be primarily focused on maintaining product/service availability.

At the strategic level, we see a shift in focus, expectations, and agenda. At this level, the focus should be outward, assuring clients and stakeholders that the entity will remain in business. The expectations for the strategic level are that the grand tactical and tactical levels will be able to manage the incident and shift work, without the need for direct intervention from above. Additional expectations are for seamless vertical communications to ensure that statements to stakeholders and media are accurate and timely. The agenda for the strategic level should be to ensure that corporate objectives and goals are being met.

For example, Jeffrey Immelt, Chief Executive Officer (CEO) of General Electric, said, "I was Chairman for two days. I had an airplane with my engines, [it] hit a building I insured, was covered by a network I owned, and I still have to increase earnings by 11 percent."[4] Because of the chain of events that ensued, neither General Electric nor its CEO could rely on the insurance operations or the jet engine division to deliver their contributions to the company's strategic earnings objective. Immelt had to turn to other divisions to increase their contributions in 2001. What may have been "mission critical" before the disaster was no longer so after September 11, 2001.

A key for all three levels is to recognize that there are indefinable variables that cannot be predicted that will cause plans to be modified as they are implemented. A pandemic will be replete with indefinable variables because of the unpredictability of human reactions to the unfolding events resulting from the pandemic. It is also important to

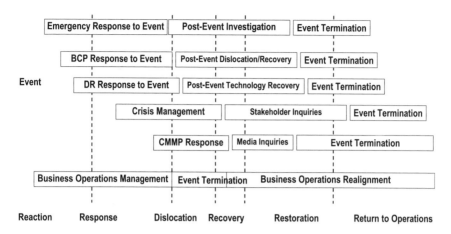

Figure 2.3. Phase—Components—Transition Points

recognize the existence of "nonlinearities." You should not try to model nonlinearities. The randomness of events precludes that. Because of the unstable nature of nonlinear events, it is very difficult for people to comprehend the nature of rare events such as a pandemic.

Figure 2.3 provides a graphic example of the relationship, or lack thereof, between the planning disciplines. Note the breaks in the linkages for ERP, BCP, DRP, CMP, and CMMP. These breaks are generally caused by the static nature of response from each discipline. The vertical lines represent the phases of an event. Each has its own characteristics. During the reaction phase, emergency response to the event is the initial response; the event controls the activities. Recall from Figure 2.1 that response capability is determined by identified capacity divided by actual capacity (on hand) at time of event. During the reactive phase, business continuity and disaster-recovery plans are implemented. The time lag can be significant depending on how well coordinated the response activities are. Business operations mostly continue unabated. These may be upstream or downstream supply chain actions and/or customer actions.

The resulting chaos, although often temporary, is generally manipulated by the media and in most instances capitalized on in the financial markets to the detriment of the enterprise's reputation and/or financial well-being.

The response and dislocation phases are often the most chaotic because of the need to draw tremendous resources to reduce the impact of the event and the relocation of the affected parts of the business to temporary locations, such as a hot site (a facility that provides temporary workstations for an organization) or alternate facilities. In the context of a pandemic, your organization may not have the ability or the luxury of a hot site or alternate facilities. You may be faced with quarantine or closure of the operation as a result of, for example, contamination.

During the recovery and restoration phases, we normally see activities that are focused on reestablishing business operations. The question that one must address in addressing pandemic preparedness is, how long will recovery take? Also, you must take a long hard look at what restoration means for your organization.

The last phase, return to operations, is generally overlooked in most planning disciplines because of the feeling that the event is over and operations are back to normal. This is a significant oversight on the part of planners. I have never seen a business return to operations as they were before the event. Things change, whether it be new equipment, upgrades to applications, or realignment of the business. A pandemic will have a greater impact on return to operations than most events. This is attributable first to the duration of a pandemic (500–800 days), with subsequent waves of outbreak that spread unevenly throughout the world. Second, you may find that demand for your business product/service does not recover completely, if ever. This makes having realignment plans as a part of your overall pandemic preparedness process even more critical.

In Figure 2.3, note that the Business Operations Management, Event Termination, and Business Operations Realignment bars touch and are overlapping. This is a result of being able to continue through the disruption and survive as an enterprise. This is not the general pattern for companies, because many do not have a continuum within business operations that allows for smooth transition from reaction to return to operations.

Pandemic: Systemic or Asymmetric Risk?

The previous section provided us with an introductory baseline to various aspects of business continuity analysis and planning. It also pointed out the complexity of a pandemic with respect to the analysis and planning efforts that have to be accomplished. When we refine our assessment processes, we also see that the complexity of a pandemic event is such that there is no one-size-fits-all approach to developing pandemic preparedness for organizations.

We will now turn our attention to some of the complexity issues that pandemic planning must address. Just because there is a pandemic does not mean that other types of disruptive events will not occur. As a matter of fact, some of the below discussion would point out that there is a greater probability for some of the cited events to occur as a result of the degradation of human capital resulting from a pandemic.

Systemic risks can be quite complex in nature and can be broken down into three categories of possible threats/occurrences/consequences that could befall an organization:[5] (1) natural, consisting of such things as drought, floods, tornadoes, earthquakes, fires, and other naturally occurring phenomena; (2) normal, consisting of such things as economic disasters (recessions, stock market downturns, and rating agency downgrade), personnel disasters (strikes, workplace violence, vandalism, and employee fraud), and physical disasters (industrial accidents, supply chain, value chain, product failure, fires, environmental, and health and safety); and (3) abnormal, consisting of criminal disasters (product tampering, terrorism, kidnapping, and hostage taking), information disasters (theft of proprietary information, hacking, data tampering, and cyber attacks), and reputation disasters (rumors, regulatory issues, litigation, product liability, media investigations, and Internet reputation). Abnormal threats/occurrences/consequences are becoming more prevalent as we see the normalization of threats such as hacking and data tampering.

Systemic risks are risks that originate in an identifiable event that threatens predictable harm to one element of the system and that, because of links between different systemic components, is (or has the potential to be) amplified in either magnitude or direction, leading to substantial damage to the system as a whole. The term is widely used in financial markets and has been defined in that context as "the risk that an event will trigger a loss of economic value or confidence in, and attendant increases in uncertainty about, a substantial portion of the financial system that is serious enough to quite probably have significant adverse effects on the real economy."[6] It is thus the linkages within a system and the possibility that certain events will have grave (and possibly unforeseen) consequences for the system as a whole, or other parts not directly connected to the original event, that make certain risks systemic. Because these links and the indirect impacts of particular events are often not transparent, or properly understood, instruments to manage and mitigate such risks may not be readily available.

There is substantial evidence to suggest that asymmetric threats pose a greater risk to the global economy today than ever before. Put simply, asymmetric threats or techniques are a version of not "fighting fair" that can include the use of surprise in all its operational and strategic dimensions.

In this section, we have touched broadly on some of the aspects of how to differentiate risks, threats, and hazards and their consequences/ probability of occurrence. In the next section, I will introduce concepts about what shapes our ability to identify risks, threats, and hazards. What you or I may consider a significant risk to someone else may be acceptable as a normal feature of the business in which they operate. We need to have a broader understanding of what constitutes risk to quantify it into a manageable and plannable parameter that can be dealt with effectively.

What Shapes Our Ability to Identify Risks?

It is important to understand that risk is a function of both probability and impact, and both can be highly subjective. We need to assess the chances of a risk occurring, as well as the magnitude of its impact and consequences, and we need to be aware of some well-known factors that inhibit our ability to make good decisions. For example, people will often judge an event as either frequent or likely to occur simply because it is easy to imagine or recall. In addition, if events are sensationalized by the media, we tend to perceive a higher frequency and assume a higher probability. In general, people will overestimate risks with which they are familiar and underestimate the unknowns. There is also something called "confirmation bias": people tend to look for evidence that confirms their own view and disregard any findings that contradict it. Similarly, people tend to place great faith in their own judgments and conclude very often that certain bad things will not happen to them. Finally, it is not uncommon for us to make estimates by starting with a value we know (the "anchor") and adjusting from that point. The fixed, mental frameworks from which we view the world color or inhibit our ability to process or accept new data or information.

To a substantial extent, risk perception and risk management are also affected by culture—the degree to which people are well informed and/or have developed some degree of resilience or tolerance to risk. One can imagine, for example, that Israelis have developed some degree of resilience to terrorism or that many inhabitants of Florida are able to block out the potential for a major hurricane to destroy their homes or livelihood. Business executives are, of course, human beings. They are vulnerable to the same kinds of forces and factors.

To better understand what shapes our ability to identify to risk, some definitions and examples of a few elements in Figure 2.1 are necessary.

Stress is just that: human stress. Expect a lot of it in a pandemic and figure it into your models accordingly. Surge refers to the sheer number of people needing services, especially medical help. Again, figure it into your planning, especially if people will be looking to your organization for needed goods and services.

Conflation, in the context of this book, can be defined as the process of two risk events, each resulting in the effects expected of it, occurring in sequence to an entity or in a geographic area, over an interval of time such that the effects of the first event cascade onto the second event, creating a potentially greater impact than if the events had occurred separately over time. The impact of the first event will expose systemic vulnerabilities in the entity or throughout the area that result in a degraded or weakened response. When the second event occurs, the entity and/or area, already weakened, has additional vulnerabilities exposed such that the cumulative impact of the separate and potentially nonrelated events is magnified. For example, on September 11, 2001, a conflation effect was created by the time interval between the planes hitting the respective towers. The additional events of the plane hitting the Pentagon and the plane going down in Pennsylvania added to the conflation effect. Another example would be New Orleans: Hurricane Katrina hit and did its damage. The city's response system was weakened and disrupted. Had Hurricane Rita, which occurred later, hit New Orleans instead of Texas, the conflation effect would have resulted in a weakened response system unable to withstand the next event. This is much like the effect that influenza and a secondary infection, such as pneumonia, would have on an individual. Your immune system is weakened in such a way that you cannot fight off another illness that you would normally have had the ability to fight.

The process of transferring attributes and effects, from one event based on one level of expected effects to a second, nonrelated event with a different expected effect, can be seen in Figure 2.4. It depicts one event sequence followed separately by the second event, resulting in a cumulative impact. Typically, the events in which conflation is to take

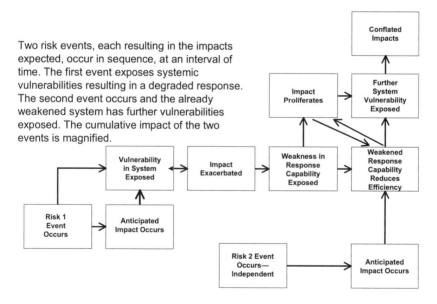

Figure 2.4. Conflation Model

place do not overlay as neatly as is depicted and generally do not share the same path of occurrence.

Conflation therefore should not be thought of as a simple process of matching events and impacts. Rather, a level of intelligence in the selection of the effects that result from multiple events occurring to an entity or geographic area over a short period of time is required.

Logically, conflation is the error of treating two distinct events as if they were one. The result of conflating events may give rise to false positives or ambiguity. For example, if the first event occurs and weakens the response system and then the second event occurs within a timeframe that is close to but not simultaneous (World Trade Center attacks on September 11, 2001), treating them as one event could result in a finding that the response system is inadequate, although in reality, the response system is adequate but overwhelmed by events that occur in such an order as to create weakness in the system. Another good example would be secondary attacks: a suicide bomber attacks, the response system acts, and then a secondary attack takes place, rendering the response inadequate and degrading the capability of the responders as they become the target. The recent assassination of former Pakistan Prime Minister Benazir Bhutto, still being investigated at the time of writing, is another example. There is speculation that a previous attack on another candidate caused a shift of responders away from Bhutto's location, thereby weakening her protection and creating a conflation effect. The false positives come from asking the wrong questions.

Confluence, in the context of this book, can be defined as the point at which things merge or flow together. Confluence, in contrast to conflation, provides a point or juncture at which events meet versus a somewhat parallel path that can occur with conflation. This is an important distinction in the context of a pandemic. While a pandemic runs its course, there are several potential conflation and confluence events that can occur that are separate and distinct from the effects of the pandemic but serve to exacerbate the effect on the entity and/or entities that have to respond to, manage, recover from, and hopefully restore operations to normal.

In a confluence situation, two risk events, each resulting in the impacts expected of it, occur almost simultaneously to an entity or in a geographic area, such that the effects of the first event meld into the second event, creating a significantly greater impact than if the events had occurred separately over time or in a conflation sequence. The impact of the first event exposes systemic vulnerabilities in the entity or throughout the area much the same as a conflation sequence, resulting in a degraded or weakened response. The second event occurs (almost simultaneous), and the entity and/or area already weakened has additional vulnerabilities exposed such that the cumulative effect of the events is magnified. The second event creates a tipping point wherein the entire response, management, recovery, and restoration paradigm has to be rethought.

The process of confluence is best exemplified by the tragedy of September 11, 2001, at the World Trade Center, where the two planes provided a confluence point, multiplying the effects of the overall event. Conflation also occurred on September 11, 2001, with the Pentagon and Pennsylvania events. Figure 2.5, entitled "Confluence Model," depicts the meeting point of two events resulting in a multiplier impact. As with conflation, typically, events in which confluence takes place do not overlay as neatly as is depicted in Figure 2.5, and generally the events do not share the same path of occurrence. Other examples of confluence would be the outbreak of a pandemic in an area with the near simultaneous occurrence of a natural disaster, such as an earthquake, hurricane, or tsunami.

The key point for planners and for management is that events will not stop occurring just because there is a pandemic. Therefore, your planning for a pandemic must not overlook the occurrence of other disruptive events and the effect that they could have on your enterprise.

As with conflation, confluence should not be thought of as a simple process of events occurring and impacts being multiplied. Rather, the

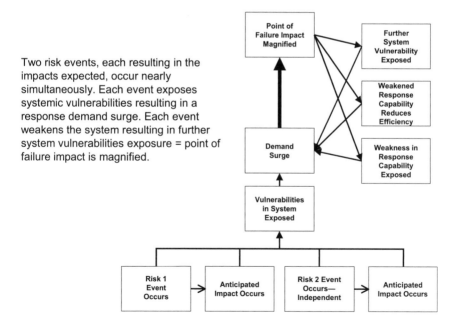

Figure 2.5. Confluence Model

same level of intelligence must be applied in the selection of the multiplier effects that result from events occurring to an entity or geographic area in an almost simultaneous timeframe.

Analysis Cycle: Active Analysis Methodology

Pandemic events are complex emergencies in which events occurring may not have an immediate direct impact on the enterprise or its operations. However, impacts may occur indirectly as a result of value chain disruption (loss of customers because of events affecting the customer, thereby creating a disruption that could lead to being put out of business).

As identified above, enterprise culture affects hazard/vulnerability perceptions. The resulting risk profile and risk acceptance level create a planning environment that is either accepting and integrative or not accepting and segmented. This leads to lack of support and plans that are an adjunct to the business rather than an integral part of the business.

The following section is a discussion of the "active analysis" system used by Logical Management Systems.[7] Based on the *LMSCARVER*™ Analysis Elements, the system provides a flexible framework for the continuous accumulation and assessment of "detectors and indicators" of change. The concept of "graceful degradation and agile restoration" is a key to active analysis, as depicted in Figure 2.6.

By "graceful degradation," I am referring to the ability of your organization to identify the event and its consequences, establish minimal stable functionality, devolve to the most robust less-functional

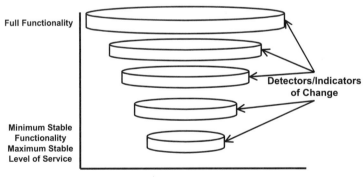

Figure 2.6. Graceful Degradation + Agile Restoration = *Resilience*

configuration (paring off service/product offerings) available in the least disruptive manner possible, and direct initial efforts for rapid restoration of services in a timely manner. "Agile restoration" refers to the ability of your organization to maintain minimal stable functionality (stay in business) and then evolve (add service/product offerings) to the next most robust functional configuration available in the least disruptive manner possible. The top ring in Figure 2.6 represents the business system and its network in full functionality (all products/services offered). The smaller rings represent successive levels of graceful degradation that the business system and its network would undergo until reaching a level of minimum functionality.

When the business system and its network reach the state of minimum functionality, the organization can conduct a campaign of agile restoration until it achieves a state of full functionality and a return to normal operations. One key to the process of graceful degradation and agile restoration is having a classification system for the business continuity plan. As Figure 2.6 depicts, detectors and indicators of change are used to facilitate the constant analysis of the state of the business system and its complex value-chain network. The detectors and indicators of change provide the early warning basis for event classification at the lowest (least severe) levels.

Now we are ready to look at an analysis tool that I have created to conduct initial business impact assessment and to practice active analysis.

Being able to achieve and maintain continuity of operations as the organization devolves and re-evolves is critical. As presented and defined below, these are the key elements of the LMSCARVER™ Analysis methodology,[8] the first step in analysis and business impact assessment.

LMSCARVER™ ANALYSIS: BUSINESS CONTINUITY TOUCH-POINT ASSESSMENT FORM VERSION 2.1

Directions: This form is designed to facilitate the evaluation of risks, threats, hazards, and vulnerabilities for your organization and to determine the consequences of organization "touch-point" degradation to your organization. A touch point can be any point at which your organization interfaces with an internal or external element that could affect it either positively or negatively. For example, the touch point "electric power supplies" can be the utility that supplies your organization power or it can be internal electric power supplies. The degree that you want to "drill down" on information is up to you, and that is the flexibility of the LMSCARVER™ Analysis methodology. Use a separate sheet for each touch point.

Part 1: Complete Part 1 by choosing a touch point for analysis (check appropriate box). This now becomes the essential element of analysis (EEA) touch point for the assessment grouping, for example, electric power supplies.

Part 2: Complete Part 2 by inserting a component that makes up a measure of effectiveness for the EEA touch point into the area of analysis box. Rank each subelement using the number scale 1 to 5, where 1 is the lowest importance and 5 is the highest importance. Provide comments as to why you rated the subelement as you did.

For example, if you have chosen the EEA touch point electric power supplies, you would have subelements consisting of source for your location, generators, and local utility.

Once a subelement is selected, insert it into the space provided and complete the *LMSCARVER* touch-point analysis, ranking each subelement using the numeric rating system. If you choose to only perform a top-level analysis, you will check the appropriate box in Part 1 and fill in the same selection name to Part 2, proceeding to complete the analysis per the above guidance. Regardless of the level of analysis that you have chosen, you must address the RTO, RPO, and MTO elements in the comments section of Part 2.

LMSCARVER™ Analysis Elements

- **Critical**: Determine the criticality of the service or product that your organization uses. This may be supplied via your organization's value chain or an external entity.

- **Accessible**: Determine accessibility by ranking the element as to the ease with which one can access the element. One needs to assess the accessibility to the item, the accessibility to alternative items that can be substituted, and the accessibility of the item to disruption.

- **Recognizable**: Determine how readily recognizable the element is.

- **Vulnerable**: Determine the total loss and/or degree of degradation that the organization can sustain.

- **Effect**: Determine what impact the loss and/or degradation presents to your organization.

- **Recovery**: Determine what your organization's recovery ability is in terms of time and costs.

- **Recovery Time Objective (RTO)**: Anticipated time to recover operation.

- **Recovery Point Objective (RPO)**: Amount of loss that can be sustained without impact to operation.

- **Maximum Tolerable Outage (MTO)**: Amount of disruption that can be sustained by the operation over time, including market share loss.

- **Cross Functional Touch Point**: A touch point of or relating to two or more functions in which a dependency for output and/or input occurs.

Part 3: Complete Part 3 by filling the consequence management significance (the end result to your organization of the event occurring and how your organization would manage these consequences) to your organization for degradation or total loss of the EEA touch-point element and its constituent subelements. Give some thought to what the consequences would be if you were unable to access or use the EEA touch point or subelement for a period of time. What duration increments would you consider as time critical, time sensitive, and time dependent? How does your organization deal with disruption?

Part 4: Complete Part 4 by defining the business ramifications/significance to your organization for degradation or total loss of the EEA touch-point element and its constituent subelements. Give some thought to what the business significance would be if you were unable to access or use the EEA touch point or subelement.

Part 5: Complete Part 5 by completing the quantitative analysis. Under the Operations Viability and Monetary Impact categories, you will see a set of numbers. These numbers generally represent time (hours, days, weeks, months). They relate to the amount of time that can pass until the impact of an event is felt. For a pandemic, you will have to determine the number of hours, days, weeks, or months until the impact is felt and insert them into the quantitative analysis. This is a subjective determination that will have to be custom fitted to your organization and its operating circumstances.

Part 6: Complete Part 6 by assessing the six criteria for customer vulnerability/exposure index and determining the impact on the enterprise of customer disruptions. Here you are evaluating your customer/client regarding how long they can stay in business if something were to happen to them or to you or a combination thereof. For example, airlines after September 11, 2001, faced a number of challenges that could have had collateral impacts for the value chain that services this area (everything from airports to baggage handling). Again, this may be a subjective assessment of your customer/client, but I have established six criteria that are color coded (Red, Blue, and Green) that you can utilize to make the determinations.

The first criterion is Staff Availability: what would happen to your customer if 40 percent of its staff did not show up to work? The second criterion, Impact to Account's Business Product/Service Demand, assesses the potential demand or lack thereof for your customer's product/service. How would your business be affected if a customer was unable to stay in business? The third criterion, Staff Furlough/Layoff, assesses the likelihood of your customer to be able to stay in business if it has to furlough/layoff portions of their workforce. What would be the impact to your business if your client furloughed a portion of its workforce with whom you perform work? The fourth criterion, Facilities Closure, assesses the likelihood of your customer to be able to stay in business if it has to close facilities. What would be the impact to your business if your client closed some of its facilities at which you perform work? The fifth criterion, Critical Infrastructure Designation—assesses whether your operations are considered to be vital to the United States' national security as defined under the USA Patriot Act. If your operations are considered vital to national security, how will your organization address the need to stay in business regardless of the effect of a pandemic on your operations? What would be the impact to your business if the government designated your business as a critical infrastructure and redirected your assets to non-revenue generating activities that are deemed critical to national security? The sixth criterion, Disclosure Requirements, assesses your client's need to report negative impacts under such legislation as the Sarbanes-Oxley Act. By conducting this type of assessment, you can shape your plans to deal with the business impacts that could cascade from your client to you.

Part 7: Complete Part 7 by establishing and defining the business case for addressing the potential impact to your organization for degradation or total loss of the EEA touch-point element and its constituent subelements.

Part 8: Complete Part 8 by establishing and defining the business case for not addressing the potential impact to your organization for degradation or total loss of the EEA touch-point element and its constituent subelements.

LMS CARVER PART 1:

PART 1: ORGANIZATION TOUCH POINTS			
✓	**Touch Point**	✓	**Touch Point**
	Electric Power Supplies		Internal Systems
	Gas and Oil Systems		Facilities
	Telecommunications Systems		Equipment
	Banking and Finance Systems		Human Resources Key Personnel
	Transportation Systems		Human Resources Staff Elements
	Water Supply Systems		Suppliers
	Emergency Services		Customers
	Continuity of Government Services		Contract Services (specify)
	Corporate Image		Stakeholders (specify)
	Operational Infrastructure (specify)		Other (specify)

LMS CARVER PART 2:

PART 2: TOUCH-POINT ANALYSIS						
Level of Analysis—check appropriate box corresponding to level of analysis						
	Strategic			Grand Tactical		Tactical
Area of Analysis:	**Lowest**			**Highest**		**Comments**
						Recovery Time Objective (RTO) **Recovery Point Objective (RPO)**
	1	**2**	**3**	**4**	**5**	**Maximum Tolerable Outage (MTO)**
C = Critical (RTO)						
A = Accessible (RPO)						
R = Recognizable						
V = Vulnerable						
E = Effect (MTO)						
R_t = Recovery Time						
R_c = Recovery Cost						
Totals						

CROSS-FUNCTIONAL TOUCH POINTS

Describe Cross-Functional Touch Points—check appropriate box and summarize cross-functional relationship

Cross-Functional Touch Points		Strategic		Grand Tactical		Tactical

LMS CARVER PART 3:

PART 3: CONSQUENCE MANAGEMENT SIGNIFICANCE

LMS CARVER PART 4:

PART 4: BUSINESS RAMIFICATIONS/SIGNIFICANCE

LMS CARVER PART 5:

PART 5: Quantitative Analysis		Time to Failure					
Business Unit	Economic Risk	Operations Viability			Monetary Impact		
		< 7	8–14	> 30	< 7	8–14	> 30

Business Unit	Critical Functions	Key Products/Services			
		Transactions		Projects/WIP	
		#	Value	#	Value

Risk Factors	Quantifiable Risk $
Financial Risk	
Operational Risk (cascade potential and effect)	
Reputation Risk	
Credit Risk	

LMS CARVER PART 6:

PART 6	Customer Vulnerability/Exposure Index		
Classification Criteria	Red	Blue	Green
Six criteria are used to determine the classification of status of Red, Blue, or Green.			
Staff Availability	40% or less staff available	Approximately 70% of staff available	Approximately 80% of staff available
Impact to Account's Business—Product/ Service Demand	65% drop in demand for product/service	40% drop in demand for product/service	Surge in demand for product/ service and/or capacity reached
Staff Furlough/ Layoff	Wide-scale lay-off/furlough of staff	Limited layoff/ furlough of staff	Recruiting temporary staff to supplement workforce vacancies

(Continued)

PART 6	Customer Vulnerability/Exposure Index		
Classification Criteria	**Red**	**Blue**	**Green**
Facilities Closures	Regional closure of facilities	Limited regional closure of facilities	No closure of facilities
Critical Infrastructure* Designation	Not designated as a critical infrastructure*	Not designated as a critical infrastructure*	Designated as a critical infrastructure*
Disclosure Requirements**	Disclosure of material change financial and operational	Disclosure of operational change	No disclosure required

* USA PATRIOT Act of 2001 (P.L. 107-56)—P.L. 107-56 states that act goes on to define "critical" infrastructure as systems and assets, whether physical or virtual, so vital to the United States that the incapacity or destruction of such systems and assets would have a debilitating impact on security, national economic security, national public health or safety, or any combination of those matters (Sec. 1016(e)).

** *Sarbanes-Oxley Act* **Section 409:** REAL TIME ISSUER DISCLOSURES—*requires management to report on a rapid and current basis information concerning operations.*

"REAL TIME ISSUER DISCLOSURE.—Each issuer reporting under section 13(a) or 15(d) shall disclose to the public on a rapid and current basis such additional information concerning material changes in the financial condition or operations of the issuer, in plain English, which may include trend and qualitative information and graphic presentations, as the Commission determines, by rule, is necessary or useful for the protection of investors and in the public interest."

Customer	Criterion 1	Criterion 2	Criterion 3	Criterion 4	Criterion 5	Criterion 6

Use additional sheets as necessary to capture all clients.

LMS CARVER PART 7:

PART 7: BUSINESS CASE FOR ADDRESSING

LMS CARVER PART 8:

PART 8: BUSINESS CASE FOR NOT ADDRESSING

If the space available is not sufficient for your write-up, attach supplemental pages as necessary.

The *LMSCARVER*™ touch-point analysis methodology is a very powerful tool that can be used at any of the three levels (strategic, grand tactical, and tactical) and can be as detailed as you deem necessary. The level of information that you gather for analysis can facilitate decision making and planning efforts to determine who needs to be involved in the planning process, what needs to be planned for, why you need to plan for it, where the business will be impacted, and for how long the impacts could last. This is not a trivial process; it is a process that requires some thought, some detail, and the involvement of skill levels within and external to your organization. The results can be the survival of your business. Please note that you will complete many of these forms for each area that you choose to assess. Doing this will form the basis for your ongoing assessment activities (active analysis).

Creating the Risk Mosaic

Our ability to identify risks, threats, hazards, vulnerabilities, and their associated consequences is of paramount importance. Unless we can accurately determine and track risks, threats, and hazards and understand vulnerabilities and consequences, we can never really achieve a complete picture of the "playing field" on which our enterprise operates. This requires bringing together seemingly unrelated pieces of information to form a comprehensive package for analysis, something I have termed "data fusion." Data fusion requires seamless communication, constant and intense scrutiny of all available data, and the ability to create a mosaic to visualize the application of information as intelligence (knowledge) to aid the decision-making process. Data fusion is the bringing together of vast amounts of information to make a decision. Most of the time, decision makers do not delve deep enough in the process to make the decision needed to solve the "right problem."

For example, Dr. Ian Mitroff cites five basic types of solving the wrong problem precisely.[9] I have observed participants in simulations that I have developed and implemented consistently solve the wrong problem precisely. One has to understand the vast amount of information that is needed to be fused to make a good decision.

A review of the five basic types of solving the wrong problem precisely is necessary. As Dr. Mitroff notes, "each type is distinct in the sense that it's a clearly identifiable instance of muddled thinking":

- Picking the wrong stakeholders
- Narrowing one's options
- Picking the wrong language of variables
- Narrowing the boundaries/scope of a problem
- Ignoring parts/systems connections

As you can see from the list above, each of the five is not necessarily independent of the others. When we assess how our organization approaches problem solving, we must address the issue of complexity in today's modern organization. The concepts of outsourcing, just-in-time supply/production, and getting back to core services work well in an ideal world, a world where nothing goes wrong, yet so many things can go awry in today's world. As mentioned previously, we can organize the assessment of risks, threats, hazards, and vulnerabilities, our mosaic basics, into three basic categories: natural, normal, and abnormal threats/occurrences/consequences.

If organizations continue to solve the wrong problem precisely, that is, not understanding the consequences of decisions that are made based on limited and/or dated source information, they will continue to operate in a reactive mode instead of a proactive mode. Corporate management must learn to develop an intelligence mosaic.

The fate of every organization depends less and less on those who can solve canned or given problems and more and more on critical thinkers, "smart thinkers," who can define and even redefine the extremely difficult problems facing it. By concentrating on the consequences of their intended actions, an organization can attain great value from the scenario. Solving the wrong problem precisely is typical: participants often focus on the event at hand instead of the consequences related to response, management, recovery, and restoration actions.

Phases of a Crisis: Will a Pandemic Be as Predictable?

We have spent some time among the trees. Now let us take a look at the forest itself. Regardless of the crisis that your organization may face, there are distinct phases that delineate the progression of a crisis. Will a pandemic be so predicable? And where are we now? As of the date of this writing, WHO is at phase 3: "Human infection(s) with a new subtype, but no human-to-human spread, or at most rare instances of spread to a close contact." What does that mean? How is it being confirmed? These are questions that beg answers. WHO reports only laboratory-confirmed cases. Does this mean that there could be a greater number of unreported and unconfirmed cases? Has H5N1 begun its mutation to a new influenza virus subtype that is causing disease in humans but is not yet spreading efficiently and in a sustainable manner among humans?

Incipient Phase of a Crisis

The first phase, or what I term the incipient phase, is characterized by warning signs of pending doom. The warning signs are clear for the observant to see. However, most, if not all of us, have a tendency to miss the subtle cues that a crisis is looming. Reading the current WHO pandemic phase 3 definition and the statistics that WHO puts out weekly about cumulative deaths (see Table 1.1 in Chapter 1) gives me pause. Do we see the incipient phase of an emerging crisis before our eyes and yet fail to take action?

During this time, the stage is set for the crisis to begin. This phase encompasses the time during which the precursors of a crisis are developed. Unsafe operating practices, failure to address known hazards, threats, and risks, and inadequate reporting mechanisms are but a few of the indicators of which we need to be cognizant. Warning indicators develop. The warning indicators may not be obvious at first but are almost always recognizable in hindsight, when it is too late. Even when warning indicators are recognized, the organization often responds incorrectly. Instead of addressing the potential issue, a more common response is shock or outright denial. Steps can be taken to avoid the looming crisis, or the issues can be ignored, inevitably resulting in the eruption of the crisis.

For example, the European Union (EU) held a two-day exercise recently to assess pandemic preparedness. "Common Ground" involved hundreds of participants, including EU agencies such as the European Centre for Disease Prevention and Control, member states, non-EU countries, and representatives from the pharmaceutical industry. The participants were responding to a series of simulated emergency events resulting from a new human flu strain that started a major pandemic in Europe. The exercise was designed to represent a period of twenty-six weeks. Twenty-six weeks is approximately 182 days, not even close to the 500–800 days a pandemic will likely play out in real life. Common Ground's timeframe (twenty-six weeks) would represent the first wave of a pandemic and the approximate time that it would take, under optimum conditions, to develop a vaccine. And that is just to develop a vaccine, not produce, deliver, distribute, and vaccinate.

The overall aim of the exercise was to test the execution and interaction of national plans and measures, as well as examine the role of the European Commission. The exercise involved crisis rooms in national health ministries and agencies, linked through early warning and monitoring secure systems. A report was prepared and the key findings were issued. The participants noted numerous failings of communication, border control, integration of response, and the supply chain, to name a few. I find it interesting that many of the assumptions of the exercise presumed ideal conditions and that a working vaccine was available, which will probably not be the case because we do not know what form H5N1 will take when it mutates to allow human-to-human transmission.

Are we in the incipient stage of a crisis? A careful analysis of the indicators suggests that we are. Are we ready for the crisis? Exercises such as the one just mentioned suggest that we are not.

Unfolding Crisis

If the indicators of the incipient phase are not recognized or are recognized and discounted, the disruptive event begins to unfold as a crisis. This is the phase in which the damage actually begins. At this point, the organization is faced with the fact that there is an unfolding crisis.

Eventually during this phase, the organization has to acknowledge that a crisis exists. Until an organization can get ahead of events, the crisis will manage the organization. It is during this time that the value of an integrated continuity and crisis management capability (organization, plans, and supporting infrastructures) becomes apparent. When an organization is not sufficiently prepared to recognize, respond to, and manage a crisis and has no documentation on which to depend, the lack of capability usually appears during the initial response and management effort. Unfortunately, the pandemic preparedness efforts to date seem to reflect a tremendous lack of understanding of the magnitude of the situation.

Transition to Recovery

After the unfolding crisis phase, we enter into a transitional phase. This phase is characterized by a reestablishing of operations and information and a return to business as usual. During this phase, the organization attempts to recover and resynchronize its operations after the actual apex of the crisis. At this point, the organization may also begin to deal with litigation as well as public and internal dissent. During the transition to recovery, the organization needs to take a long, hard look at itself, determine what went wrong, and devise preventative steps to ensure that similar instances do not occur in the future.

Because we are in the incipient stage of a pandemic, we have time to analyze our operations and to determine what it will take to return to a business-as-usual state. We can perform simulations that will give us data to analyze and a basis for developing plans for addressing the long-term impacts of a pandemic. If we wait until this stage, which should occur during the last 100–120 days of the pandemic situation, there may be just too much damage done to be able to return to normal operations. Markets may cease to exist for companies, constituencies may cease to exist for many governments.

After the Crisis: Restoration

The final and most desirable stage of a crisis is the post-crisis or restoration phase. During this phase, the crisis has been rectified and the organization has returned to relatively normal operations. However, in some unfortunate cases, the stricken organization may never get to this phase. In the case of a pandemic, we may see a completely new paradigm emerge as markets adjust to new realities. For some sectors, business may revive. For others, it may be a long process to restore operations to pre-pandemic levels. This is readily apparent in the history of the Black Death. In the fifty years after the Black Death, the medieval world's traditional winners and losers exchanged places. Will we see the North American and European nations become losers and the South American, Asian, and African nations become winners as a result of a plague? One of the things that European society experienced after the Black Death was an imbalance in food prices (lower because of less demand) and labor costs (higher because less available). Western economies are heavily dependent on Asian, South American, and African economies for cheap labor, production of goods, and energy sources. What happens if the balance is suddenly disrupted?

Of course, it should be the goal of every organization to reach this phase from the onset of the crisis. The sooner this phase is reached, the less damage will result. If a crisis proceeds beyond the incipient phase, the goal should be to find the quickest, most effective way of reaching the post-crisis phase and resolving the crisis.

Concluding Thoughts

As this chapter concludes, I would like to emphasize some key points regarding pandemic preparedness. First, no matter what we do to prevent a pandemic from occurring, the best we can hope for is to delay one, not to prevent one. Second, preparation should be focused on a broad array of disruptive events, not on the specific aspects of the pandemic from the standpoint of the medical consequences.

In the area of planning, whether you are planning for a pandemic or any disruptive event, you need to identify emerging issues, develop your ability to analyze issues, and assess decision-making processes. Figure 2.7 offers a perspective for developing "decision analytics" as a

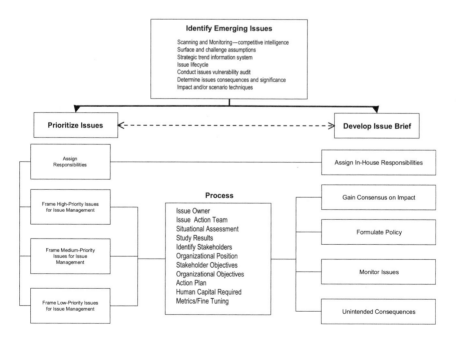

Figure 2.7. Active Analysis—Create a Mosaic

tool from which the enterprise can benefit before, during, and after a pandemic or similar mass-disruption event. As depicted in the top box of the figure, the ability to identify emerging issues early allows you to use more decision aids to determine the potential for impact that the emerging issue has. As you move to the left column, prioritization of issues once identified allows for assignment to a responsible party for monitoring, framing into categories of high, medium and low priority. This leads to the center box, which depicts some of the main processes that can be used to fine-tune and monitor issues so that, when you develop issues briefs (right column), you can develop a consensus regarding potential impact. From there, you can develop policies and plans that will allow you to minimize the negative affects and maximize the positive affects while you continue to monitor the issues and conduct analysis on potential unintended consequences based on proposed actions that could be taken to address the issue. It also makes good business sense to have a system in place that allows the enterprise to interpret vast amounts of information (data) and turn it into intelligence that can be used to create competitive advantage. The use of predictive modeling and scenario-based simulations can afford the enterprise opportunities to strengthen distinct capabilities, break down information-sharing inhibitors (silos), and support strategic initiatives.

Hopefully, you can differentiate your enterprise from its competitors in such a way that you create the competitive advantage needed to survive a pandemic and, more importantly, the long-term effects of a pandemic.

Increase your knowledge management through the use of active analysis[10] to ensure that your enterprise has the best possible information available to it before a pandemic. This will ensure that your business decisions regarding pandemic preparedness are well defined and supported by intelligence that is useful, not by hype that can create undue panic, chaos, and confusion.

Last, you have to be patient. It takes a long time to develop the infrastructure, information-gathering capability, and analytical team to make sense of the data. Maximize the human capabilities of your enterprise to make strategic use of information.

In the next chapter, we will investigate more tools that can be used to prepare your organization and its extended value chain for a pandemic or other widespread disruptive event.

The Pandemic Settles In

Giving up the illusion that you can predict the future is a very liberating moment. All you can do is give yourself the capacity to respond to the only certainty in life—which is uncertainty. The creation of that capability is the purpose of strategy.

—Lord John Browne, Group Chief Executive, BP

As we have seen, the first wave of a pandemic will be chaotic. The human toll could be significant but relatively short term in its impact. How long with the first wave last? The simple fact is that no one knows. Past history is somewhere around eight to twelve weeks. The long-term toll will be the high economic cost that will further worsen the human suffering. For many businesses, this could mean a significant erosion of the customer base as they face a lack of demand for products and services. However, some businesses could find a significant increase in demand for products and services. Your quandary may be that you have insufficient human resources available to meet the demand. Can you successfully realign your business offerings to protect your revenue stream? What "re-purposing" of your business could help you create opportunity from the crisis? There are risks and costs associated with any program of action, but they are far less than the cost of comfortable inaction.

For government at all levels, the erosion of the tax base will create tremendous stress on the system. Remember that government makes its money on taxation and fees. All the services that we are accustomed to having, from waste removal to public health, depend on a steady flow of tax money. If you are a local or state government, thinking that a declaration of a "state of emergency" will get you federal aid, think again. A pandemic may be so widespread that the federal government will not be able to render any financial aid. Even if it is able, it may have to crank up the printing presses to create the money that is needed. That will inflate the currency and possibly send us into a worldwide depression with high inflation.

So, if you, as a business person or private citizen, choose to leave preparation and problem solving to the government, think long and hard about this decision. In all events, there is a potential for actions and consequences that have significant downside and, conversely, significant upside potential. Having a program in place that provides flexibility in determining the probability of the event and the spectrum of consequences that could result from the event gives your enterprise (whether government or business) a head start.

Will a pandemic unfold in accordance with your plans? No. However, if your enterprise does not have a plan or if you have relied on someone else for your well-being, you place your fate in the illusion of stability. This illusion of stability lowers our perception of the risks we could face. Underestimating how risky a pandemic actually will be could be catastrophic for you, your enterprise, and society as a whole.

The first two chapters of this book have focused on analysis techniques, such as active analysis. Now we will turn our attention to preparedness steps. I have organized this chapter into two parts. The first part presents a scenario of what might occur during the 180–320-day timeframe of my projected 500–800-day pandemic. The second part provides tools that can be applied to facilitate your planning efforts. The tools are designed to build on the risk-analysis tools presented in Chapters 1 and 2. Once you have completed your analysis activities and have a baseline impact assessment, you can move to the next step, developing your plan. Planning is an activity that should be participative; you need the input of those who will activate the plan and implement the steps that you document in the plan.

PART 1: SIX MONTHS IN

Paralysis: 180–320 Days

We left off in Chapter 2 at day 180 of the pandemic. As the world settles into the reality of the outbreak, adjustments are made. The UN, WHO, CDC, and other entities set out to contain the outbreaks that continue to materialize. Businesses readjust to the realities of a changed and changing operating model. It is no longer business as usual. Supply chain adjustments are being made, albeit slowly and sporadically as a result of disruption of transportation systems. Service center operations (such as call centers) are being reconfigured to adjust to the need to focus on geographical areas currently less affected by the pandemic.

Assets mobilized by WHO, the international community, governments, and industry, after adjusting their status and effectiveness, begin to help. Death tolls, for example, show signs of leveling off and even declining in some areas. (However, this may be a false positive in that pandemics have been shown in the past to be cyclical in the manner that death tolls rise and fall.) Yet in this phase, a paralysis takes effect as economies, affected by the reaction of governments (border closures or quarantine), become bodies at rest, not bodies in motion.

The world begins to realize that the energy required to regenerate global economic motion will have to be massive.

Some countries reopen their borders. This action does not instantaneously restart stagnant economies, as many hope. Unlike a light switch being turned on, merely reopening borders will not generate pre-pandemic levels of commerce. Restarting an economy cannot be accomplished instantaneously. One of the things that we are told to do when power goes out is to turn off electric appliances. Why? The simple fact is that, when power is restored, if all appliances are on, the stress on the system may cause an overload surge, creating a more severe outage than the initial incident. Thus, the global economy will be faced with a vexing problem: how to restart an intricate and complex system, that has evolved over time, in a way that it can manage the stresses associated with the jumpstart.

Sector Analysis: 180–320 Days

The financial sector is faced with the task of regaining the confidence of the investing public. Stock markets and commodity markets are experiencing tremendous delays and spot closures attributable to the absence of clearing and settling personnel. Replacement staff is becoming more and more difficult to find, and the right skill sets are not easily developed. Many exchanges are discussing merging settling and clearing operations, but it is likely to take more than nine months to accomplish the systems integration that is necessary. Further exacerbating the problem is the lack of support staff necessary to accomplish the systems integration. Banks and other financial institutions still face solvency issues, some of them terminal to the institutions most severely affected. Institutions such as the World Bank, International Monetary Fund, and Asian Development Bank may be forced to suspend normal operations until donor nations are economically viable. This is a complex issue, because many donor nations are dependent on developing nations to support their economic engines. Developing nations cannot fuel their own economic engines because of the debilitating effect of the pandemic on their populations. Stock, commodity, and finished goods prices could fluctuate dramatically as access to commodities and transporting them are disrupted, as well as the activities of publicly traded companies. The financial sector will require large infusions of cash from central banks that have no revenue base as a result of expenditures and loss of tax base support. Markets could enter a recessionary period.

The manufacturing sector is faced with attempting to restart operations without access to normal streams of raw materials, some of which are imported and/or are dependent on transportation systems still affected by local outbreaks of the flu. Firms once dependent on outsourcing and parts made overseas are forced to seek local sources. This requires that cottage industries be started. Although creating a localized economy, the inception of cottage industries could further delay the recovery of the global economy because of the limitations of local resources, workforce, and goods and services demands.

The service sector is faced with much the same situation as the financial sector. Many restaurants are closed because of loss of staff, lack of demand, and inability to procure products. How does this sector create volume demand?

The telecommunications sector is faced with loss of connectivity issues caused by loss of and/or sporadic disruption of support infrastructure, including electrical power. Telecommuting, once a panacea for business continuity planning, is proving to be more difficult than imagined because of the inability of people to replicate the office environment in the home setting. Additional strains on the telecommunication system continue as stress on residential infrastructure increases.

The insurance sector faces the overwhelming task of claims processing with limited human resources. This affects healthcare providers dependent on insurance payments to continue operations. The ability of some insurers (life, health, and workers compensation) to pay claims becomes more doubtful as time goes on.

The healthcare sector faces less patient volume than in the previous six months. However, there is the issue of healthcare supplies becoming increasingly difficult to acquire because of transportation system impacts and offshore production facilities being unable to ship supplies.

The energy sector faces supply issues (raw materials), transformation issues (refining raw materials into useable energy), and transportation issues. The key question to answer for this sector is, "How will production centers get finished products to users, while replenishing depleted reserves and a depleted workforce?" Commodity prices will fluctuate because of demand for basic raw materials that now have to be generated locally.

The utility sector faces infrastructure strains caused by an aging infrastructure that is not designed to meet the types of demand placed on it. More brownouts and blackouts occur as utilities are forced off the grid to meet local demand with limited local supplies of fuel.

The agriculture sector faces localization caused by transportation issues. Seasonal demands for food products change the market for food distribution and retail operations. A key question for this sector will be, "How to meet local demand when localization of production has not been accomplished?" The United States continues to suffer regional spot outages. The absence of agricultural products inspectors throughout the world is beginning to have serious consequences on the movement of all agricultural products, including meats. There is reluctance to accept products that have not gone through the traditional inspection process.

The education sector faces limited capability to reopen because teacher shortages and fearful parents may keep students away from educational institutions. Additionally, the government may commandeer facilities to house units that have been called to active duty in support of operations to mitigate the effects of the pandemic.

The high-technology sector faces continuing high demand for access and support related to the Internet. Support services could reach marginal levels because of continued workforce disruption.

By the time that we enter the tenth month (320 days) of the pandemic, the impact on the global economy will have reached all sectors. Although disruption in the chaotic sense is possible, the gradual localization of economies is more likely to be the case. It should be noted that we have not factored in any naturally occurring phenomena, such as hurricanes or other natural disasters, that are likely to exacerbate local economic difficulties and strain even more local and national responders.

Speculation and fear could therefore be replaced by paralysis, despair, and retrenchment during this timeframe.

PART 2: PANDEMIC PREPAREDNESS PLANNING TOOLS

Part 2 presents a structure for the pandemic taskforce that includes its composition and main areas of focus. Plan components and additional risk-analysis tools are also presented. This section is not meant to be prescriptive. Rather, it is designed to provide you with examples that you can use for your organization. The discussion on assessment and risk analysis emphasizes the need to build an assessment system that is dynamic and constantly used rather than one that is a one-time or periodic process that can only provide limited information based on the time that it was conducted. The tools presented here focus on the pandemic taskforce and its activities.

Pandemic Preparedness Steps

To effectively address a pandemic, the enterprise, whether it is business or government, must be prepared for a wide variety of contingencies and consequences that result from reaction to overreaction, as the pandemic unfolds. A premise that can be used to begin the process of developing a preparedness program is to determine how long it will last. Generally, pandemics have a cycle of recurring waves of outbreak that last between eight and twelve weeks. Over the course of a pandemic, there may be multiple waves over a period of eighteen to twenty-four months, or approximately 500–800 days.

The WHO and the DHHS have each created classification-type systems that are designed to facilitate an understanding of a pandemic cycle. WHO uses a six-phase cycle, and DHHS uses a six-stage cycle. This may be confusing, and it gets more so when we actually look at the phases/stages compared with each other. By the way, the stages and phases do not correlate to any timeframe with regard to waves of outbreak. I highly recommend that you visit the DHHS and WHO websites (www.dhhs.gov, www.panflu.gov, and www.who.int) to download the phase/stage matrices.

WHO phases 1 and 2 relate to DHHS stage 0. This can be termed the "inter-pandemic period." WHO phase 3 relates to DHHS stages 0 and 1. To avoid confusion, DHHS stage 0 is very broadly defined as "New domestic outbreak in country at risk," and therefore it transitions WHO phases 1, 2, and part of 3. WHO phases 4 and 5 relate to DHHS stage 2. WHO phases 3–5 and DHHS stages 0–2 constitute the "pandemic alert period." We are currently in WHO phase 3, which means that we are in either DHHS stage 0 or 1 depending on how you define the situation in the country that is experiencing an outbreak.

WHO phase 6 relates to DHHS stages 3–6 and can be termed the "pandemic period." There is one very important point to be made here: there is no set time period for any of the WHO phases or DHHS stages. Second, WHO phases apply worldwide, and DHHS stages apply only to the United States. If you are totally confused, you are not alone; many organizations have taken the WHO phases and DHHS stages and created their own internal six-element matrix that is, again, slightly different from those of the WHO and DHHS.

Key objectives of pandemic preparedness include, but are not limited to, the following:

- Prepare your enterprise to continue operations at acceptable levels when faced with a pandemic outbreak.
- Define/develop trigger points to initiate response, management, recovery, and restoration steps.
- Train employees to minimize pandemic penetration throughout the enterprise.
- Refine/develop corporate policies and procedures to address pandemic operational issues.

- Develop document-required preparedness measures to enhance existing business continuity plans to address pandemic issues.

- Exercise preparedness through a tiered system of drills that validate preparedness strategies and enhance capabilities and knowledge within the enterprise.

It may be quite useful to create a pandemic preparedness working group or taskforce to accomplish the necessary tasks across the enterprise. The taskforce should have a charter and defined parameters for operation to ensure that it will maintain its focus. One of the key areas of focus for the taskforce will be to develop strategies for realigning your enterprise to capitalize on available human resources and the demand for products/services.

In most organizations, this will require amending contingency plans (which, again, include business continuity, emergency-response, and disaster-recovery plans) to ensure preparedness for major business disruptions that are caused by the pandemic. Shaping strategy in the face of uncertainty is one of the biggest challenges that the taskforce will face. I recommend that a senior executive be named as the taskforce sponsor. Second, the taskforce should be scheduled to provide periodic updates on the current worldwide situation, preferably in senior management briefings with a summary report to document progress on the taskforce's activities. In this way, the taskforce can maintain its momentum and senior management can be better informed and more aware.

Figure 3.1 provides a graphic of influencing factors of which the taskforce should be aware and prepared to address.

The taskforce should be a central coordinating point for collecting, reviewing, and distributing relevant pandemic materials (e.g., World

Figure 3.1. Facing Uncertainty

Health Organization, federal government, CDC, and other sources of information). This requires that the taskforce reshape current BIA models, refocusing methodologies and outputs to reflect a more comprehensive and truly integrated analysis that addresses strategic, grand tactical, and tactical assessments as defined in the *LMSCARVER*™ analysis tool presented in Chapter 2. What will be required if your enterprise is forced to realign its product/service offerings as a result of the disruption created by the pandemic? How will your enterprise address the effect that failure to achieve financial goals and objectives will have? Failure to achieve financial goals and objectives, because of market conditions, competition, client-base erosion, or reputation damage, has a far greater business impact on the enterprise.

The taskforce should be able to operate with relative independence within the enterprise to enable it to meet its goals and objectives. Again, I strongly recommend executive leadership sponsorship and regular project status meetings and reports to facilitate knowledge sharing throughout the enterprise and so that senior managers can provide guidance to the taskforce on their courses of action.

In a recent issue of *Chief Executive*, Elaine Eisenam wrote the following:

> There is a major trap that leaders can inadvertently set for themselves when they assemble their teams, whether the team is their direct reports or their boards. That trap is bringing in weak people. In this respect, weak does not mean unskilled or untalented. Weak means hiring men and women, whose role it is to support your views. These individuals are the quintessential "yes men" who will tell the naked emperor that he is wearing a custom suit.[1]

Heed this warning well. The taskforce must be unafraid of presenting "bad news" to executive leadership. Executive leadership, conversely, must be able to deal with bad news by formulating strategies and guidance that turns bad news into opportunity.

Let us further define the scope for the pandemic preparedness taskforce. Many contingency planning programs consist of three major components: business continuity, disaster recovery, and emergency response. Business continuity plans are generally based on ensuring that the business can maintain its operational capability when faced with a crisis situation. Disaster recovery plans are generally based on the ability to recover and restore systems and data. Emergency-response plans generally center on initial response, life safety, and security actions.

Pandemic preparedness should focus on the people side (both internal and external) of contingency planning, ensuring an integration of business continuity, disaster recovery, and emergency response that facilitates assurance of long-term business survivability. I have always felt that a comprehensive plan that incorporates people, technology, and physical structures into a single plan is the most effective way to approach the planning process, be it for a pandemic or any other type of disruptive event.

Taskforce Composition

Personnel responsible for management and support of pandemic preparedness activities should represent, at a minimum, the following functions:

- Taskforce chair: overall direction of pandemic preparedness efforts and coordination of taskforce activities. Taskforce chair interfaces with executive management.
- Business planning (e.g., strategic): development of strategic, grand tactical, and tactical planning portion of pandemic preparedness documentation.
- Legal representative: development of legal review processes to ensure that all elements of pandemic preparedness documentation comply with legal constructs and do not put the enterprise at risk.
- Human resources representative: development of human resources portion of pandemic preparedness documentation.
- Operations representative(s): development of operations (product/service) portion of pandemic preparedness documentation.
- Public relations representative: development of media/public relations portion of pandemic preparedness documentation.
- Internal communications representative: development of internal communications portion of pandemic preparedness documentation.
- Marketing/sales representative (customer facing): development of marketing/sales and customer relations portion of pandemic preparedness documentation.
- Procurement/logistics representative (supplier/vendor facing): development of supplier/vendor assurance portion of pandemic preparedness documentation.
- Finance/treasury operations representative: development of financial budgets, financial impact statements, and risk management portion of pandemic preparedness documentation.
- Facilities operations representative: development of facilities protection, decontamination, and alternate facilities/relocation plans portion of pandemic preparedness documentation.
- Information systems representative (disaster recovery): development of information systems portion of pandemic preparedness documentation.
- Security representative (physical security, life safety): development of physical security, and life safety and facilities protection portion of pandemic preparedness documentation.

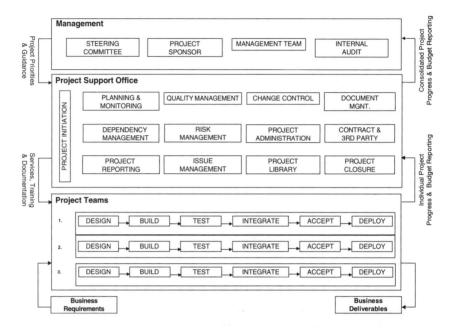

Figure 3.2. Project Management Office

- Contingency planning representative: development of business continuity considerations portion of pandemic preparedness documentation.

Figure 3.2 depicts a typical project management structure that would be implemented for developing pandemic preparedness.

Once the project management structure is in place, the project teams and areas of focus can be defined. It should be noted that, for smaller organizations, the project management structure will have to be sized accordingly. It is important, however, to ensure that all of the functions are addressed in your plans no matter the size of the organization.

To establish a framework for focusing the energies of the project teams, regular taskforce meetings need to occur. To ensure that the meetings are successful, an agenda needs to be developed and followed for each meeting.

Taskforce Areas of Focus

Six areas of focus that I feel are essential to address in a pandemic preparedness plan are strategy, policies, communications, training, resources, and outreach. Each will be discussed in the following paragraphs. Please note that the six areas of focus must be addressed by each element of your taskforce with respect to its area of operation. For example, human resources will have a different set of information for each of the six areas of focus than security. This reflects each taskforce element's different responsibilities. Each of the taskforce elements will have a strategy, policies for their area, communication requirements, training requirements, resource requirements, and outreach requirements. The goal of the planning process is to identify the unique needs and requirements and to then meld them into a cohesive plan that allows for coordinated implementation by the diverse representative groups of the taskforce.

The six areas of focus are universal in that private- and public-sector organizations throughout the world will have to address them in some manner to achieve pandemic preparedness.

The typical components of a pandemic preparedness plan consist of seven elements: human capital, facilities, operations, legal, business partners/suppliers (value chain), customers, and government. We will discuss these elements of the pandemic preparedness plan in detail in subsequent chapters. Although I consider these seven elements to be generally reflective of most enterprise structures from a high level, there may be modifications necessary or other areas that you need to address for your enterprise because of the unique aspects of the enterprise.

Strategy: The first component of pandemic preparedness and of any contingency planning is strategy. A strategy is a long-term plan of action designed to achieve a particular goal. Strategy comprises three subdivisions: strategic, those items that are related to corporate strategy, the meeting of goals and objectives, and ensuring that the business survives; grand tactical, those items that are related to business unit operations, regional operations, and division operations (also referred to as operational), focusing on lessening the impact and preventing events from cascading uncontrollably; and tactical, those items that are related to departmental, team, and smaller functions, generally localized response, management, recovery, and restoration actions. Two key elements for resilience: (1) A common set of functions performed at all three levels is the first element. These common functions include the following: leadership, focusing on decision making; planning, focusing on short- and long-term business implications; operations, focusing on affected and unaffected operations; logistics, focusing on support to ensure the continuity of operations; finance, focusing on expediting financial processes and tracking expenditures; administration, focusing on human capital, policies, and compliance; infrastructure, focusing on internal and external infrastructure operations required to support business operations; and external relations, focusing on government, stakeholders, and value chain interfaces. (2) The second element is seamless vertical and horizontal communication. This is possible through an organizational vertical structure consisting of the three subdivisions summarized above (strategic, grand tactical, and tactical) and the use of common terminology.

Corporate policies: The second component of pandemic preparedness is policy, consisting of all policy modifications required and/or new policies created to address pandemic preparedness issues. The policy process includes identifying different alternatives, such as human resource management programs or spending priorities. Although policies may already be well established, it will be necessary to review and modify them to ensure that they are adequate for addressing a pandemic.

Communication: The third component of pandemic preparedness is communication. Communication is usually described along three major dimensions: content, form, and destination. Developing a communication strategy and refining the messages to be communicated in the pre-pandemic, pandemic, and post-pandemic periods need to be coordinated by the pandemic taskforce. Communications consist of internal (e.g., employee, contractor) and external (e.g., government, stakeholders, media) communications regarding pandemic information as it applies to operations. Communications considerations should also address external relations (e.g., alliances, partners, customers, vendors).

Training: Training, the fourth component, refers to the acquisition of knowledge, skills, and competencies. The training programs that will be developed can be categorized into formal classroom presentations, computer-based programs, and action-based learning (drills and exercises) that are developed and implemented to ensure preparedness and to educate employees on actions being taken to ensure continuity of operations.

Resources: The fifth component is resources. It consists of current human and facilities resources, technical assets, and projected needs to address a public health emergency, such as an influenza pandemic.

Outreach: The sixth and final component is outreach. Outreach consists of all efforts to coordinate, liaise, conduct joint operations, cooperate, and maintain lines of communication with all applicable external parties (i.e., federal, state, and local authorities, customers, providers).

Pandemic Preparedness Plan Components

Once the taskforce is chartered and the six areas of focus are established and defined, the pandemic preparedness documentation process can begin. To facilitate management and maintenance of the documentation, it has been convenient to subdivide the material into four components. The four components are strategy, pandemic guidelines, business unit/operational level supplements, and tactical supplements (business continuity plan appendices). These four components are a natural subdivision and a way of creating manageable parts for a very large and complex set of documentation. Additionally, the full set of documentation can be organized in such a way that only the applicable parts for the level within the organization get the material that they need for implementation. For example, at the corporate level, a complete set of the four components (strategy, guidelines, business unit/operational-level supplements, and tactical supplements) will be useful to executive decision makers. At the department level, the tactical supplement may be all that is required because it will be tailored specifically to the needs of the department that has to implement it.

In subsequent chapters, we will discuss each of the components in detail. These form the basic documentation that is derived from the analysis that has been accomplished in the first phase of pandemic preparedness. The analysis should continue on an ongoing basis (active analysis); this will enable the enterprise to continue to develop and refine the pandemic preparedness documentation. It also ensures that the most current guidance is incorporated into the pandemic preparedness documentation. Many organizations are developing a separate pandemic preparedness plan as a stand-alone document. I highly recommend that pandemic preparedness materials be integrated into existing plan structures. This will eliminate confusion, and you will find that much of the pandemic preparedness activities that you undertake can readily be applied to lesser catastrophic events with great effect for the organization.

For example, I had a client that was developing its pandemic preparedness capabilities. One of its divisions experienced a devastating ice storm that literally shut down all of its offices in the geographic area affected. This, in turn, forced it to shift work to other geographic divisions outside of the affected area. It also had to deal with stranded employees who, as a result of weather, were stuck in the closed offices because they were unable to travel (almost like being quarantined). This lasted for more than a week.

In effect, the client implemented its pandemic plans, addressing all six elements: strategy, policies, communication, training, resources, and outreach. It had to modify current strategy to continue to meet business goals and objectives. Policies were modified to address pay for employees unable to get to work. Communication with employees, clients, and other stakeholders had to be accomplished in a coordinated manner. Training was essentially done on the job, because personnel were required to fill roles and accomplish functions that they did not normally perform. Resources were allocated and reallocated to meet the need to address closed offices and work that had to be shifted to other areas. Outreach was essential to ensure that customer needs were being met and to facilitate the needs of employees who could not get to work.

Analysis, Assessment, and Risk Intelligence

Creating a risk-intelligent organization is based on the ability of the organization to acquire and use information to its maximum benefit. The taskforce must be able to define "risk intelligence" and communicate it throughout the enterprise. To accomplish this, the taskforce may want to consider developing a simple survey as a precursor to implementing the analysis tools presented in Chapters 1 and 2. I find that it is useful to do this to ensure that the taskforce speaks with "one voice," that members have an understanding and agreement on what things mean. Seamless communication is dependent on a common terminology.

The following twelve-question Crisis Management Survey, developed by Logical Management Systems (© 2007), seems to work well in achieving a level of understanding for the taskforce. An example of a completed questionnaire is also provided. The questionnaire responses should be treated as confidential, proprietary information.

Table 3.1. Crisis Management Survey

1. What is a "crisis" for your company?

2. What is the single highest probable failure factor for your business?

3. How will your company pay for its next crisis?

4. What does your current business interruption insurance policy cover?

(Continued)

Table 3.1. (*continued*)

5. Do you know what contingent business interruption insurance is?

6. Should a crisis materialize for your company, how will it achieve its strategic goals and corporate objectives?

7. How would a crisis reshape your company?

8. Does your corporate culture embrace contingency preparedness as a way of doing business, or is this perceived as an adjunct to the business of your company?

9. Has your company addressed human capital utilization during a crisis?

10. How critical are your customers to your company's crisis preparedness?

(*Continued*)

Table 3.1. (*continued*)

11. How critical is your value chain (suppliers, vendors, contractors, third-party service/product providers) to your company's crisis preparedness?

12. Are your product/service offerings immune to a crisis?

Table 3.2 is an example of a typical response to the questions and an analysis of the answers.

I find that it is useful to create a level of understanding within the taskforce and executive management. You might use the twelve questions to facilitate initial meetings with executive management. In this way, you can integrate pandemic preparedness into the overall business of the business and not have it be an adjunct to the business of the business.

Figure 3.3 depicts how this integration can be achieved. A key is to develop an understanding of the business structure and how the continuity model can facilitate the achievement of enterprise goals and objectives. The left side of the figure represents the normal business operational hierarchy and structure for an organization. From bottom to top, we see that the division of activity corresponds to the center titles (Implementer through Integrator). The right side of the figure represents the breakdown of how business continuity should be structured to ensure that it is part of the business and not an adjunct to the business. Again, see that the center titles correspond to activities that would be carried out at different levels in the organization.

Risk, Threat, Hazard, Vulnerability, and Consequence Analysis

In addition to focusing on the potential effects of a disruption caused by a pandemic, your enterprise needs to factor in the potential effects other disruptive events can have. For most enterprises, the output will be

Table 3.2. Crisis Management Survey Example

1. What is a "crisis" for your company?

A crisis is any <u>critical incident</u> that involves death, serious injury, or threat to people; damage to environment, animals, property, and/or data; disruption of operations; threat to the ability to carry out mission; and/or threat to the financial welfare and image of our company. A crisis is an unexpected event or series of events that spiral out of control, interrupt normal operations, and cause intense and unwanted public scrutiny that harms or threatens to harm an organization's reputation.

Analysis:
> While the above definitions are good, they are process focused and therefore have limitations. Recognizing that a "crisis" is any event that threatens the existence of the enterprise or the ability of the enterprise to conduct its normal operations offers a broader, less process-focused perspective.

> The following does not attempt to define "crisis"; rather, it focuses on goals and objectives instead of problem identification:

> > All initiatives taken to assure the survival, growth, and resilience of the enterprise—this means *not merely thinking about the plannable or planning for the unthinkable, but learning to think about the unplannable*

2. What is the single highest probable failure factor for your business?

Terrorism, technology failure, natural disaster, etc.

Analysis:
> What about competition? A competitor will put you out of business faster than a natural or manmade event. In "Management and the Activity Trap," George S. Odiorne points out that many organizations become so enmeshed in activity that they lose sight of their goals and the activity becomes an end in itself. Unquestioningly continuing activities from past years, lacking clarity about objectives, and losing sight of the enterprise's overall purpose will often lead to failure of the enterprise. Why not take the most important problem and really analyze it?

3. How will your company pay for its next crisis?

Insurance; in the form of business interruption insurance

Analysis:
> Can you afford the inevitable delays in getting cash when it is truly needed? Do you know what will be excluded from your claim? If you are to survive the crisis, your enterprise has to be able to meet customer and marketplace demands. If you cannot provide the products or services, you will not have the customers for long.

4. What does your current business interruption insurance policy cover?

Not sure. I have not read the policy and do not know where it is located or what coverage we have.

(continued)

Table 3.2. (*continued*)

Analysis:
> Find the policy and read it carefully. Then check and see if you are really insured against the potential losses you could encounter.

5. Do you know what contingent business interruption insurance is?

Not a clue.

Analysis:
> Contingent business interruption (CBI) insurance is a special coverage rider in addition to a business interruption policy. Swiss Re publishes an excellent document that explains contingent business interruption and other special covers. Get a copy and read it to see if you need to add CBI or other special covers.

6. Should a crisis materialize for your company, how will it achieve its strategic goals and corporate objectives?

Not sure. I guess that we will adjust them based on the situation.

Analysis:
> Is your plan focused on "mission-critical activities" versus "mission-critical goals and objectives"? The "business of the business" has never been part of the planning process, because planners never recognize they are engulfed by the company's activities rather than its objectives. Until planners understand and recognize the difference, the company they support will be limited in its business resiliency capability.

7. How would a crisis reshape your company?

Not sure; we might have to divest some assets and restructure.

Analysis:
> What is required is a change in focus or reference points for planning. Instead of focusing entirely on point-specific and event-linked plans (natural, technology disaster, etc.), focus on planning that addresses the business aspects (what could happen if your product or service is no longer in demand or your organization loses a key customer, etc.).

8. Does your corporate culture embrace contingency preparedness as a way of doing business or is this perceived as an adjunct to the business of your company?

Planning for contingencies is like regulatory compliance; it is something that you do but do not integrate into business operations.

Analysis:
> Have a compelling story—state a business case for the value of planning. Know what drives the business, how "core business" is defined, and what can threaten it. Communicate what the organization is putting at risk and the value that a business continuity plan provides in reducing the risk exposure.

(*continued*)

Table 3.2. (*continued*)

9. Has your company addressed human capital utilization during a crisis?

Current plans do not identify the consequences of loss of personnel.

Analysis:
>Traditionally, HR has had a limited role in crisis management activities. This role has been mainly to address "humanitarian assistance" (Employee Assistance Programs, etc.) aspects of crisis response. However, when we start to rethink the role that HR plays in today's global environment, we see that HR's crisis management role is more than humanitarian assistance.

>HR should focus on a comprehensive structuring of initiatives designed to establish and maintain resilience between and among all the touch points of the enterprise. Eight key areas must be taken into consideration:

>>**Management**—Decision making regarding the human capital aspects of the handling of the event.

>>**Planning**—Short term and long term; effect on human capital needs (to include succession planning, intellectual skill sets, training time, etc.) that could result from the event.

>>**Operations**—Explain how staff degradation levels, availability of human capital (resource pools), etc., will affect business operations.

>>**Logistics**—Worksite, temporary worksites, and supporting logistics—equipment, extended logistics support necessary to keep human capital available (hotels, meals, etc.).

>>**Infrastructure**—Internal and external to support human capital during the event.

>>**Administration**—Support factors such as policy changes, etc.

>>**Finance**—Short-term dislocation and long-term dislocation, budgets, payroll, etc.

>>**External Liaison**—Communication to stakeholders regarding the human factors considerations that the event has created.

10. How critical are your customers to your company's crisis preparedness?

Customers are not critical to company preparedness.

Analysis:
>Customers are the lifeblood of the enterprise; without them there is no enterprise. The marketplace will define your enterprise. Therefore it is imperative to involve customers in your planning process.

11. How critical is your value chain (suppliers, vendors, contractors, third-party service/product providers) to your company's crisis preparedness?

Third-party entities are not included in our contingency planning process as they are outside the scope of our plan.

(*continued*)

Table 3.2. (*continued*)

Analysis:

> If customers are the lifeblood of the enterprise, your value chain enables you to meet their demands. Unless you have a monopoly, you cannot survive without the participation of the value chain in your planning process.

12. Are your product/service offerings immune to a crisis?
Not sure.

Analysis:

> When was the last time that you bought a box of carbon paper for your typewriter? The advent of the computer ended the era of the typewriter and subsequently ushered in the death of an industry segment that was not in competition with the computer—carbon paper manufacturing.

> Ask yourself, will my product/service continue to be in demand in a changing marketplace? Becoming a risk-intelligent organization, one that learns as much as possible about the nature of risks, threats, hazards, and vulnerabilities, allows you to develop continuity strategies that facilitate the survival of the enterprise.

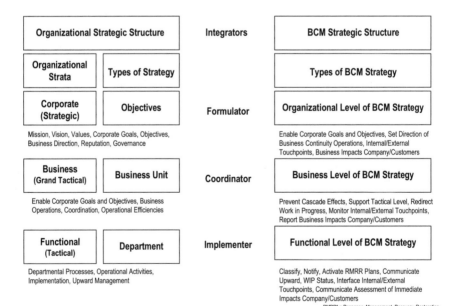

Figure 3.3. Business Contingencies—A Continuity Model

a matrix like the one below that summarizes the typical events that could occur. Although responsibility for developing and maintaining the matrix will generally reside in the business continuity area, all elements of the organization are involved in the development and update of the matrix.

In Chapters 1 and 2, we presented information on traditional analysis you need to perform as you begin to develop the business continuity plan. Doing active analysis is necessary to develop a baseline of information, but it also has certain limitations. We do not know exactly what the future will bring.

Traditional analysis creates undecidability attributable to the inability to predict all behavior in a dynamic environment. Therefore, one should adopt an active analysis methodology, such as that developed by LMS.[2] The advantages that can be realized by adopting this methodology and maintaining an active analysis process are as follows: uses static analysis as a basis, includes touch-point complexity factors, is dynamic-based on creating a mosaic, and time factors (time critical, time sensitive, and time dependent) act as drivers.

Termed "futureproofing" by LMS, the active analysis process is designed to create a mosaic that enhances decision making by identifying behavior patterns in a dynamic environment. Five key assumptions were used as a basis for the developmental framework of the futureproofing methodology: (1) The modern business organization represents a complex system operating within multiple networks; (2) there are many layers of complexity within an organization and its value chain; (3) because of complexity, active analysis of the potential consequences of disruptive events is critical; (4) actions in response to disruptive events need to be coordinated; and (5) resources and skill sets are key issues.

Based on the above assumptions and the results of the baseline analysis (static analysis), one realizes that the timely identification and classification of, communication and response to, management of, and recovery from a disruptive event are critical. Uncertainty will decrease with the passage of time, as will available options for response, recovery, and restoration. This is contrasted with increasing numbers of issues and higher costs associated with response, recovery, and restoration efforts. As such, an organization should seek to continually analyze situations so as to develop a clear picture of the current state of the business system network. Referred to as "data fusion: constructing a mosaic" by Logical Management Systems, this is a process of getting enough bits and pieces of information in place to transform seeming chaos into recognizable patterns on which decisions can be made.

The end result should be an analysis that informs us of not only what natural, manmade, and technological threats, risks, hazards, and vulnerabilities the enterprise faces but also the potential impacts on performance that relate to business operations. For pandemic preparedness, it is

Table 3.3. Risk, Threat, Hazard, Vulnerabilty Analysis

Risks/Threats/Hazards/Vulnerabilities Potential Events (RTVH*)	Probability (H,M,L)*	Impact (H,M,L)*	Effect (LT, ST)**
Bomb Threat			
Bomb Event			
Customer Injury on Premises			
Data Entry Threat/Employee Error			
Disruption of Courier/Mail Delivery Service			
Earthquake			
Executive Succession			
Explosion			
Fire			
Fraud/Embezzlement			
Health Event (Employee Life Safety)			
Heating/Cooling Failure			
Hurricane			
Kidnapping/Extortion			
Lightning			
Loss of Critical Personnel			
Medical Event—Public Health Related			
Natural Gas Leak/Carbon Monoxide			
Pandemic			
Power Failure			
Robbery/Assault			
Severe Weather Conditions			
Snow/Ice			
Software Failure/Virus			
Tampering with Sensitive Data			
Telecommunications Failure			
Terrorist Act			
Tornado/Wind Damage			
Unauthorized Access/Vandalism			
Water Damage/Rain Storms			
Weapons of Mass Disruption (Chemical/Biological)			
Weapons of Mass Destruction (WMD) (Nuclear)			
Workplace Violence			
Additional Vulnerabilities Not Listed Here			

*H, M, L = High, Medium, Low. **ST, LT = Short Term, Long Term.

imperative that we expand our analysis of our enterprise to include nontraditional areas of analysis.

Exercise 1: Determining Pandemic Risk Tolerance Level

What is your pandemic risk tolerance level? Figure 3.4 provides an example of what could occur to an organization during a pandemic. I have used an 800-day timeframe because it allows flexibility in determining risk tolerance triggers.

The value of conducting this type of exercise is that you can vary the severity and develop some interesting projections on product/service demand and staff impact. Then you can begin to factor in stress and fatigue factors and assess where your enterprise is in pandemic preparedness.

What is your pandemic risk tolerance level? Figure 3.5 provides a form that can be used as a basis for determining the risk tolerance level of your enterprise. Why not take some time right now and give the exercise a try?

Concluding Thoughts

In this chapter, we have discussed some basic pandemic preparedness steps. I have attempted to keep this discussion on a more strategic level, focusing on business and economic issues that will present

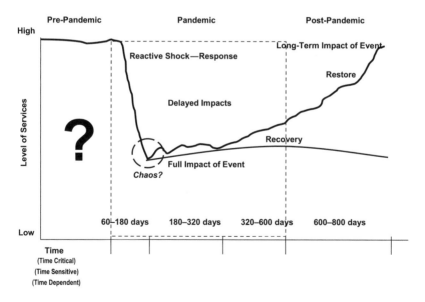

Figure 3.4. Plan—Respond—Manage—Recover—Restore

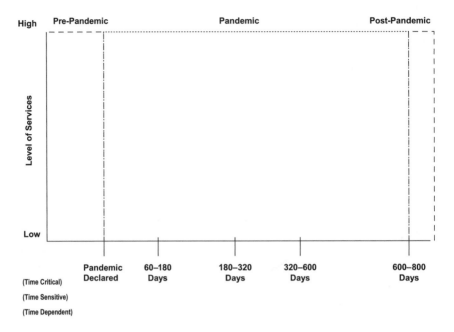

Figure 3.5. Plan—Respond—Manage—Recover—Restore

themselves during a pandemic rather than on which mask works best
or what you should or should not be stockpiling. I have stayed away
from the issue of stockpiling because I learned at a conference that I
recently attended on pandemic planning and preparedness that governments can and will step in during a pandemic and relieve you of your
stockpiles for the greater good of the community. Eminent domain is a
legal construct that I urge all businesses to become extremely familiar
with. This is not meant to condemn government or to discourage stockpiling by the private sector; rather it is to provide you with an understanding of the magnitude of the event we are facing. In the next chapter,
I will present some tools for documenting pandemic preparedness.

Global Reaction to a Pandemic

It ain't what you don't know that gets you into trouble. It's what you know for sure that just ain't so.

—Mark Twain

When will the second wave of the pandemic strike? A better question is, will there be a second wave? Or a third? A second wave of infection or outbreak has traditionally occurred after an indeterminate time interval. This is the difficulty with pandemic planning and preparedness. One does not have a strict timetable with which to work. We can only look at past pandemics and estimate the number of waves of outbreak or the interval between waves. It is generally accepted that a wave may last eight to twelve weeks, but there is no guarantee that the next pandemic will follow the patterns of previous pandemics. Table 4.1 provides some illuminating figures.[1]

Despite the grim numbers, a word of caution: currently, the H5N1 virus has not mutated to a form that would allow human-to-human transmission. Many such viruses do not mutate, or, if they do mutate, they are potentially less lethal in their human-to-human transmissibility form. There is not current methodology to accurately determine what form a mutated H5N1 virus (one that allows human-to-human transmission) will take.

PART 1: THE AFTERMATH

In his book *The Black Swan: The Impact of the Highly Improbable*, Nassim Nicholas Taleb[2] presents what he calls the "ludic fallacy" (*ludic* comes

Table 4.1. Number of Episodes of Illness, Healthcare Utilization, and Death
Associated with Moderate and Severe Pandemic Influenza Scenarios*

Characteristic	Moderate (1958/68-like)	Severe (1918-like)
Illness	90 million (30%)	90 million (30%)
Outpatient Medical Care	45 million (50%)	45 million (50%)
Hospitalization	865,000	9,900,000
ICU Care	128,750	1,485,000
Mechanical Ventilation	64,875	742,500
Deaths	209,000	1,903,000

* Estimates based on extrapolation from past pandemics in the United States. Note that
these estimates do not include the potential impact of interventions not available during
the twentieth-century pandemics.
Source: Department of Health and Human Services, Department of Homeland Security Pandemic preparedness plans and reports.

from *ludus*, Latin for games). Taleb defines the ludic fallacy as "the
attributes if the uncertainty that we face in real life have little connection to the sterilized ones we encounter in exams and games." In
essence, the gaming that we may do, developing scenarios and extrapolating statistics from past events (historical evidence), may not reflect
the uncertainty that we encounter in the real world as the event (in this
case, an influenza pandemic) emerges.

Gaming, in this case scenario-based planning, results from attempting
to apply "rules" that we can use to calculate odds and probabilities. In
real-life situations, we do not and cannot know the odds. As Taleb says,
you have to discover them. The sources of uncertainty are not defined.

This is a key point for pandemic preparedness efforts. Currently,
much of the planning and effort being expended by the public sector
and, in many instances, the private sector is focused on initial response:
getting patients cared for. Exercises are conducted in which volunteers
by the hundreds are "vaccinated" to demonstrate the capability of public health departments and hospitals to handle a surge. This may be an
interesting exercise; however, it is an exercise in futility: (1), because
there will be no vaccine initially because the influenza strain will be
novel and resistant to current vaccines (that is why it will become a
pandemic), and (2), because we cannot be certain that the mass of sick
individuals will all appear at one time for treatment.

The availability of antiviral medications will most probably be limited
and may not be effective against the novel strain of the virus that causes
the pandemic. Therefore, sick individuals will be receiving whatever is
at hand until a vaccine can be developed to deal with the virus. It is
generally assumed that an effective vaccine will take up to six months
to develop. Once developed, the vaccine must be produced in sufficient
quantity and then distributed worldwide. The process of production

and distribution could take eighteen months or more, and there is no guarantee that production and distribution will be without incident. You can read that as uninterrupted and without any seizure of cargo by desperate people or countries.

Reactive or Proactive?

Will your enterprise be reactive or proactive? Reactive enterprises may not fare well in the face of a pandemic. Reactive means that your enterprise will let events control it. Events can have a great influence on how we react if we are unprepared or unaware of them. Taleb uses the example of the black swan in his book. The military uses terms such as "known unknown" and "unknown unknown" to describe how we can categorize risk and probability and what cannot be currently estimated because we have not thought of it yet. In retrospect, we generally find that we really did know a lot, but by then it will be too late.

A proactive approach does not necessarily mean stockpiling items. Being proactive means that you have developed situational awareness. Situational awareness is being able to put pieces of information from a variety of sources, some seemingly disparate, to create a mosaic. The mosaic gives you a clearer picture of the situation, one that can be constantly assessed. This allows for the development of contingency strategies that can be modified and adapted as they are implemented. For example, let us look at some of the legal issues that your enterprise may face.

Know the Law

Private-sector firms should investigate in detail the legal requirements that the enterprise has as an employer under various regulatory requirements to ensure a safe workplace. These include compliance with the Occupational Safety and Health Administration General Duty Clause, Health Insurance Portability Accountability Act of 1996, Privacy Act (personal information that is considered sensitive), and the following legal constructs: constructive knowledge, constructive notice, negligence, and foreseeability. A good law dictionary will come in handy during pandemic planning. Knowledge of the legal requirements can facilitate contingency strategy development, help to create education programs for your employees, and ensure that you have a defensible position when your enterprise is sued for failure to provide a safe workplace. For publicly held and some privately held companies, the Sarbanes-Oxley Act governance and disclosure requirements will come into play.

Numerous federal and state statutes authorize relevant public health actions to address pandemic influenza. Section 319(a) of the Public

Health Service (PHS) Act (42 U.S. Code 247d), for example, authorizes the DHHS secretary to declare a public health emergency and "take such action as may be appropriate to respond" to that emergency consistent with existing authorities. Appropriate action may include making grants, providing awards for expenses, entering into contracts, and conducting and supporting investigation into the cause, treatment, or prevention of the disease or disorder that presents the emergency. The secretary's declaration also can be the first step in authorizing emergency use of unapproved products or approved products for unapproved uses under section 564 of the Food, Drug, and Cosmetic Act (21 U.S. Code 360bbb-3) or waiving certain regulatory requirements of the department, such as select agents requirements or—when the president also declares an emergency—waiving certain Medicare, Medicaid, and State Children's Health Insurance Program provisions.

Under the Robert T. Stafford Disaster Relief and Emergency Assistance Act (42 U.S. Code 5121 et seq.), FEMA/Department of Homeland Security is authorized to coordinate the activities of federal agencies in response to a presidential declaration of a major disaster or emergency, with DHHS having the lead for health and medical services. The president may also declare an emergency under the National Emergencies Act (50 U.S. Code 1601 et seq.).

The PHS Act provides additional authorities for core activities of DHHS that will be needed to plan and implement an emergency response. For example, sections 301, 319F-1, 402, and 405 of the PHS Act authorize the DHHS secretary to conduct and support research. Section 351 of the PHS Act and provisions of the Federal Food, Drug, and Cosmetics Act authorize the secretary and the Food and Drug Administration to regulate vaccine development and production. Infrastructure support for preventive health services such as immunization activities, including vaccine purchase assistance, is provided under section 317 of the PHS Act. Section 319F-2 of the PHS Act authorizes the secretary, in coordination with the secretary of Homeland Security, to maintain the Strategic National Stockpile.

Section 361 authorizes the secretary to make and enforce regulations necessary to prevent the introduction, transmission, or spread of communicable diseases from foreign countries into the United States or from one state or possession into any other state or possession. CDC administers these regulations as they relate to quarantine of humans. Diseases for which individuals may be quarantined are specified by executive order; the most recent change to the list of diseases that can be quarantined was the April 1, 2005, Executive Order 13375, which amended the Executive Order 13295 by adding "influenza caused by novel or reemergent influenza viruses that are causing, or have the potential to cause, a pandemic" to the list.

Other provisions in Title III of the PHS Act permit DHHS to establish quarantine stations, provide care and treatment for persons under quarantine, and provide for quarantine enforcement. Section 311 of the PHS Act provides for federal-state cooperative activities to enforce quarantine and plan and perform public health activities. Section 311 also authorizes the secretary to make available the resources of the PHS to help control epidemics and deal with other public health emergencies. DHHS may also engage in certain international activities under Section 307 of the PHS Act.

Statute 42 U.S. Code § 97 provides that the secretary of Health and Human Services may request that Customs, Coast Guard, and military officers aid in the execution of quarantines imposed by states. The secretary also has the authority to implement disease control measures in Indian country, if necessary (25 U.S. Code 198, 231; 42 U.S. Code 2001). Indian tribes, like states, are sovereign entities with police power authority to enact their own disease control rules and regulations. Tribal law should be consulted as well if you are within tribal territory.

Furthermore, DHHS has broad authority to coordinate vaccine development, distribution, and use activities under Section 2102 of the PHS Act, describing the functions of the National Vaccine Program. The secretary has authority for health information and promotion activities under Title XVII and other sections of the PHS Act. DHHS can provide support to states and localities for emergency health planning under Title III of the PHS Act. Both federal and state statutes may apply to specific interventions that would be implemented to control a pandemic.

Creating a Mosaic: Putting Pieces Together

Just being aware of the legal issues is not sufficient to ensure that compliance will be achieved. We must incorporate the legal requirements into our planning efforts. Additionally, there are numerous planning considerations that do not have legal/regulatory drivers. Two articles, one by Paul Reynolds, BBC News Online world affairs correspondent, and the other by Steven Minsky, a business process management consultant, offer some perspectives on risk vulnerability coverage. I have summarized the six coverage vulnerabilities that they present as they might apply to an influenza pandemic. If we tie these and the legal issues together, we can see that the mosaic begins to materialize. The six coverage vulnerabilities are as follows: overestimation, a determination to overemphasize information, leading to a false conclusion; underestimation, business analysts or leadership completely misreads the probability that an event will occur; overconfidence, bad assumptions based on our own certainty on how we would handle the situation; complacency, something is going to happen although we are not sure what or when, and no action is taken; ignorance, when there is virtually no intelligence, and we are at the mercy of events; and failure to join the dots, failure to make connections between bits of intelligence to make a coherent whole (mosaic).[3] We will now look at each in detail.

Overestimation is generally driven by media hype, and overemphasis on information presented can create false conclusions or, as I refer to them, false positives. An excellent example of a false positive is this statement, taken from an article in *CSO* magazine:

> About two-thirds (67 percent) of *Fortune* 1000 executives say their companies are more prepared now than before 9/11 to access critical data in a disaster situation. The majority (60 percent) say they have a command team in place to maintain information continuity operations from a remote location if a disaster occurs. Close to three quarters of executives (71 percent) discuss disaster policies and procedures at executive-level meetings, and 62 percent have increased their budgets for preventing loss of information availability.[4]

Because we are asking the wrong questions precisely, we are getting the wrong answers precisely; as a result, we are creating false positives. A false positive is created when you ask a question that has an answer that appears to satisfy the intent of the question. We often do not understand the information that we are getting because we frame the questions that we ask in such a way that the answers provided are satisfying but do not really answer the true question. For example, a study was conducted by Swiss scientists for a Swiss bank recently that revealed that a "normal flu virus" could survive for up to two weeks on used banknotes under the right circumstances. Does this mean that all banknotes will react in the same manner? No, but it is an indication that banknotes should be analyzed to determine what characteristics they have that will react with a normal flu virus. U.S. banknotes may use different paper or different ink, and these could react differently with the virus. However, a false positive is created if you ask whether banknotes will react to a normal flu virus and get a positive answer that is based on limited information availability.

Another example of a false positive leading to overestimation is the WHO report of confirmed human cases of avian influenza. This information is provided in a weekly table that the WHO publishes, providing statistics on the current situation regarding H5N1 and human cases (for an example, see Table 1.2). This table can be very misleading for the reader who looks only at the numbers, because they would lead you to believe there is a low probability of an influenza pandemic occurring. However, when you read the footnotes to the table, you will see that the WHO only reports laboratory-confirmed cases.

Establishing objective criteria is the first defense against overemphasizing or becoming blinded by your own convictions or those of others, either positively or negatively. Enterprise risk management procedures

establish a standard and easy-to-understand methodology to systematically identify, qualify, and quantify risk. Look at three criteria: impact,
likelihood of occurrence, and estimated effectiveness of preparations.
They can help you create an objective estimation of the risks you face.

Underestimation has almost the same result as overestimation, except
that you may find yourself in the reactive state that the event actually
happened. Not paying attention to or downplaying the indicators can
result in an underestimation of the probability that an event will occur,
the impact that it will have, and the estimated effectiveness of your ability to respond. The media facilitates underestimation of occurrence by
picking up and then dropping an issue, such as H5N1, as a "hot" news
item. It is more interesting to cover the celebrity going to jail or the poli-
tician citing how poorly the current administration is performing than
to continue coverage of H5N1 and the culling of poultry or the death of
one or two individuals who became infected. Wait until the media
decides to "hype" the issue because it has again become newsworthy
(and then overestimation of a bad outcome may take root).

Most enterprises tend to be overconfident when it comes to their ability to respond to disruptive events. This may be the result of embedded
culture, having survived disruptions in the past, or assuming that
adequate planning has been accomplished. The issue with an influenza
pandemic is simple: most of us have never faced it, therefore we do not
have any idea, other than historical accounts, as to what it will be like.
History, at best, gives us a retrospective view. We must realize that the
world today is vastly different from 1918 and even 1968 when the last
pandemic occurred. As such, we are probably overconfident that our
healthcare system can solve the problem before it becomes widespread.
We may be so overconfident with our successes that we fail to analyze
accurately what caused them. We should also take heed that few if any
researchers study the traits present in failure; this is partially because of
the lack of documentation on the traits of failures. Although there are
numerous studies on specific causes of failure, they may fail to
adequately determine all the influencing factors that resulted in the failure. This is attributable to the lack of interest in publishing information
on failed experiments. We focus on successful outcomes but fail to
document the failed outcomes because there is generally not much interest in research or other efforts that yield no results. Imagine trying to
sell a weight-loss product that does not "guarantee" results. Your ad-
vertisement would not make it to the TV screen.

Complacency must be feared. You do not have to take action on every
risk, but you do need to quantify and measure your current risk and
compare it with your thresholds of acceptable risk to decide whether to
monitor and take action if the risk is adequate. Using software to stand-
ardize the process and capture risk issues helps formalize the process
and target issues for follow-up. Software helps manage the workflow of

assigning roles and responsibilities as well as follow-up notifications and tracking. However, you must be careful with software so as not to become too dependent on it. It is only as good as the programmer who developed it. You may not capture all the risks or manage all the workflow unless they are all contained in the database that is created. Complacency can also occur from too heavy a dependence on the output of software programs. In his book *Management and the Activity Trap*, George Odiorne discussed how processes can become activity traps:

- Processes and procedures are developed to achieve an objective (usually in support of a strategic objective).
- Over time, goals and objectives change to reflect changes in the market and new opportunities. However, the processes and procedures continue on.
- Eventually, procedures become a goal in themselves—doing an activity for the sake of the activity rather than what it accomplishes.[5]

We have a tendency to become complacent because we are in a comfort zone. We need to acknowledge this and focus our attention on what needs to be done to address the potential issue (influenza pandemic) and see also that, by addressing this issue, we can build a framework that will allow us to recognize opportunities and potential pitfalls much earlier and therefore be better able to respond to them. W. Edwards Deming (widely recognized as the father of quality control) may have summed it best: "Having lost sight of our goal, we redoubled our efforts."

Deming recognized the folly in working for the sake of procedure rather than finding the goal and making every effort to achieve it. Too often today, contingency planning reflects the "activity trap." The "business of the business" has never been part of the planning process, because planners never recognized they are engulfed by the company's activities rather than its objectives. Until planners understand and recognize the difference, the company they support will be complacent with its capabilities to respond, manage, recover, and restore its operations based on a false assumption that the markets served and the products/services offered will always be in demand.

Ignorance is also to be feared. New and novel viruses emerge. Viruses survive by mutating. We can look at history, but it will be of little help when we are faced with something that is new; it is an unknown with which we have no experience. With the emergence of H5N1 as a potential threat, there is more need for active analysis and constantly scanning the horizon for news of the new. Remember Taleb's words: "In real life you do not know the odds; you need to discover them, and the sources of uncertainty are not defined." We need to ensure that our enterprise takes into account information that does not necessarily relate to it. For example, Microsoft or Yahoo could have purchased Google but failed to see how Google fit into their business models. Both have since begun to look for acquisition targets that do not seem to relate to their businesses. There are many instances of not being able to take into account information that appears unrelated. All one has to do is study the history books and the numerous times in war that we have failed to see what is right there; the surprise offensive in the Ardennes in 1914, the invasion of the Soviet Union, and Pearl Harbor all are examples of failure to recognize information that is seemingly not related to the situation.

Failure to join the dots is a problem for most organizations. Joining the dots is what creating a mosaic is about. Too many enterprises are silo based: everyone stays in their own knowledge/discipline/division silos, which makes sharing information very difficult as a result of a perceived lack of need to communicate with other areas.

Many times there is a dependency between a risk in one business area with a risk in another business area, or there is a compound risk of two separate but identical risks in separate areas occurring at the same time that can be worse than either risk individually. Aggregating this information up to interactive monitoring systems (dashboards) and flexible reporting that can filter and present risk segmented by risk or by risk dependencies is invaluable in seeing the big picture. Intelligence entities do this well for the most part. Creating and implementing an active analysis program that is focused on issues management comprise one way to expand the role of your risk management department and get them more involved in providing information to the operational elements of the organization. Active analysis creates situational awareness in the organization. Situational awareness is the ability to identify, process, and comprehend the critical elements of information about what is happening and apply this information to the focus of the organization. Simply stated, it is knowing what is going on around you.

Why do businesses fail? Because they are unprepared to deal with changes in how they operate. These changes are generally brought on by innovation and/or urgency. The drivers for change can be internal, external, or a combination thereof. These drivers are controlled or uncontrolled, predictable or unpredictable. They are often overlooked, leading to a failure to anticipate. RTO and RPO mean relatively little compared with customer tolerance level (CTL) and MTO. CTL can be determined by how many delays or disruptions to service a customer is willing to put up with before finding another vendor. MTO is predicated on how long a customer can be without your service and/or product before they seek alternatives.

What does a business require to not fail? Recognize that most disruptive events that occur in business will not trigger the activation of an organization's business continuity plan, regardless of the severity of the event, unless the business continuity plan is integrated into the way the organization does its business. To succeed, a business must have the following: the ability to anticipate change; the ability to recognize information that is of value; the ability to be innovative/responsive in the face of rapidly changing business circumstances; the ability to recognize complexity impacts, because complex processes can become cumbersome, often leading to the creation of activity traps (doing a process for the sake of the process instead of what the process should accomplish); and the ability to recognize and change processes that no longer accomplish what they were initially designed to do as a result of changing business circumstances.

At the current level of planning that constitutes most business continuity plans today, the use of the word "strategy" is a misnomer. Rather than misuse the term strategy, use the term "execution." This is because most business continuity plans that are developed focus on executable steps for the recovery of systems, whether they are processes, applications, hardware, or work space (including buildings). Few business continuity plans actually focus on strategic issues. This is often attributable to the fact that they are designed to be implemented after the fact, not in a preventative manner.

Transparent Vulnerabilities

As a transition to the next section, I will close here with a brief introduction to what I term "transparent vulnerabilities." Transparent vulnerabilities are so obvious that they are easily overlooked: we see them when they are pointed out; we recognize them when we are aware of them; and we fail to acknowledge them, leading to potentially significant consequences when the vulnerability is realized.

Examples of transparent vulnerabilities include the following: lack of depth in skill sets within an organization (e.g., agricultural inspectors, underwriters, mailroom, cleaning staff); planning assumptions that are not validated; human reactions affecting decision making; and false positives created by asking the right question and getting an answer that does not reflect the reality that exists.

We fail to see the vulnerability because we discount it. For example, agricultural inspectors are critical to ensuring that produce gets to market, yet this is not a career path that many choose to pursue. Hence, there is a lack of depth in the skill set. If a pandemic strikes and agricultural inspectors are ill and cannot work, produce may not get to market. This in turn creates "availability risk," which means food may not be available to consumers. The time to replace a product will have an impact on its value. For example, if crops are deemed contaminated, the time to replace is a complete growing season.

Dependencies are not fully realized or clearly understood in most planning processes. For example, Internet access may be limited to priority of service based on need; access restrictions may be imposed, certain IP addresses may be blacklisted, and there is the last-mile consideration (infrastructure not capable of supporting numerous new users; other considerations are maintenance and operability of the infrastructure with a degraded workforce, for example attributable to sickness).

In the next section, I will draw examples reflecting the complexity of issues that we could face in a pandemic. The aspect of complexity creates a high potential for the cascade of negative effects to mutate as they migrate through the various sectors. This is going to be one of the great challenges for business and government during a pandemic: literally, learning to manage what we do not know.

Phase 3—Worst Case: Collapse (320–600 days)

Chapter 3 left us at 320 days. As the pandemic continues seemingly unabated, the world suddenly becomes larger as localization takes root. Realizing that surviving the pandemic will require a rethinking of business strategies, many sectors see a reverse in trend as large, integrated companies are forced to downsize and localize. As the world settles in to this new reality, more adjustments are made. The United Nations, WHO, CDC, and other entities, although still combating outbreaks, are less effective because of local constraints put in place.

Governments, businesses, and consumers readjust to the realities of changes in economic models. Goods and services revert more and more to reflect the localization brought on by disruptions to transportation channels. Although it is no longer business as usual, some local economies begin to revitalize as access to raw materials or changes in demand are compensated for by readily available products. Supply chain adjustments continue to be made as countries dependent on external resources are seeing the balance of power shift. Consumer societies are being forced to face sobering realities.

Death tolls may again begin to rise as local efforts to stem the continued pandemic and deal with normal medical issues are faced with lack of materials (e.g., vaccine and medicines) caused by the impact of the past 320 days of the pandemic.

In this phase, paralysis might give way to collapse as localization changes the economic model. Collapse is not to be viewed as a return to the Stone Age; rather, it is a collapse of global trading systems and a refocusing of these systems to address a more local and/or regional marketplace. The economies (bodies at rest) slowly create localized movement. This movement is limited because of the impact of the pandemic, local restrictions, and the localization of good and services that may lead to a change in consumer mentality.

The world begins to realize that the energy being expended on localization could form the basis for the regeneration of the global economy.

Trade talks between consumer and supplier nations dominate the day. Financial concerns in the transportation industry are of major focus as trade routes are dependent on getting national and international transportation systems recovered. This action revives and expands local economies but does not instantaneously return us to the pre-pandemic days.

The global economy is still faced with answering this significant question: "How to restart an intricate and complex system that has evolved over time such that it can manage the stresses associated with its functioning?" Furthermore, the global economy may begin to question which country should lead and manage this undertaking.

The following tables, from the U.S. Congressional Budget Office, provide some evidence of what has been done to determine some of the demand issues during mild and severe pandemic scenarios.

Table 4.2 depicts mild and severe pandemic impacts on economic sectors.

It is important to understand the impact of demand on today's complex worldwide economy. One thing that is often overlooked is what happens to healthy workers who are in economic sectors in which demand has dropped significantly, creating a surplus of workers. Will they be able to readily transfer their skills to sectors hit hard and regain lost earning power? Will they require significant training to accomplish new tasks? Will jobs be out of reach because of an inability to relocate resulting from government or self-imposed travel restrictions? Will fear of exposure keep people from doing anything except subsistence activities?

Table 4.2. Assumptions Underlying Estimates of the Supply-Side Impact of an Avian Flu Pandemic

Economic Sector	Gross Attack Rate (%)		Weeks Out of Work		Case Fatality Rate (%)	
	Severe	Mild	Severe	Mild	Severe	Mild
Nonfarm Business	30	25	3	0.75	2.5	1.14
Farm	10	5	1	0.25	2.5	1.14
Household	30	25	3	0.75	2.5	1.14
Nonprofit Institutions	30	25	3	0.75	2.5	1.14
Government	30	25	3	0.75	2.5	1.14

Source: Congressional Budget Office.

Note: Gross attack rate is the percentage of the population that is infected with a disease. The case fatality rate is the percentage of persons who eventually die from the disease or complications.

Table 4.3 illustrates mild and severe pandemic scenario impacts on demand from economic sectors. The Congressional Budget Office study addresses primarily the United States, failing to acknowledge that we are essentially a consumption economy that gets most of our goods from overseas suppliers. We need to assess what the lack of demand will have for the long-term global trade.

Note that the severe scenario described in Table 4.3 is a pandemic that is similar to the 1918–1919 Spanish Flu outbreak. It incorporates the assumption that a particularly virulent strain of influenza infects approximately 90 million people in the United States and kills more than 2 million of them. The mild scenario describes a pandemic that

Table 4.3. Assumed Declines in Demand, by Industry, in the Event of an Avian Flu Pandemic

Economic Sector	Percent (%) Decline Severe Scenario	Percent (%) Decline Mild Scenario
Private Industries	10	3
Agriculture	10	3
Mining	0	0
Utilities	10	3
Construction	10	3
Manufacturing	10	3
Wholesale Trade	10	3
Retail Trade	10	3
Transportation and Warehousing		
Air	67	17
Rail	67	17
Transit	67	17
Information (Published, Broadcast)	0	0
Finance	0	0
Professional and Business Services	0	0
Educational/Healthcare		
Education	0	0
Healthcare	−15	−4
Arts/Entertainment/Accommodation/Food		
Arts and Recreation	80	20
Accommodation	80	20
Food Service	80	20
Other Services Except Government	5	1
Government		
Federal	0	0
State and Local	0	0

Source: Congressional Budget Office.

resembles the outbreaks of 1957–1958 and 1968–1969. It incorporates the assumption that 75 million people become infected and about 100,000 of them die from illness or complications.

What is missing from the table above? Frankly, a lot. What about water transport or Internet firms (perhaps contained within the category "Professional and Business Services")? Also not taken into account is the impact of declining U.S. demand for foreign goods from countries that depend on the United States for much of their trade. What about foreign aid? Will it be curtailed or will the United States continue to have the same presence on the world stage as it does today?

Sector Analysis (320–600 days)

The financial sector may shrink as international conglomerates are forced to divest and localize. This sector is still faced with regaining the confidence of the investing public. Banks and other financial institutions still face solvency issues. Governments and institutions such as the World Bank and International Monetary Fund are faced with controlling inflationary trends. The recessionary period could have an extended life because of reluctance on the part of consumers.

The manufacturing sector is still faced with access to normal streams of raw materials issues and dependency on transportation systems that remain affected by local outbreaks of the flu. Cottage industries begin to grow in strength and vitality. Localized economies reflect some of the robustness of the global economy but are still limited because of resources, workforce, goods, and services demands.

The service sector may dwindle as the workforce is assimilated into the manufacturing sector to survive. Volume demand is still the major issue.

The telecommunications sector recovers as it localizes much as the utility sector. Cellular communications are in high demand because fixed infrastructure is still faced with loss of connectivity issues as a result of loss of and/or sporadic disruption of support infrastructure such as electrical power. Telecommuting begins to adjust to the realities of infrastructure availability.

The insurance sector continues to be buffeted by the overwhelming task of claims processing with limited human resources. This continues to affect healthcare providers dependent on insurance payments to continue operations.

The healthcare sector faces sporadic jumps in patient volume as the pandemic hits a second wave of outbreaks. Healthcare supplies become increasingly difficult to acquire because of production constraints.

The energy sector continues to face supply (raw materials), transformation (refining raw materials into useable energy), and transportation issues. Commodity prices continue to fluctuate based on spot demand.

The utility sector continues to face infrastructure strains as demand begins to increase as workforces return to some office functions. Brownouts and blackouts are a regular occurrence and are now viewed as part of life versus a crisis situation.

The agriculture sector sees localization develop unique markets for products. Seasonal demands for food products are unchanged. The United States continues to suffer regional spot outages.

The education sector faces limited capability to reopen because teacher shortages and fearful parents may keep students away from educational institutions. Government use of commandeered facilities continues.

The high-technology sector faces continuing high demand for access and support related to the Internet. Support services could reach marginal levels because of continued workforce disruption.

By the time that we enter the twentieth month (600 days) of the pandemic, the impact on the global economy will have changed the operations of all sectors. Localization of economies has become the norm and is creating a baseline of inertia that could propel the recovery of the global economy. Again, remember that none of this factors in any naturally occurring phenomena such as weather-related and natural-disaster situations, either of which are likely to exacerbate difficulties in the local economies.

Paralysis, despair, and retrenchment are replaced with local revitalization and rediscovery during this timeframe.

PART 2: PANDEMIC PREPAREDNESS PLANNING TOOLS

Part 2 of this chapter presents a planning template that I have found useful for developing a structure that facilitates planning and identification of commitments that are contained in the planning documentation. The examples are focused on human capital. However, you can easily modify the templates to include the other areas of focus that the pandemic taskforce could be charged with addressing. A discussion of Logical Management Systems' *AUDITRAK*™ program is provided as an example of how you can organize your planning materials into a structure that enables clustering of components into areas of analysis and supporting information elements. Last, this section delves into some tools for "commitment identification" and tracking. It will be important for your organization to identify its commitments and to track the completion and/or monitoring of commitments to ensure that they are accomplished over time.

Pandemic Preparedness Documentation

Let us turn our attention back to pandemic preparedness efforts in your organization. To achieve a standard of focus for pandemic preparedness, I have found it useful to create documentation that serves to enable thought on the part of the personnel who are developing the strategies, materials, and training programs.

This usually takes the form of a template package consisting of six areas of focus, accompanied by supporting documents that are used to capture and record information. The six areas of focus for each template package, outlined in Chapter 3, are strategy, policies, communications, training, resources, and outreach. The responsibility of the pandemic taskforce is to bring together this information and to create a planning format that can be fitted to the organization and its extended value chain. The challenge will be to ensure that there is consistency within, between, and externally with the downstream (customers and stakeholders) elements, as well as the upstream (suppliers and vendors) elements. This is an iterative process. It does not stop; rather, it continues to build and change to reflect new information and changes in the situation. The following examples are provided to illustrate the template format and describe the instructions for use of each form:

- Template use: The interviewer/developer uses the template when preparing information related to a specific element of the enterprise, for example, human capital or public relations.

- Documentation status: This is required for the final documentation package.

- Instructions: Complete all the forms contained in this template. A copy should be retained in your files, and a copy of all documentation should be forwarded to the pandemic preparedness taskforce for incorporation into the overall pandemic preparedness plan/documentation. Please note that your pandemic preparedness planning should be incorporated into existing contingency plans and not treated as a stand-alone process. Existing plans need to be updated to include the planning concepts that are contained in the pandemic planning materials. Careful documentation of considerations will facilitate accurate planning for the pre-pandemic, pandemic, and post-pandemic requirements for the enterprise. Should you require assistance, contact the pandemic preparedness taskforce.

- Contents: The package contains the following master forms:

  o Essential Elements of Analysis Worksheet Form (Table 4.4)

  o Questionnaire Form (Table 4.5)

  o Resource Allocation Form (Table 4.6)

  o Scenario Form (Table 4.7)

  o Evaluation Form (Table 4.8)

  o Commitment Identification/Tracking Form (Table 4.9)

The examples below will be used in subsequent chapters to illustrate how one might populate the information that is gathered in the analysis stage.

In 1994, I created Logical Management Systems' *AUDITRAK*™, an assessment tool used to evaluate the state of crisis management programs. In subsequent years, *AUDITRAK*™ has evolved into an assessment tool for the evaluation of business continuity, crisis management, emergency preparedness, and crisis media management. The following definitions are provided for the essential elements of analysis (EEA) form that has been modified from the *AUDITRAK*™ package to address pandemic preparedness requirements.[6]

Table 4.4. Essential Elements of Analysis Form

	Pre-Pandemic	Pandemic	Post-Pandemic
Strategy			
Strategic Plan			
Grand Tactical Plan			
Tactical Plan			
Corporate Policies			
Regulatory Compliance			
Operationally Specific Policy			
Other Policy Considerations			
Communication			
Employee			
Third Party			
Other Considerations			
Training			
Employee			
Third Party			
Other Considerations			
Resources			
Staff Augmentation			
Equipment			
Budget			
Outreach			
Internal Touch Points			
External Touch Points			
Other Considerations			

Table 4.5. Questionnaire Form

Pre-Pandemic Planning		
Question	**Yes**	**No**
Has XYZ developed a pandemic contingency plan supplement to existing business continuity plans?		
Has XYZ identified personnel to staff a crisis management team(s) in the event of a pandemic?		
Has XYZ developed position function, duty, and task procedures for the crisis management team(s)?		
Has XYZ developed an exercise schedule for the crisis management team(s)?		
Has XYZ conducted an assessment of all areas of its business to determine the impact of a pandemic on operations?		
Are all applicable regulatory (HIPAA, OSHA, etc.) guidelines referenced or addressed in your planning?		
Has liaison with multilateral health organizations been established?		
Do XYZ's plans incorporate the latest available information?		
Has XYZ developed individual department plans?		
Does XYZ have operations located in multitenant facilities (risk of exposure may be greater in a multitenant facility)?		
Has XYZ prepared a succession plan for senior executives and managers?		
Has XYZ developed a repopulation of the workforce strategy and plan?		
Has XYZ established a plan for contacting family members and/or employees (at home, etc.)?		
Has XYZ considered the operational and economic impact of a pandemic?		
Has XYZ evaluated budgets in accordance with the potential economic impact of a pandemic?		
Does XYZ have a strategy for how supplies and essential products are to be stockpiled?		
Does XYZ maintain a plan for a backup Emergency Operations Center (EOC) site?		

Policy Issues during a Pandemic		
Question	**Yes**	**No**
Does XYZ have a plan for the rapid recruitment of additional workers during the pandemic?		
Does XYZ have a plan that will support telecommuting?		
Does XYZ have a plan for employee compensation?		

Continued

Table 4.5. (*continued*)

Has XYZ assessed what employee sick leave or other absences would do to operations during a pandemic?		
Has XYZ surveyed its employees regarding family issues if a pandemic occurs?		
Has XYZ developed a supplement addressing stakeholder and public relations issues during the pandemic?		
Does each XYZ office have a line of succession for key positions at the facility?		
Have XYZ employees had their roles and responsibilities during a pandemic explained to them and documented?		
Does XYZ have a plan to implement resource controls during a pandemic?		
Does XYZ have a plan on how to identify and preserve essential records?		
Does XYZ back up all essential records at an offsite location?		

Protecting Employees during a Pandemic		
Question	**Yes**	**No**
Does XYZ encourage staff to receive flu shots?		
Does XYZ provide funding to pay for employee annual flu shots?		
Is XYZ capable of providing flu shots on site at all facilities?		
Does XYZ have proper sanitizing equipment?		
Does XYZ have hand sanitizers in common areas?		
Do all XYZ facilities have a quarantine procedure?		
Have all XYZ facilities coordinated with local authorities to determine how XYZ will be affected by a quarantine order?		

The EEA form (Table 4.4) has been created to assess the six areas of focus against a time matrix consisting of three periods: pre-pandemic, pandemic (consider here the waves that may occur), and post-pandemic. It is important to note that previous pandemics have ranged from 500 to 800 days in duration. A look at history can provide value in preparing the EEA form. Table 4.6 depicts the form in its basic format. Customize the subheadings to fit your organization.

The second form is designed to be a thought generator for the pandemic taskforce. It is a questionnaire that can be used to assess the current knowledge base of the enterprise regarding pandemic preparedness.

Table 4.6. Human Capital/Resource Allocation Form

OBJECTIVE 1: ESSENTIAL FUNCTIONS	Output

OBJECTIVE 1: ESSENTIAL FUNCTIONS

Identify and prioritize priority and secondary human resource essential functions

Identify functional interdependencies that support division essential functions

Identify required staffing to support essential functions

OBJECTIVE 2: MINIMIZING LOSS

Develop HR policies, plans, and guidance

Develop and maintain local-level HR pandemic response plans and implementation plans

OBJECTIVE 3: EXECUTING SUCCESSION/ DELEGATIONS OF AUTHORITY

Develop HR leadership succession plan

Review and distribute HR delegations of authority(ies) guidance

OBJECTIVE 4: MITIGATING OPERATIONS INTERRUPTIONS

Develop and maintain HR guidance for mitigating disruptions to essential functions

OBJECTIVE 5: ALTERNATE FACILITIES

Develop alternate facility guidance for HR needs

OBJECTIVE 6: PROTECTION OF ASSETS

Develop an HR vital records and databases management plan

OBJECTIVE 7: XYZ RECOVERY

Develop an HR repopulation plan procedure

OBJECTIVE 8: RESTORATION

Develop HR guidance for a timely and orderly restoration to reestablish full service without interruption of essential functions

Identify vendor/contract support, as required

OBJECTIVE 9: TRAINING AND EXERCISES (T&E)

Develop a schedule to provide training, drills, and exercises to support the implementation of HR pandemic plans

Table 4.7. Human Capital/Resources Scenario Form Proprietary—Confidential
XYZ Pandemic Plan Scenario Form

Scenario Type	Activity	✓	Comments
Pre-Pandemic	Response:		
Pandemic	Management:		
Post-Pandemic	Recovery:		
	Restoration:		
	Combination:		

Scenario Information:

I. Highlights:

Highlights of the current situation.

II. Summary of Current Situation:

Separate paragraphs for each category below. Additional categories may be created to supplement the below categories.

A. Corporate: Detailed analysis of the current achievement of corporate objectives in relation to stakeholder—subscriber, group, member (downstream value chain) demands with comments on projected activity in the next [insert a timeframe].

B. Business Unit: Detailed analysis of the current business unit activities with comments on projected activity in the next [insert a timeframe].

C. Business Unit Team(s): Detailed analysis of specific facility level situations with comments on projected activity in the next [insert a timeframe].

D. Upstream Value Chain: Customer/Supplier/Vendor Analysis: Detailed analysis of situation with comments on projected activity in the next [insert a timeframe].

E. Special Considerations: Detailed analysis of the special considerations, such as disruptive events, pending regulations, geopolitical trends, issues that could affect HR continuity with comments on projected activity in the next [insert a timeframe].

Proprietary—Confidential

The third form is designed to be an outline generator for the pandemic taskforce. It addresses the nine objectives that can be used to develop pandemic preparedness plans for the enterprise. The example below depicts human capital/resources.

The fourth form is designed to allow the pandemic taskforce representatives to develop various scenarios that may play out in a pandemic situation. This form can be used to develop drills and exercises.

Table 4.8. Human Capital/Resources Evaluation Worksheet Form

Human Resource Evaluation Worksheet	
Resource	**Comment**

Additional Comments

Date:
Name:
Pandemic Plan:
Business Function(s):

The fifth form is designed to facilitate the identification of required resources that will be needed during the pre-pandemic, pandemic, and post-pandemic periods. Remember that resources can be defined broadly; everything from people to capital (cash) should be listed.

The sixth form is designed to be completed after the other forms and pandemic preparedness documentation are developed. This form should be quite useful because it focuses on the identification of commitments, the status of the commitment, and related information. It is important that the enterprise address the commitments that it makes in its pandemic preparedness efforts. Each commitment represents a potential legal obligation that must be fulfilled. For example, if your enterprise commits to procuring hand sanitizer but fails to actually

Table 4.9. Commitment Identification/Tracking Form

Task Description	Task Owner	Start Date	End Date	Status	Comments
Items on commit-ment tracking list Documentation	Name or Initials	Scheduled	Scheduled	O = open C = closed	
Review					
Review					
Review [INSERT ITEMS AS NECESSARY]					

COMMITMENT IDENTIFICATION/TRACKING FORM

☐ Use: Document commitments identified.

☐ Documentation Status: Required in the final documentation package.

☐ Instructions: Complete the following form identifying the task owner, start/end dates, status, and any comments associated with the task to be completed. Biweekly status meetings with task owners to ensure that tasks are being addressed and completed should be scheduled. Completed tasks should be validated during the next drill/exercise (as applicable).

procure the hand sanitizer, there could be a legal liability for failure to ensure a safe workplace.

Table 4.9 below highlights the commitment identification/tracking methodology that has been used successfully in the past.

Concluding Thoughts

In this chapter, we have presented tools for organizing the pandemic planning effort. The decisions required of the pandemic taskforce to enable a broader approach to planning necessitate broader oversight and an understanding of global perspectives that most organizations do not generally focus on in the planning process. Management can provide assistance to the taskforce by facilitating the development of broader-based enterprise risk management activities that include strategy management.

Ability to execute the pandemic plan will be the most important driver of organizational performance during the pandemic timeframe. Organizational strategy is important; strategy execution in a pandemic will be critical. Strategy must be linked to strategy execution.

5

The Danger of Reassortment

Reassortment of viruses means that viruses of different types exchange genetic material resulting in a genetically different virus. In the case of bird flu, the fear is that a person could be infected with two viruses at the same time (co-infected), a virulent bird flu virus and a common human flu virus resulting in the exchange of genetic information between the two. The exchange of genetic material could result in a deadly virus that is as easily transmissible from one person to another as the common seasonal flu viruses.

— Centers for Disease Control[1]

Reassortment, as the quotation above suggests, is a simple concept to understand but one whose impact can be devastating.

Although the medical definition of reassortment is important to understand because it could lead to new viruses, there is another kind of reassortment that is also of critical importance: reassortment of our social and economic systems as a result of the impact of the pandemic event. Although we do not know what the impacts will be and can only speculate about their effects, history suggests that we could see many grand-scale changes and shocks to the socioeconomic structure that we currently have. For those who want to look back, I suggest that you look at the Great Plague as an example of societal and economic change.

Previous pandemic events have been studied, and there is an indication that multiple waves occur, during which there are varying degrees of human impact. The human factor is what I will focus on in this chapter. It is important to note that few, if any, contingency plans (e.g., business continuity, disaster recovery, emergency response, risk management) ever really focus on human factors. This is partially attributable to the fact that human factors are difficult to plan for.

What are human factors? For our purposes, human factors are those that deal with and relate to critical decision making, resource allocation, skill sets, and moral/ethical issues. Concerns range from the trivial (getting your iPod to work) to areas of such vital importance as providing equipment to assist anesthesiologists in monitoring patients. If the importance of the latter task is not immediately obvious, consider that 98,000 people die in surgery every year in the United States alone and that most of these fatalities are caused by avoidable human error.[2]

Humans are the focus of a pandemic. A pandemic does not kill or create health effects for machinery, computers, information, or industry. A pandemic is a result of the infection of living things, both humans and animals. At the time of writing, poultry and wild fowl have suffered well over 200 million deaths as a result of H5N1 infection. Although the human toll has been much less, the potential is growing with each outbreak that the H5N1 virus will mutate into a form that is easily transmissible from human to human. Should this occur, the shocks to our global socioeconomic structure could be immense. However, it is we who will feel the reverberations from a pandemic, directly and indirectly. This is what our planning should focus on. Although a pandemic may last for the 500–800 days that I use as a marker for this book, the socioeconomic consequences will occur over a far greater timeframe. The pandemic might be over as far as sickness and death, but the socioeconomic consequences will last for years, perhaps decades. That is what this book is about: getting people to understand that a pandemic is not about hospital responses (although they are important) but is about economic consequences that will be with us for decades after the pandemic ends.

Reducing human error during the pandemic timeframe (500–800 days) and the post-pandemic period of recovery, restoration, and conditional realignment of socioeconomic systems (perhaps a decade) will be critical to the survival of your enterprise. We will be in a weakened state on a global basis, which will provide a fertile field for opportunists, for either the good or the bad. This is probably the most important element of pandemic planning. Having a plan to survive the pandemic is important from a tactical and grand tactical point of view. Your organization must be able to continue executing its operations to survive. However, unless you address the strategic issue of human factors (human capital, decision making, succession, and skill sets), your organization may be unable to emerge from the pandemic period into the post-pandemic period positioned to leverage its successes.

The remainder of this chapter is focused on the various aspects of the human element. I realize that this will not be a comprehensive discussion into all aspects of human capital, decision making, or human factors. My intent here is to introduce some of the key issues regarding how humans influence the contingency planning process and how we are influenced by our decisions, both conscious and unconscious.

DO YOU FEEL COMFORTABLE ANSWERING THESE QUESTIONS?

Can you answer the following ten questions with a level of comfort that the human factors issues have been addressed in your current contingency plans? When you read the questions, read them with human factors in mind; I think you will find that your answers may change.

Table 5.1. The Unrecognized Influence of Human Factors on Contingency Planning

Question	Response
Has your organization established written standards for managing long-term business disruptions?	
Does your organization have succession, chain of command, or other sequential authority, decision rights, etc., plans?	
Has your organization developed a repopulation of the workforce plan?	
Is your organization dependent on external resources to support its critical business functions?	
Has your organization identified time-critical functions that, if disrupted, would create a crisis?	
Has your organization identified time-sensitive functions that, if disrupted, would create a crisis?	
Has your organization identified time-dependent functions that, if disrupted, would create a crisis?	
Could the loss of a core business function have a cascading effect throughout your organization?	
Does your organization have a contingency plan that addresses the loss of critical external infrastructures?	
Does your organization have a contingency plan that addresses the loss of critical internal infrastructures?	

(Continued)

Table 5.1 (*continued*)

Question	Response
Does your organization have adequate funds in reserve, or access to capital resources to be able to operate for a period of 30 days? Does your organization have a contingency plan that addresses the management of the consequences of an event (short term to long term)?	

Market research indicates that only a small portion (5 percent) of businesses today have a viable contingency plan, but virtually 100 percent now realize they are at risk. By seizing the initiative and getting involved in all the phases of crisis management, HR professionals facilitate the development and implementation of processes that can mitigate or prevent major losses.

THE ROLE OF HUMAN RESOURCES IN PANDEMIC MANAGEMENT

Traditionally, the human resources department has had a limited role in crisis-management activities, mainly addressing the humanitarian assistance aspects of crisis response. However, when we rethink the role that human resources will play in a pandemic, we see that the human resources' pandemic management role is going to be more than humanitarian assistance.

The role of human resources in preparing for, during, and in the aftermath of a pandemic should focus on a comprehensive structuring of initiatives designed to establish and maintain resilience between and among all the touch points of the enterprise. Figure 5.1 depicts the common functions at the three levels: strategic, grand tactical, and tactical. Although each level has different focus and agenda issues, the commonality of functions is essentially the same.

Each organization must develop variations on the simple model depicted in the graphic. However, every organization must also have an intimate understanding of the human side of crisis management to create resilience. This depends on aligning three spheres: interest (the assets and capabilities of others can affect your courses of action), influence (your assets and capabilities can affect the courses of action of others), and responsibility (your organization's mission, vision, and values). A plan will not provide resilience; resilience is realized only through the sustained, collective actions of an organization's human

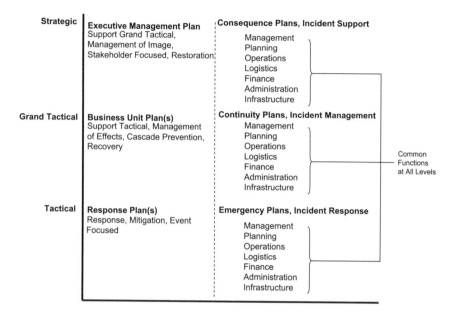

Figure 5.1. Common Functions Addressed at All Levels of Crisis Management

resources, who must respond to, manage, recover from, and restore the organization's capabilities when a crisis strikes.

Below, in summary form, is a list of nine practices, tools, and techniques that can be adapted to a variety of situations. Using these as a guide, human resources professionals and emergency-response planners can engage the entire organization in the crisis-management process.

(1) Focus on human factors systematically. Any crisis creates people issues. Dealing with these issues on a reactive basis puts the organization at risk. To be successful, communications channels must be responsive. This requires data collection, analysis, collation, and effective distribution of information, to inform and enable strategic decision making.

(2) Communicate "top down and bottom up." Because crises are inherently unsettling for people at all levels of an organization, CEOs and their leadership teams must speak with one voice. The executive team also needs to understand that communication comes up through the organization, and this chain consists of individuals who are going through stressful times and need to be supported. Seamless vertical and horizontal communications consisting of common terminology and clearly defined goals is critical.

(3) Engage every level. As a crisis progresses, it affects different levels of the organization and the value chain. HR personnel can be instrumental in assisting management in identifying leaders throughout the

company to ensure that appropriate crisis response is implemented. This will prevent "crisis cascades" through the organization.

(4) Establish a value proposition. Although corporate management knows that having a comprehensive program for business continuity is a worthwhile expense, most organizations have not dedicated the resources to developing and maintaining such a program. Articulating a formal case for a establishing a comprehensive program provides valuable opportunities to create alignment at all levels in the organization and with external partners. In doing so, follow three steps. First, confront reality. Second, provide a road map to guide behavior and decision making. Third, communicate to internal and external audiences, in terms that matter to the individuals. These three steps not only can be used to convince management of the value of a continuity planning program, but they can serve as a check and balance for the development of your program. For example, confronting reality is essential in developing realistic assessments and analysis (business impact assessment; risk, threat, vulnerability, and hazard analysis). Confronting reality is also valuable when communicating the focus of the continuity program to management and staff, i.e., there is a threat of a pandemic, but we have to convince management and staff that preparations to address the potential threat are of value.

One way to do this is to recognize that pandemic planning is not just for pandemics. You can use the tools presented here to develop and/or expand existing programs. On the second point, a roadmap to guide behavior and decision making, it is essential that management and staff see a light at the end of the tunnel. You need to get the buy-in of the organization. One way is to demonstrate that there is a defined path and that execution of the pandemic plan is not contingent on a pandemic being declared. You can execute a pandemic plan for a variety of wide-area disaster situations. For example, recently a client had to close offices because of an ice storm that affected multiple states. Usually, the outage from this type of event lasts a day or two; this one lasted more than a week before the offices could reopen. The employees also had to deal with extended power outages that affected their home lives. Hurricane Katrina is another example of how an area-wide event can affect behavior and decision making. Without a roadmap, you will eventually find what you are seeking, but it may not be what you need. The last point, communication, is critical for success in any circumstance. Without effective communication, things have a tendency to grind to a halt or just move along without any understanding of what is needed.

(5) Make business continuity a way of doing business, not an adjunct to the business. Creating ownership and internalizing the processes for crisis management must become ways of doing business instead of adjuncts to the business. This requires creating a critical mass among the work force. You want more than mere buy-in or passive agreement.

Ownership by leaders willing to accept responsibility for making continuity an integral element of their sphere of influence is often best created by involving people in identifying problems and crafting solutions.

(6) Communicate commitment. Top down and bottom up means that leaders make a commitment to ensuring that others understand the issues and see the direction as clearly as the leaders do. HR professionals can reinforce core messages through regular, timely communications targeted to provide employees the right information at the right time and to solicit their input and feedback.

(7) Assess the cultural landscape. It is critically important to understand culture at each level of the organization. Assessing organizational culture can have major benefits in internalizing crisis management processes and reducing resistance to change. This is the sphere of responsibility; your corporate mission, vision, and value statement is a driver for this element, defining an explicit desired culture.

(8) Prepare for the unexpected. No crisis or business continuity program ever goes completely according to plan. In a crisis, people react in unexpected ways. HR professionals need to communicate to the organization that we are no longer able to merely think about the plannable or plan for the unthinkable, but we must learn to think about the unplannable. Whether a natural or human-induced disaster, surprise is the key element in an organization's failure to anticipate effectively; effective communications through HR can facilitate the organization's willingness and ability to respond to crisis situations supported by solid decision-making processes.

(9) Personalize the message. Crises affect both the organization as a whole and the individual on a very personal level. People will react to what they see and hear around them and need to be involved in the crisis-management process. People matter; people are the key factor in an organization's success or failure in a crisis. It can be very tempting to focus on the planning process rather than address critical human issues. However, involving human resources as an integral element of the crisis-management program can make the program more responsive and less reactive.

The two tables below outline human factors issues that may become major concerns for companies and governments as they deal with the succession of waves of illness that a pandemic may bring. For convenience, I have subdivided the tables; they can be easily combined into one table for analysis.

The first, Table 5.2, identifies five factors: personnel availability, skills availability, geopolitical impacts, transport options, and logistics support. These are categorized on the vertical axis against the three levels that I have used to stratify enterprises and government organizations: strategic, grand tactical, and tactical (corporate, business unit, and department, or federal, state, and local). From a planning perspective,

Table 5.2. Human Factors Issues

Human Factors	Personnel Availability	Skills Availability	Geopolitical Impacts	Transport Options	Logistics Support
Strategic (Corporate)	Determine staff needs and resource allocation over time Set corporate goals and objectives Identify policy	Do skills inventory of what is needed long term	Ensure long-term viability of enterprise presence	Determine if commitment to provide transportation for staff is necessary. Provide for service-level agreements	Determine if temporary housing (hotel, etc.) for staff is necessary Provide for service-level agreements
Grand Tactical (Division—Business Unit)	Identify affected and unaffected staff Manage corporate goals and objectives Develop and enforce policy	Do skills inventory of what is needed short-term	Identify potential to cascade to other locations	Develop transportation plans in accordance with current strategy	Develop temporary housing plans in accordance with current strategy
Tactical (Department—Work Group)	Identify staff on hand at event inception Implement corporate goals and objectives Implement policy	Do skills inventory of what is needed immediately	Manage impact at the location where the event is occurring	Execute transportation plans in accordance with current contracts/obligations Identify air, land, and water transport available and accessible at location	Execute temporary housing plans in accordance with current contracts/obligations with vendors (hotels, etc.)

these factors should be addressed by the pandemic taskforce as part of the process that was described in Chapter 1. There, I described five steps or elements for developing a pandemic planning program. Pandemic planning is predicated on having a concept in mind for how to address the availability of people, their skill sets, and the broader issues, such as geopolitical events, that are generally beyond the purview of the typical contingency plan. Remember that a pandemic is an event of such magnitude that we have very little in recent memory with which to compare it.

Table 5.3 identifies four additional factors: personal factors, resilience issues, internal interfaces, and external interfaces. These are also categorized on the vertical axis against the three levels that I have used to stratify enterprises and government organizations: strategic, grand tactical, and tactical (corporate, business unit, and department or federal, state, and local).

The value of these tables is that they facilitate a useful categorization of issues you will need to deal with based on considerations that take into

Table 5.3. Human Factors Issues

Human Factors	Personal Factors	Resilience Issues	Internal Interfaces	External Interfaces
Strategic (Corporate)	Accept duty to accommodate	Graceful degradation—agile restoration	Identify stakeholders	Provide service-level agreements
Grand Tactical (Division—Business Unit)	Understand possible staff degradation and plan availability of replacement human capital with intellectual skill sets necessary to continue the business operation	Ability to offset affected operations, staff degradation, and/or permanent loss and prevent cascade effects on nonaffected elements of the business	Chart operational elements of the enterprise	Identify external third-party organizations that provide support to operational elements of the enterprise
Tactical (Department—Work Group)	Identify family status issues	Ability to continue operations	Create location-specific structure for operating in a crisis	Identify availability of external sources of service and/or product

account the human portion of the continuity equation. This leads to easier active analysis and greater situational awareness, which in turn aid decision making and decision execution. Furthermore, the tables will help you identify critical points that should be addressed before the onset of the pandemic. If you do not consider these factors before the onset of a pandemic, you will have (avoidable) trouble as the pandemic unfolds.

DECISION MAKING UNDER DURESS AND UNCERTAINTY

Professor Hossein Arsham said, "Decisions are at the heart of leader success, and at times there are critical moments when they can be difficult, perplexing, and nerve-racking."

Effective decision making during the pre-pandemic, pandemic, and post-pandemic periods will be challenging. I have included certain decision-making models in this chapter, specifically those that aid decision making under duress. Models have a powerful influence on individuals and on society because our view of the world is determined by our set of assumptions about it.

Decisions, decisions, and more decisions! The fear of making serious decisions is a new kind of fear, called decidophobia, proclaimed by Walter Kaufmann at Princeton University in 1973. The fear of making the wrong decisions is well-known to any responsible manager, but, as Eleanor Roosevelt said, "You gain strength, courage, and confidence by every experience in which you really stop to look fear in the face." Effective and timely decision making (the ability to execute corporate-, division-, and department-level strategies effectively) will be determined by who is available to make decisions. In previous chapters, we presented methodologies for business impact assessment, the basis of your contingency plan. A disruptive event can create widespread breakdowns in the decision-making process. To gather information efficiently and to subsequently analyze, interpret, and communicate it effectively, standardized terminology should be adapted in all contingency plans developed by your enterprise. Terminology is generally regional and is predicated on public and private sectors determining a common set of terms. The National Incident Command System provides widely accepted terminology that can be readily applied.

The goal is to provide seamless communications both vertically and horizontally throughout your enterprise. To this end, each plan needs to create guidelines that allow flexibility in the decision-making process.

Figure 5.2 depicts the typical progression of decision making from decision rights (the rules) through decision inventories (the checklists) to the clustering of decisions (decisions are assigned to people who have appropriate information and perspective) as a business continuity plan

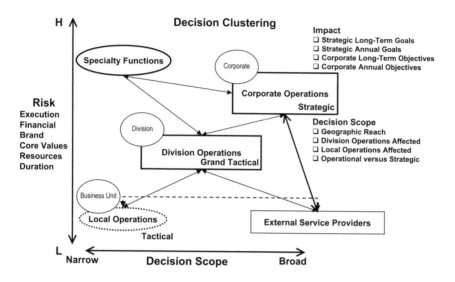

Figure 5.2. Decision Clustering Urgency Index

is activated. At the lowest level (tactical), representing local operations, the decision scope and decision authority are generally narrowly defined. This is attributable to the focus of the operation, the agenda, and the expectations. In a typical crisis situation, the tactical focus is on mitigation, the agenda is directly related to the event that is occurring, and the expectations are that assistance will come from above. The difference that we will face with a pandemic is that expectations may not be able to be met. This is attributable to the fact that a pandemic has a widespread effect, with the general upward support levels potentially being affected as heavily as the lowest levels in the organization.

At the next level (grand tactical), the decision scope and decision authorities are generally broader and have greater latitude. Again, in a typical crisis situation, the grand tactical level is focused on minimizing the impact of the event, preventing cascade effects, and maintaining workflow by workload shifting. The agenda at this level consists primarily of support to the affected entity and coordination of work-arounds. The expectations are for the next level (strategic) to address the longer-term support requirements that the event has evoked.

At the strategic level, the focus is generally external in nature. It is on stakeholders, customers, and other value-chain components. Generally, this is attributable to the distance from the event in terms of hierarchy of structure and the broader-based decision scope and authority. In a corporate environment, this is the "C" suite. The agenda at this level is on how to meet corporate goals and objectives now that the event has disrupted the flow of operations. The expectations are for seamless vertical communications (again, common terminology is a great asset) and seamless horizontal communications. Seamless communications facilitate decision making and provide a platform for common understanding.

This explanation is presented in its simplest form for space considerations and because organizations vary in terms of the amount of autonomy (decision scope and authority) that is allowed. The advent of a pandemic may cause alterations to the model, driving greater decision scope and authority lower into the organization because of the nature of widespread illness and the impact of actions by authorities (government at all levels) on the ability of an organization to support its operations in the traditional hierarchic form. We sometimes see this occur for short durations during events that have a wide-area impact (Hurricanes Katrina and Rita, for example), but generally, the increase in decision scope and authorities at the lower levels are short lived.

FACTORS AFFECTING DECISION MAKING

Humans have an innate characteristic: we constantly think about the future, and we are generally wrong about how things will turn out! Consider all the predictions of calamity that would befall us as a result of Y2K. What we fail to understand in our predictive dabbling is that human nature, the complexity of the world, and the nature of organizations come into play. Plans have a tendency to fail, as Nassim Nicholas Taleb writes in *The Black Swan: The Impact of the Highly Improbable*, because planners have a tendency to "tunnel," that is, to neglect sources of uncertainty outside of the plan itself. Unexpected events almost always push us in one direction regarding decisions: fewer options over time resulting in higher costs, greater reactivity to subsequent events, and longer duration of disruption within the enterprise.[3]

To overcome this limitation, we, as planners, must strive to be less narrow minded; we must take into account external uncertainties that are outside of the realm of our planning focus. This is the "unknown unknown," as Taleb refers to it. This limitation is difficult to overcome for most, because "unknown unknowns" are too abstract for us to think about or talk about intelligently. We cannot depend on the accuracy of our plans as a measure of what will unfold in the future, because we cannot truly understand the future. This is actually not horrible news. Plans provide a framework for decision making.

Figure 5.3 depicts how little we truly know and how limited the value of our current projections is because of the inability to understand the future.

You must reduce uncertainty

"Because we are asking the wrong questions precisely, we are getting the wrong answers precisely; and as a result we are creating false positives."

Geary W. Sikich, 2003

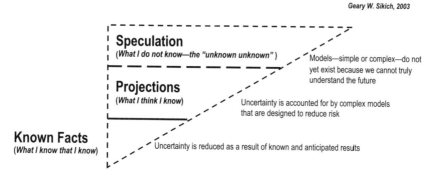

Speculation
(What I do not know—the "unknown unknown")

Models—simple or complex—do not yet exist because we cannot truly understand the future

Projections
(What I think I know)

Uncertainty is accounted for by complex models that are designed to reduce risk

Known Facts
(What I know that I know)

Uncertainty is reduced as a result of known and anticipated results

Seemingly disparate information must become useable. Information has to be transformed into intelligence.

Figure 5.3. Before You Make a Decision…

An interesting approach that was introduced in an article published by Vladimir A. Masch in the *Journal of Evolutionary Economics* presents the concept of risk-constrained optimization (RCO).[4] RCO is an ensemble of special models, procedures, and algorithms to generate, evaluate, and help in executing good alternative strategies. RCO is a system for planning under uncertainty that searches for the most acceptable compromise between improving results and reducing risk in our decisions. However, one problem with special models and models in general is that they do not necessarily work. Studies have shown that many practitioners' models fare no better than the predictive ability of the general public. In his book *Blink: The Power of Thinking without Thinking*, Malcom Gladwell presents the concept of rapid cognition, about the kind of thinking that happens in a blink of an eye. Your mind takes about two seconds to jump to a series of conclusions. It is in that moment of decision that those instant conclusions move us forward.[5]

THIRD WAVE PANDEMONIUM?

When we finally emerge from the throes of the pandemic, what will the socioeconomic situation look like? This is a good question to ask when you start your planning process. First, you will be able to use this question to assess your enterprise now. Are our products/services going to be in high demand during a pandemic and/or in the aftermath of a pandemic? Will we have to deal with a significant drop in demand that could warrant closure of the enterprise? Second, you can use this question to make adjustments to your strategy (goals and objectives) to fine-tune them as the pandemic progresses. The six considerations presented below are framed in a general way to allow you to fit them to your particular organization and its specific market sector. Additionally, these six considerations are valuable for the planning efforts that you are undertaking and can be readily applied to general business continuity planning. Six considerations for your planning should be as follows:

Interconnectedness: We live in a highly interconnected socioeconomic milieu. Cascading effects from events happening far from your location can create havoc if you are not prepared for them. Will China and India be so hard hit that much of the outsourced services we have become dependent on will be so degraded that it causes significant turmoil here? Will the Middle East erupt with violence threatening oil supplies? Will the United States still be able to act as the world's policeman? One of the cascading effects of the devastation from Hurricane Katrina was higher oil prices caused by closed refineries.

Asymmetry: A known threat is replaced by an unknown threat. Asymmetric threats are a version of "not fighting fair." These can include surprise, unplannable and unpredictable events, and impacts to your touch points that have not been anticipated. Not fighting fair also includes the prospect of an opponent designing a strategy that fundamentally alters the markets in which you compete. In this case, you have known opponents (e.g., your competition) and the unknown (a mutational virus with as yet unknown virulence).

Speed, the Compression of Time: As the authors of *Blur: The Speed of Change in the Connected Economy* point out,[6] "Connectivity, speed and intangible values are the new driving forces in business today. Traditional business boundaries are blurring as everyone becomes electronically connected. The traditional rules governing the conduct of business are blurred as businesses are redefined, products become services, services become products and business lines change constantly." It is projected that it will take less than one month for a pandemic to reach every corner of the globe. Today, just-in-time processes leave little leeway for business or government. How dependent are you on an extended supply chain?

Blinders: Salient facts are often not noticed at the time because of limitations on your planning focus. The business of the business has never been part of the contingency planning process, because planners never recognized they are engulfed by the company's activities rather than its objectives. Until planners understand and recognize the difference, the company they support will be limited in its business resiliency capability.

Expectations: Output expectations are continuous and impose on leadership a never-ending need to mobilize resources to maintain support. This requires assessment and commitment of real resources, at satisfactory levels, that create genuine costs that any complex organization must bear. Output failure occurs when authorities are unable to meet the demands of the supported population or do not take anticipatory actions to counter adversities. How will a pandemic affect output expectations? You may have all the output capacity that you require but lack the resources (human) to deliver your product or service.

The Value of Intelligence: Thomas C. Schelling, in the foreword to *Pearl Harbor: Warning and Decision*, by Roberta Wohlstetter, wrote, "Whether at Pearl Harbor or at the Berlin Wall, surprise is everything involved in a government's (or in an alliance's) failure to anticipate effectively."[7]

The above applies equally to businesses. If you leave things to chance or await help from others (read that to mean government at any level), you will be in for a surprise. Active analysis needs to be an integral element of your pandemic preparedness program. Misinformation or inadequately provided information can lead to unanticipated risks that develop rapidly and distort responses.

The time is now for making the kinds of serious decisions that will shape the future of your enterprise in the event of a pandemic. Serious business decisions ultimately shape, guide, and direct our future. These decisions generally occur at the strategic level and involve goals and objectives, but they are carried out at the grand tactical and tactical level of the enterprise. A structured, well-focused approach to the decision-making process lessens uncertainty over decision making and decision rights (the level of authority for making decisions), and can facilitate seamless communications (vertically and horizontally) within the organization.

Decision making regarding pandemic preparedness is not a risk-free process. The outcome of many decisions that you make in the pre-pandemic, pandemic, and post-pandemic periods will be influenced by other parties. Does your enterprise purchase Tamiflu or some other antiviral drug? What is the shelf life for these products? Will the government confiscate them for the greater good of the community? One of the characteristics of decision analysis is that "good" decision making does not necessarily bring about good outcomes. How prudent will your decision making be?

I have often found it useful to break down the decision process, as depicted in Table 5.4.

Making the correct decisions is not only about what we want to do; it is also about what we have to do. One must distinguish between facts and media hype. At the time of this writing, H5N1 is not being splashed all over the news but that does not diminish its relevance as a

Table 5.4. Decision-Making Model

#	Process Step	End Point Result
1	Define the decision.	Describe what you need to decide.
2	State alternatives.	Compile a list of decision alternatives.
3	What are the objectives?	Compile a list of the desired objectives. State them in terms of what is preferred by you in the final outcome.
4	Which alternatives best meet the objectives?	Evaluate each objective. Rank alternatives, one relative to another, by your opinion as to how well each would meet a single objective. Create an alphabetical or numerical ranking (A = best, B = second best, etc.).
5	Which objectives are most important?	Judge the value of the objectives using the same ranking system as used for alternatives.
6	Apply relative value.	Combine judgment steps 4 and 5.
7	Identify the best choice.	Add numbers across each row for alternatives.
8	Make the decision.	Review the results; satisfy yourself that these are your best judgments.
9	Implement the decision.	You have to have conscious dedication to implement the decision. Once your decision has been implemented you need to see it through. This does not mean blind dedication; rather, it means that you have "situational awareness" and are able to shape the outcome of your decision.

threat that we should take seriously. Failing to carefully prepare for a pandemic is doing a grave disservice to your enterprise. This means making sound decisions and understanding the facts. It is this approach to decision making that makes the business successful, but it is important to note that progress may not come easily.

CREATING MANAGEMENT AWARENESS AND EMPLOYEE BUY-IN

Creating awareness in management and getting buy-in from employees regarding the seriousness of pandemic preparedness are a challenge. Just speaking to management and all staff, including human resources professionals, is not enough. There is no concrete set of actions to offer. Buy-in is acceptance, and no amount of talk or coercion can get people to buy in if they do not believe. The challenge is to offer communications that are believable and that are supported by all levels within the organization. This takes some research and perhaps setting up a central clearinghouse for information.

Awareness is very much based on media hype, and, as of this writing, H5N1 is not the top of the charts for media focus. I was in Croatia in June 2007 speaking at a conference for emergency managers and was astounded to see how much coverage Paris Hilton was receiving for her stay in jail. This was headline news on CNN International. Sentencing, jail, breakdown, release, court circus; it was running on CNN for almost a week! H5N1? What's that? Is it a new sports car? I am keenly aware of the challenge faced by contingency planners of getting management awareness of an issue that is not a "hot button" item.

Consider the following:

Sometime in 200?—In response to The World Health Organization's raising of its Pandemic Alert Level from 3 to 4 (evidence of increased human-to-human transmission), U.S. Centers for Disease Control and Prevention today announced that the death of a businessman recently returned from a trip that included stops in Hong Kong, India, China, Japan, and Canada has been attributed to the human-to-human transmissible strain of the avian influenza virus. In related events, although bird flu has not been declared present yet, Indian health authorities have established an Isolation Ward Set at JN Hospital in Imphal, India, to meet flu eventualities. The Imphal state health department has started taking up special precautionary measures against any possible outbreak of avian influenza by maintaining a ten-bed isolated ward at JN Hospital in Imphal for the treatment of patients, according to a highly placed official source.

Or, consider this, from the Associated Press (May 29, 2007):

A man with a form of tuberculosis so dangerous he is under the first U.S. government-ordered quarantine since 1963 had health officials around the world scrambling Wednesday to find about 80 passengers who sat within five rows of him on two trans-Atlantic flights.

There is every reason to believe that the first news release is plausible. This is because it is partially true. Indian authorities did set up an isolation ward at JN Hospital in Imphal to treat patients (*Imphal Free Press*, July 24, 2007). The second scenario, although seemingly incredible, is totally true!

Here is another example. The graphic below (Figure 5.4) was extracted from a U.S. government report, "A Line in the Sand: Confronting the Threat at the Southwest Border." What does drug smuggling have to do with pandemic preparedness? The fact that we know cartel smuggling routes and cannot shut them down is indicative of how porous the U.S. border is and should give you reason to be concerned. First, what about the routes that have not been identified? Second, from a pandemic planning standpoint, what will the

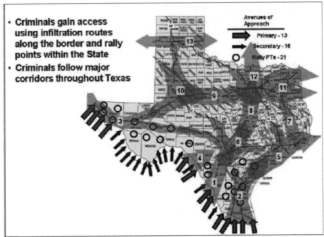

· **Criminals gain access using infiltration routes along the border and rally points within the State**
· **Criminals follow major corridors throughout Texas**

Avenues of Approach
Primary - 13
Secondary - 16
Rally PTs - 21

Drug and human smuggling routes from Mexico into the United States

Figure 5.4. Smuggling Routes

Source: "A Line in the Sand: Confronting the Threat at the Southwest Border"—Prepared by the majority staff of the House Committee on Homeland Security Subcommittee on Investigations—Michael T. McCaul, Chairman.

United States do about the influx of ailing individuals from south of the border who will inevitably seek medical aid during the pandemic? Third, this is just Texas; New Mexico, Arizona, and California also border Mexico. The report not only describes overland routes but also provides some interesting information about the increasing coordination between Mexican drug cartels, human smuggling networks, and United States–based gangs.

The Laredo Port of Entry is the busiest and most heavily traversed land port of entry on the southwest border, handling approximately 6,000 commercial vehicles a day. Forty percent of all Mexican exports cross into Laredo, Texas, where Interstate 35 connects directly to Dallas, and from there throughout the United States. U.S. Border Patrol Chief John Montoya describes this port of entry as "the key ingress into the United States."

"It's called a gateway city, not only into Mexico but into the United States as well." The very conditions that make the Laredo Port of Entry so attractive to legitimate commerce also make the city ideal for the illicit drug and human smuggling trade. In a pandemic, we can expect our borders to be inundated with individuals seeking medical treatment because they are sick, because they are caring for someone who is sick, or because they are feeling threatened and are seeking aid.

"What about Canada?" I can hear some of you asking. Well, the situation is not much better in some respects. Take, for instance, Saint Clair

County, Michigan; Port Huron is a relatively small midwestern town. However, Saint Clair County and Port Huron can boast the following:

- #1 entry point for carriers of hazardous, radioactive, and flammable materials between Michigan and Canada (Blue Water Bridge, Canadian National Rail Tunnel, Marine City, Michigan to Sombra, Ontario Ferry, Algonac, Michigan to Walpole [First Nation] Ferry, and St. Clair County International Airport).
- #2 entry point in the United States for hazardous materials imports.
- #2 busiest northern border crossing in America.
- #3 entry point for the entire North American continent.
- The Blue Water Bridge is the crossing for 4,800 commercial trucks and 12,000 passenger vehicles daily and 5.8 million commercial and passenger vehicles annually.

Why are these last two examples important from a pandemic preparedness perspective? The simple answer deals with economics. The United States, Canada, and Mexico have come to the realization that they cannot close borders during a pandemic because of the economic impact on the three trading partners. The three countries recently signed a trilateral agreement to provide mutual aid and support to each other in the event of a pandemic. Thus, border closures will most likely not occur. The more complex answer deals with humanity. Although reports of the spread of avian influenza A (H5N1) virus have diminished, the world is very much at risk of an influenza pandemic.

There is still a good deal of debate among scientists and health experts as to whether the conditions for sustained human-to-human transmission of the H5N1 strain will ever materialize. However, health experts are not debating the "what if" question; it is more a debate centered around when and whether it will be the H5N1 virus. The twentieth century saw three pandemics, starting with the 1918 Spanish Influenza. The origin of this pandemic has always been disputed and may never be resolved. Next there was the 1957 Asian Influenza (H2N2) and finally the 1968 Hong Kong Influenza (H3N2). Sooner or later in the twenty-first century, an outbreak is expected.

Yes, we can prepare, but the truth is that no amount of hand washing, hand wringing, public education, or gauze masks will do the trick. The keystone of influenza prevention is vaccination. It is unreasonable to believe that we can count on prophylaxis with antiviral agents to protect a large, vulnerable population for more than a few days at a time, and that is not long enough. How long will they be given? To whom? What are the risks in mass administration? All of this is unknown. But vaccination against what? We do not know. Perhaps against H5N1. But do we not already have a vaccine? No, we do not; no vaccine of adequate antigenic potency is available in sufficient supply.

An outbreak of influenza can spread quickly. Figure 5.5 shows how easily an exceptionally high number of people can become infected over a relatively short period of time.

In *The Histories*, written in 450 BC, Herodotus makes the following statement:

> If an important decision is to be made [the Persians] discuss the question when they are drunk and the following day the master of the house ... submits their decision for reconsideration when they are sober. If they still approve it, it is adopted; if not, it is abandoned. Conversely, any decision they make when they are sober is reconsidered afterwards when they are drunk.[8]

What a strange way to make decisions, you might say. Perhaps it is, but there are even stranger methods of human choice. One is simply to avoid making decisions at all, to pretend an event will never occur. Another is to decide to let someone else, such as the government or your employer, worry about keeping you safe in the event of a pandemic. What I have advised clients in the past is to establish a clearinghouse function for pandemic-related information. This would include web-based intranet portals for staff and Internet portals for clients, vendors, suppliers, and other interested parties. The clearinghouse functions as a repository for information and as a screening mechanism to filter information that is not exactly correct. Furthermore, you can make

Spread of Contagion

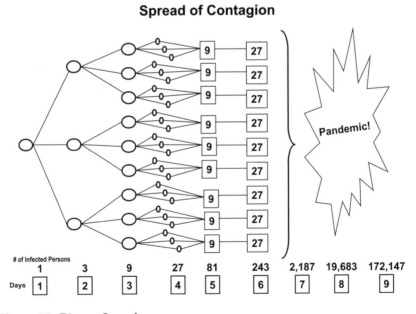

Figure 5.5. Disease Spread

the portals interactive to allow for questions and contact information to be exchanged.

Are we prepared to address a crisis as large as a pandemic? Do the public and private institutions of our society, with their traditional structures and organizational behaviors, have the requisite integrity to manage the crisis as needed? The answer seems to be not yet.

Can we depend on the federal government to bail us out? Reflecting on the current state of response capabilities in the aftermath of Hurricane Katrina and projecting forward to the possible response to a pandemic, what do you think? The aftermath of Katrina indicates that there is much to be done regarding the ability of government to respond effectively.

Should you depend on your employer for your personal well-being in the event of a pandemic or a terrorist event such as a "dirty bomb" incident? Remember, market research indicates that only 5 percent of businesses today have a viable contingency plan.

The journey from buy-in to personal preparedness is not a long one. Government has preached personal preparedness since the Cold War. We are, depending on where you live and the season, reminded that it is "hurricane preparedness week," earthquake preparedness week," or some other type of personal preparedness week. Individuals should have their own personal preparedness plan. Perhaps by applying the following eight essential elements of analysis to your personal preparedness you can take steps in the direction of ensuring your personal safety. (Astute readers will recognize the eight essential elements as the incident-management system described previously.) Remember, having such a plan will be useful not just for a pandemic but for natural disasters and terrorist incidents as well. Eight key areas that must be taken into consideration for personal safety are as follows:

Management: Consider what decisions you might have to make and how you will handle the event. No crisis ever goes completely according to plan. In a crisis people, react in unexpected ways. Whether a natural or human-induced disaster, surprise is the key element in the failure to anticipate effectively.

Planning: Identify short-term and long-term considerations for you and your family. Plan for long-term sheltering; avoid being herded into a "Superdome" situation. Assess the worst-case scenario and work backward to a preparation level with which you are comfortable.

Operations: Identify how you will function if your home or workplace is affected by an event.

Logistics: Identify and acquire essential and supporting logistics for survival. Assess your food and water situation in your home and your workplace; do not count on being able to leave either. Get first aid items beyond the norm, for example, antibiotics, face masks, and gloves. Get a shortwave radio or National Oceanic and Atmospheric

Administration/FEMA radio and/or a radio that can communicate with local authorities.

Infrastructure: Identify internal and external infrastructures that will support you and your family, and develop a backup for external infrastructures that may not be available (get that generator!).

Administration: Keep a current set of critical documents available in a secure location and include a copy on an electronic medium. Keep a log of the entire event for future potential litigation.

Finance: Keep some cash on hand and plan for short-term dislocation and long-term dislocation.

External liaison: Communicate with others in your community and local government regarding current plans and considerations. If New Orleans is an example, human civility will deteriorate quickly; panic will be beyond what we saw with Katrina. In a pandemic or terrorist scenario, you will potentially have injured people, people getting sick over a period of days, and people who want to leave but cannot because of quarantined conditions.

PREPARE THE BUSINESS CASE TO GET BUY-IN

Below are some worksheets that I have found useful in preparing the business case for pandemic preparedness. Each has three examples of areas on which you may want to focus (or adapt them to your situation).

Table 5.5. Critical Decision-Making Area, Worksheet 1

Critical Decision-Making Areas	Decisions—Timeframe	Consequences—Potential
Management (leadership/decision making) 1 Workforce assessment 2 Product/service delivery assessment 3 Workspace assessment		
Planning (tactical, grand tactical, strategic) 1 Tactical (emergency response) 2 Grand tactical (cascade effect) 3 Strategic (corporate objectives)		
Operations (affected/nonaffected) 1 Tactical (event mitigation) 2 Grand tactical (cascade prevention) 3 Strategic (corporate objectives impact)		
Infrastructure (internal/external) 1 Facilities/equipment 2 Systems/applications 3 Utilities/support services		

Table 5.6. Critical Decision-Making Area, Worksheet 2

Critical Decision-Making Areas	Decisions—Timeframe	Consequences—Potential
Logistics (immediate/long term) 1 Alternate workspace 2 Temporary housing 3 Supplies/consumables		
Finance (cost tracking/sources of funds) 1 Cost tracking 2 Financial impact creditworthiness 3 Source of emergency funds		
Administration (resource management) 1 Human resource assessment 2 Documentation/recordkeeping 3 Altered work schedules		
External relations (stakeholders/media /image) 1 Customers 2 Value chain 3 Media/image		

RECOVERY, PART 1: EVERY TIME HISTORY REPEATS ITSELF, THE PRICE GOES UP

The pandemic will gradually subside, relieving healthcare systems that are, by this time, grasping for survival. The world enters a very slow and potentially torturous recovery mode. This recovery period can be projected to occur in three distinct parts: recovery, restoration, and realignment. Recovery will be a return to some semblance of business. Restoration will be a return to the pre-pandemic socioeconomic conditions (of course, this is highly improbable in the short term) that we have now. Realignment will be a reshaping of almost everything that you can think of, from health care to the global powerbase.

Joseph Tainter, in his book *The Collapse of Complex Societies*, cites four concepts that would lead to an understanding of collapse:[9]

- Human societies are problem-solving organizations.
- Sociopolitical systems require energy for their maintenance.
- Increased complexity carries with it increased costs per capita.
- Investment in sociopolitical complexity as a problem-solving response often reaches a point of declining returns.

Taking these four concepts and projecting them into the pandemic scenario, we see that societies that increase in complexity do so as a system. The interlinked parts are forced in a direction of growth, and the touch points (not directly linked) are required to adjust accordingly.

If we consider the last point made by Tainter, that increasing complexity often reaches a point of declining returns, we can project that, at this stage of the pandemic, attempting to maintain the status quo regarding our complex global economy may actually delay the recovery from the pandemic.

The economic stakes at this stage are going to be very high. Governments, businesses, and consumers will have to work hand in hand to realize the revival of the global economy. Although localization has provided a basis for a surviving the pandemic, new growth on a global scale will be slow in coming. This may partially be attributable to fear that a return to the norm might just invite a recurrence of the pandemic to areas that are considered virus free.

If the pandemic does indeed cost the United States the staggering sum of $675 billion, as cited by Senator Bill Frist,[10] what will be the impact on the global economy? If the Congressional Budget Office estimate is correct, that direct and indirect costs would reduce U.S. economic production by 5 percent, what will that mean on a global basis?

The U.S. economy is part of a complex global economy. Will we have the wherewithal, as nations, to fight off the temptation to "go it alone"? Each cog (nation-state) in the global economy is like the links in a gigantic supply chain. Where a country fits into that chain is of critical importance to the recovery process. Although the U.S. economy is capable of generating $12 trillion in gross domestic product, will it be at the head, middle, or end of the value chain? A value chain is a network of suppliers, vendors, production, distribution options, and customers; it procures, transforms, distributes, and consumes products/services. Value chain continuity is the ability to maintain the value chain in a state of continuous operation in the face of discontinuity threats, such as a pandemic. Three questions need to be answered:

- Where does your company rank on its supplier's list of priority clients?
- How will your company meet corporate goals and objectives when a value chain disruption occurs?
- How would a value chain disruption affect your clients and the markets that you serve?

We can answer these three questions by creating a scale. On a piece of paper, draw a vertical line. This line represents the investment cost. Draw a horizontal line that intersects with the vertical line. The horizontal line represents where organizations enter the value chain. The cost of investment is predicated on where you are in the value chain. If you are a consumer (an importing country) much like the United States is, then your cost of investment is related to the availability of alternate sources for the product or service that you consume and how near you are to the delivery point(s) for the product/service. The converse holds for the supplier side of the equation. If you are at an early entry point in the horizontal line of the value chain, the likelihood that you will get paid if a disruption occurs is good, if that disruption occurs after you have completed your input to the value chain.

Think of how many parts go into, say, a jet engine. There are probably thousands. One company does not make all the parts. Parts are made to specification and enter the value chain at various points on the horizontal access. If an incident occurs at some point along that line of entry points, the suppliers awaiting entry are going to be negatively affected. This can be a minor inconvenience or a major crisis depending on how much of the supplier's business is represented by the customer. If 2 percent of my business is represented, I have 98 percent of my revenue coming from elsewhere. If 98 percent of my revenue comes from this source, then I have to address a potential crisis resulting from a delay in revenue realized or complete loss of revenue. The effect can cascade throughout the entire value chain, creating significant impact on the customer expecting delivery of the completed product that has been ordered.

I have highlighted below the effect of three elements that are considerations that should be taken into account when answering the three questions posited above: order of occurrence, randomness, and impact of the highly improbable.

- Random occurrences can lead to chaotic reactionary responses (pandemic is a random occurrence).
- Chaotic reactionary responses can lead to ineffective solutions (e.g., closing borders).
- Ineffective solutions can create potential for cascading (by closing borders, economic activity is negatively affected).
- Cascade effects can lead to a multiplication of impact effects (critical items produced in countries that export cannot get to where they are needed).
- Multiplication of impact effects can lead to higher potential of uncertainty of effectiveness (many of the consumable supplies that hospitals will need in a pandemic are manufactured outside of the United States. No supplies leads to limited patient care).

Being a consumer in the post-pandemic economy may be a difficult situation if the consuming nation does not have a strong financial standing and/or readily acceptable trade alternative (i.e., monetized commodities).

If you are a supplier (an exporting country) much like the countries rich in natural resources or those that manufacture for the global market, you have to determine where along the supply chain your entry point is. However, being a supplier in the post-pandemic economy may be as difficult as being a consumer if other suppliers (i.e., shippers) have breakdowns caused by financial woes brought on during the pandemic.

Your investment (your country's economy) is going to reflect the degree of damage that the pandemic does to your population and the economic infrastructure that that population supports.

Therefore, as former Senator Frist points out, "A severe pandemic, CBO [*Congressional Budget Office*] says, would lead to an 80 percent drop in economic activity for the entertainment, arts and dining sectors, the disappearance of a quarter of all retail sales and a severe curtailing of travel. Agriculture and manufacturing would take heavy hits as well. Pandemics dry up world trade."[11]

Restarting a complex global economy may initially create a cost-benefit curve that looks very promising at first, because the easiest, most general, most accessible, and least expensive solutions will be the ones that are attempted first. As these solutions realize maximum value and essentially are exhausted, continued economic stresses will require additional investments in complexity. The question will be, "Where do the governments, peoples, businesses of the world come up with the money to pay for investments in complexity that return the global economy to the status quo?" Realize that, in the 500–800-day timeframe that we envision, a lot of the cash reserves of the world's economies will have been spent fighting the pandemic. There is no way to predict an answer to this question.

SECTOR ANALYSIS: 800–1,100 DAYS, THE POST-PANDEMIC TIMEFRAME

Although the pandemic might be over as far as sickness is concerned, the socioeconomic consequences will last for years, decades perhaps. That is what this book is all about: getting you and others to understand that a pandemic is not just about hospital response. It is about immediate and long-term economic consequences and effects.

The financial sector may face solvency issues as a result of people choosing alternative savings methodologies and/or just not having any income to save. Governments and institutions, such as the World Bank and International Monetary Fund, could face extinction, severe restructuring, and/or loss of power with regard to controlling the flow of capital.

The manufacturing sector is now faced with raising capital to expand beyond the local markets, because access to raw materials and transportation systems will require capital to be expended to grow.

The service sector may continue to wither as the lack of workforce, assimilated into the manufacturing sector, is no longer available and demand volume remains low.

The telecommunications sector recovery could be the most robust if the infrastructure that supports it (i.e., the utility sector) can provide needed support. Again, capital, or lack of it, will be a key factor. Telecommuting may become the norm as adjustment soon creates a viable resource base to support telecommuters. However, it should be pointed out that information processing may take a back seat to agriculture and manufacturing.

The insurance sector will have to be deconstructed and reconstructed in a different model. Social Security, Medicare, Medicaid, and other government-sponsored entitlement programs could be faced with extinction as a result of the expenditure of funds during the pandemic's phases and the now readily apparent loss of a significant portion of the working population attributable to death, illness, loss of employment, and loss of employment sectors.

The healthcare sector will have to be deconstructed and reconstructed much the same as the insurance sector. Expect government intervention and possibly a national healthcare system being created.

The energy sector will continue to face supply (raw materials), transformation (refining raw materials into useable energy), and transportation issues. Commodity prices continue to fluctuate based on spot demand.

The utility sector will continue to face infrastructure strains as demand begins to increase as workforces return to some office functions. This will be reflected in the lack of depth of skill sets in the utility sector. You cannot train a person in a short time to do the complex tasks that utility workers perform. Brownouts and blackouts are a regular occurrence and are now viewed as part of life versus a crisis situation.

The agriculture sector faces a transformation from localization to globalization, but transportation will play a defining role in the regrowth of complexity in this sector. Seasonal demands for food products are unchanged. The United States continues to suffer regional spot outages.

The education sector continues to have to address limited capability to operate because teacher shortages at educational institutions are most likely to continue. Again, we see that the depth of skill sets comes into play. Government use of commandeered facilities most likely will continue.

The high-technology sector may see a drop in demand as the pace of innovation is altered and/or permanently slowed. Support services could reach marginal levels attributable to continued workforce and support infrastructure (utility and telecommunications sectors) disruption.

By the time that we enter the twenty-fourth month (800 days) of the pandemic, the recovery will be well underway, albeit reflective of the altered operations within all sectors. Localized economies may limit expansion by virtue of finding that they do not want to participate in a global economy that has become fraught with vulnerabilities.

CONCLUSION

Enabling effective business continuity processes across geographically dispersed operations and myriad value chain touch points requires that HR professionals become an integral part of the process and implement formal performance measures needed to ensure internalization of continuity plans and processes often distributed across diverse organizations, lines of business, groups, departments, geographies, and value chain touch points. This requires extracting, analyzing, and communicating information; internalizing processes; and exercising controls to enable a 360-degree, three-dimensional view of organizational performance when crisis strikes. Eight key areas that must be taken into consideration for determining human factors impacts are as follows:

- Management: decision making regarding the handling of the event
- Planning: short term and long term
- Operations: affected and nonaffected
- Logistics: worksite and supporting logistics
- Infrastructure: internal and external
- Administration: support factors
- Finance: short-term dislocation and long-term dislocation
- External liaison: communication to stakeholders regarding disposition of the event and human factors considerations

6

After the Shock: Potential Risks for the Global Economy

It must be considered that there is nothing more difficult to carry out, nor more doubtful of success, nor more dangerous to handle, than to initiate a new order of things. For the reformer has enemies in all those who would profit by the old order, and only lukewarm defenders in all those who would profit by the new order. This lukewarmness arising partly from the fear of their adversaries, who have the laws in their favor; and partly from the incredulity of mankind, who do not truly believe in anything new until they have actually experienced it.

—Niccolo Machiavelli, *The Prince*

Have you given thought to how you might realign your enterprise? Would it be along product/service lines? Would it be along geographic boundaries? Would it be a "virtual" enterprise instead of based on the "bricks-and-mortar" concept? What models are available? Has anyone done this before? In a previous chapter, I referred to a pandemic as an asymmetric threat. Once we have made it through the 500–800 days that the pandemic will take to run its course, is there any reason to believe that we will return rapidly to the socioeconomic situation of pre-pandemic days? The potential for disruption to the global economy is tremendous, and the impacts could be deep and last longer than the pandemic itself.

As you will recall, asymmetric threats or techniques are a version of not fighting fair, which can include the use of surprise in all its operational and strategic dimensions and the introduction of and use of products/services in ways unplanned by your organization and the markets that you serve. Not fighting fair also includes the prospect of an opponent designing a strategy that fundamentally alters the market in which you operate.

As the impact of the pandemic subsides and experts consider that there is no threat of additional waves of outbreak occurring, countries will move into a prolonged recovery, restoration, and realignment phase. Although the objective will be to return to pre-pandemic levels of socioeconomic functioning as soon as possible, the pace of recovery, restoration, and realignment will depend on the residual or cascade effect that the pandemic has had. Countries and companies will have to determine whether there are ongoing demands for products/services. What will the public and private sectors do if there is a lack of demand for products/services? What about backlogs? The survivors will have to overcome a lot of stress and fatigue. Medical systems will not be able to return to pre-pandemic levels of service rapidly, which means that elective surgeries and other treatment options will remain at minimal levels. Strained staff and organizational fatigue, coupled with continuing supply difficulties throughout the world, should make economic recovery even more difficult.

Therefore, do not expect a gradual return to normality. Shape your expectations for a long and difficult road to restoration of pre-pandemic socioeconomic standards. Contingency plans at all levels within government and private industry should recognize the potential need to prioritize the restoration of services and to phase the return to normal in a managed and sustainable way.

RECOVERY EFFORTS: GLOBAL ECONOMIC IMPACT

My colleague John Stagl and I transcribed some notes as we were preparing to discuss the economic consequences of a pandemic at a luncheon in Chicago in 2006. We had come to the conclusion at the time that a pandemic will have a domino effect worldwide. We all know that a pandemic will create a unique set of conditions that affect society, the business markets, and medical support systems. One of the differentiating characteristics of a pandemic, unlike any other disaster, is its widespread impact. We have already seen that this impact has occurred without human-to-human contagion occurring. The economic consequences to the poultry industry have been dramatic.

However, let us turn our attention to the human-to-human aspects of the post-pandemic period. Although we know that the medical community will be one of the hardest hit areas, it is by no means the only area that will suffer extensive near-term and severe long-term impact. The medical impact, in fact, will probably be among the most short-lived (i.e., in terms of deaths). The degradation of medical systems will last much longer. In the post-pandemic periods, people will perhaps have to alter their lifestyles to do with fewer medical services. This is a key point to understand, and it is not just the medical systems that are going to feel the impact. Just about everything that we have come to depend on in our modern society will suffer from the impact of the pandemic. The medical situation (deaths, illness, and long-term health issues) will be amongst the myriad points of disruption that will continually cascade to other areas until some balance is achieved and we can return to some form of stability.

The longer-term ramifications will be felt economically throughout the world. The key point to note is that the reverberation and cascading effect will be painfully uneven. Some countries will fare better than others. Some industries will fare better than others. Some companies will fare better than others. Collectively, however, each will feel the impact of the other as if they were dominos falling, creating a cascade effect. An analogy would be to compare the cascade effect of a pandemic to a tsunami wave. The initial wave may be hardly noticeable. However, as it ripples out, it gains strength until it surges over the land, causing devastation and destruction. Current thinking about pandemic generally starts with the recognition of the illness and a projection on its societal impacts. We know the following:

- People are affected.
- Society is unprepared.
- Governments are unprepared.
- Private-sector enterprises are unprepared.
- Medical institutions will be affected.
- Economic sectors worldwide will be affected.
- Medical support systems are affected.
- Social behavior will be susceptible to significant degradation.

However, what we do not know and can only speculate about is the scalable variables brought about by random chance. Biological variables (mortality and morbidity rates as a result of the pandemic) can be estimated based on the lethality of the avian flu virus (currently at almost 60 percent versus the Spanish Influenza virus, which was around 2–3 percent). With scalable variables, as Taleb says in *The Black Swan: The Impact of the Highly Improbable*, "the longer you wait, the longer you will be expected to wait."[1] This is as a result of the scalability of random events: randomness runs counterintuitive to conventional logic and the normal bell curve deviations that we are used to.

So, here are some purely speculative projections as to what the post-pandemic recovery, restoration, and realignment may look like. I have

based some of what I am about to project on limited historical evidence
from the plague and Spanish Influenza. I use the term "limited" to reflect
the differences in technology, population, education, and industrializa-
tion that were present at the time of the plague and Spanish Influenza
(the latter a mere eighty-nine years ago as of this writing in 2007).

Here are some fast facts (courtesy of Maplecroft Index, August 2007)
to ponder as we get ready for our journey into post-pandemic
speculation:

- Nearly 2 billion people (mostly in developing countries) do not have access
  to electricity.
- Nearly half the world's population (3 billion people) have never made a
  phone call.
- Enabling digital inclusion is most urgent in Africa, a continent that houses
  1 in 8 people (12 percent) and has only 1 in 40 fixed-line telephones (2.5
  percent), 1 in 30 mobile telephones (3 percent), 1 in 70 personal computers
  (1.5 percent), 1 in 150 Internet users (0.7 percent), and 1 in 500 Internet
  hosts (0.2 percent).
- Developing countries now account for almost half (49 percent) of total telephone subscribers in the world, up from just 19 percent in 1990.
- Globally, only 650 million people have personal computers. In the developing world, figures average about 1 in 100 people but can be as high as 8 in
  100 in Argentina or as low as 0.18 in 100 in Burundi.
- In 1990, only twenty countries were connected to the Internet. In 2003,
  there were 209.[2]

The facts above, when taken into the context of a pandemic, allow for
some interesting speculation. If nearly 2 billion people survive without
electricity, is that an indication that they also manage without medical
treatment? Probably. Developing countries are likely to suffer during a
pandemic, and, in the post-pandemic period, they will continue to suffer as developed nations turn their attention inward in attempts to
rebuild shattered economies. Nearly half the world's population have
never made a telephone call. If I have never made a telephone call, is it
not just as likely that I have very little knowledge of what is going on in
the world outside of my immediate location? This is also another indi-
cator that developing countries do not have the infrastructure to support the response to a pandemic. Much of the economic activity that is
termed "growth" is occurring in developing nations, the same nations
that do not have the infrastructure to deal with a pandemic. These are
the same nations that will see economic development potentially dry up
as a result of the inability of developed nations to continue to pour
money and skilled human capital into the development effort. The main
point that should be taken from these fast facts is that we are extremely
unprepared for a pandemic, especially in the developing world, and

that the long-term economic ramifications could make the subprime mortgage crisis pale in comparison.

Consider these aspects of predicting the future. In the material that follows, I have calculated a possible error rate of 100 percent. I could be completely wrong. What I am writing is pure speculation based on a random event occurring at some time in the future. However, I have cleverly, I hope, not cast my forecast with any date-specific timeframe and therefore could be 100 percent right—eventually! Forecasting without incorporating an error rate uncovers, according to Taleb, three fallacies. All arise from the same misconception about the nature of uncertainty. The first fallacy is that variability matters. I agree; that is why I am not taking my projections too seriously and casting them with a date. I also propose a range of possible outcomes. Second, he states that there is the fallacy of failing to take into account forecast degradation as the projected period lengthens. Here again, I agree; we do not realize the full extent of the difference between near and far futures. H5N1 is extremely lethal at present. Viruses mutate to survive. I would speculate that the influenza virus that creates a pandemic will be far less lethal than the current strain of H5N1. This, however, also allows for the virus to spread faster and longer and to infect more people because we stay alive longer and can pass it to many others over time. Finally, Taleb offers his third, and according to him possibly the most grave, fallacy, which concerns a misunderstanding about the random character of the variables being forecast. We do not realize the consequences of the rare event. It is the lower bound of estimates (worst-case scenario) that matters when engaging in a decision. The worst case is far more consequential than the forecast itself. Remember,

A black swan is a highly improbable event with three principal characteristics: it is unpredictable; it carries a massive impact; and, after the fact, we concoct an explanation that makes it appear less random, and more predictable, than it was.[3]

The following are the initial, albeit speculative, impacts that we can attribute to a pandemic:[4]

Business (all forms of private enterprise) impact

- Reduction in workforce leads to a reduction in output capacity.
- Reduction in consumption (people staying at home) leads to a decrease in demand.
- Reduction in revenue leading to less profit, leading to less taxes being paid.
- Lack of consumption demand leads to employees being laid off, leading to loss of benefits (e.g., healthcare insurance).

- Reduction in disposable income leads to additional consumption declines and consumption focused on necessities (healthcare insurance may become a luxury).
- Redistribution of family asset spending to necessities only:
  - Food
  - Medical (if you can pay health insurance, you still have deductibles; will the influenza be covered under your existing plan?)
  - Housing
  - Private transportation, if possible.
- More layoffs as a result of a worldwide sloughing off of demand and some countries closing borders as they attempt to isolate themselves.
- Business bankruptcies: medium and small businesses will feel the pain because they have limited cash reserves. Large enterprises will suffer as a result of loss of consumers and suppliers (how dependent is your business on the small- to medium-size supplier/vendor? Or is your small/medium-size business heavily dependent on a customer (large enterprise) that may experience a drop in demand putting your operations at risk?

Medical support systems (all medically related endeavors)

- Doctors are in demand for patient diagnosis and office visits.
- Hospitals are overwhelmed with patients.
- Virus patients must be isolated from other patients.
- Isolation supplies become limited, if available at all.
- Respiratory equipment is in short supply, for secondary pneumonia.
- Committees will decide who gets respirator support and who does not.
- Limited supplies of medication (no vaccine for six to nine months).
- Hospital and public pharmacies must increase security for medications.

The value of investments fall (anything that can be monetized)

- Redistribution of family assets and reduced investing.
- Companies need cash for operations versus reduced investments.
- Investors seek "safe havens" for investing, with no Third World investments.
- Reduced capacity to process investment activity, with up to 40 percent of staff sick.
- Stock and bond markets behave erratically, leading to less and less investment in publicly traded stocks and bonds.
- Private equity investments in companies drop.

Commodity markets

- Demand becomes erratic, leading to reduced trading.
- Open-pit operations are limited because of physical concerns and exposure to others in the trading pit.
- Electronic trading (heavier now than ever) becomes erratic as power supply systems and the Internet are less consistent and clearing/settling operations are degraded.
- Commodity delivery becomes erratic, and agricultural inspectors become a chokepoint because of illness, mortality rates, and inability to meet demand for services.
- Investors seek safe havens for investing, with little to no Third World investments.
- Reduced capacity to process investment activity, with 30 percent of staff sick.

Business assets depleted

- Lack of investment.
- Redistribution of company assets to cover current expenses.
- Growth is replaced with survival strategies.
- Revenue continues to slip.
- Unemployment grows.
- National disposable income declines.
- Human capital (talent, an overlooked asset) is not easily replaceable, and there are long lead times to train, less loyalty, and more dependence on technology.

Personal financial trouble increases

- More unemployment.
- Loss of personal disposable income.
- Increased demand for government services (at all levels).

Government impact

- Substantial drop in revenues (tax base drops).
- Quarantine and isolation requirements will use most of government assets.
- Limited ability to provide traditional support services.
- Increased demand for services.
- Social unrest ferments, with a "someone has to help us" mentality.

Bankruptcies

- Business failures increase to unprecedented levels.
- Increase in personal and commercial bankruptcies.
- Backlog in court processing of bankruptcies.
- Creditors wait longer for assets from courts.
- Creditors see drop in assets from bankruptcies.
- Creditors become more restrictive in loaning money and extending credit.
- Credit and loan availability drops.
- More companies fail as a result of lack of loans and credit.

Creditors fail

- Delays in bankruptcy processing and asset distribution result in lender failures.
- Bankrupt company assets are not redistributed into the market.
- Business market contracts because of operational asset decline.
- Lender failures compounds bankruptcy backlog and asset distribution.

Opportunities

- Large numbers of qualified, trained individuals available for employment.
- Companies prepared to identify these people will grow stronger and faster.
- Substantial number of opportunities will exist as a result of company failures.

Let's take a look at one sector, transportation. Within that sector, take the slice dealing with passengers and cargo. Just on the basis of moving people and stuff, you can already project the complexity of the issue. The business impact of a pandemic to the airline industry and related industries that support the airlines is potentially huge. The world's airports move billions of passengers and millions of tons of cargo involving millions of aircraft movements. What was your estimate that a person, who knew that they had a highly infectious form of tuberculosis, would be capable of flying internationally on several flights as happened in 2007? Now, take that projection and add the variability factor and random character of the event and think about the consequences in the context of flying from any airport with a case of influenza. There were almost 2 billion passengers traveling in 2006; that is roughly 3 million people every day flying from one city or one country or one continent to another. The potential is obvious for someone with an infectious disease, unwittingly perhaps, carrying it from one part of the world to another.

Air New Zealand had an unexpected downturn in revenue of 11 percent when cities with SARS were transformed by the SARS outbreak. Sherry Cooper from Toronto explains:

> During its four-month run in Toronto, ending in June, SARS killed fewer than 50 people. Even China and Hong Kong, the two places hardest hit by the virus, suffered "only" 648 deaths in total. On April 23, the WHO sent out a warning against all unnecessary travel to Toronto, Beijing, and China's Shanxi province. Travel to and from Toronto plummeted overnight. Overall SARS cost the city's hotel industry more than $125 million Canadian; more generally, the tourism industry in the province of Ontario lost more than $2 billion Canadian in income and jobs.[5]

The *Wall Street Journal* reported the following in 2007:

> This summer, rampant flight cancellations and delays are forcing many travelers to languish, sometimes for hours, before they can board their flight. Unfortunately, that's nothing compared with what may await them on the plane.... Between flights ... the cleaning tends to be cursory. American says it picks up trash and cleans seat-back pouches between flights, but it doesn't wipe down tray tables or vacuum while at the gate unless there's an obvious mess that must be addressed. ATA Airlines also says it doesn't wipe down tray tables between flights unless there's a clear need because of the limited ground time.[6]

I am sure that after reading this, you are probably thinking about carrying disinfectant wipes with you on your future travels. If the above examples are common practice, the spread of viral illness could extend the post-pandemic meltdown for the transportation industry, or the industry could be required to use more stringent cleaning standards to their fleets of aircraft. This is only one example of only one segment of one industry sector!

BUSINESS IMPACTS: HOW LONG CAN YOU SURVIVE?

Impacts can be immediate and expensive. It is therefore prudent that your pandemic planning efforts consider the dynamic nature of the world's markets as part of your overall strategy. This makes good business sense. It can be readily applied to situations other than a pandemic. With this broader perspective in mind, your pandemic preparations can be leveraged into greater management awareness and, perhaps, more of a competitive edge for your enterprise. This is true for public-sector entities, too. Government can be more competitive and forward thinking and gain leverage with the constituents (taxpayers) whether they are individuals or businesses.

One key issue that businesses face with a pandemic that is different from other disasters is that multiple locations could be affected simultaneously. This is complicated by loss of personnel that could occur for several reasons: sickness, caring for sick individuals, school closures, and fear of contamination at the workplace. Most of the current business continuity models are based on the recovery of technology and facilities. Few address the human component, and whether they do, they are not doing it very well. First and foremost, make sure you have a basis for ensuring that communication and information flows seamlessly vertically and horizontally throughout the enterprise. This means that you have to have common terminology within and with all the external touch points (customers to vendors) that is clearly understood by all. Most organizations come up short when an analysis of the communication and information flow is undertaken. The general finding is that fragmentation and a lack of seamlessness exist. Some examples (not exhaustive) of how seamless communication can be ensured include the following:

- Common terminology: if we both know what we mean, then we can communicate.
- Decision aids: if we have the same criteria to assist us in decision making, we can, at least, assess situations with a common understanding of the potential impacts.
- Clearinghouse, knowledge repository: if we can access a base of knowledge, then we have a greater chance of understanding operational elements within our organization and external to our organization.
- Rely less on technology as the end-all solution: technology works well only with the interface of the human element and the absence of disruptive situations (e.g., natural disasters and technology glitches).

Additionally, most organizations lack a common set of decision aids such as have been introduced in this book to facilitate the clustering of decisions into categories that can be addressed at various management levels to ensure support of the affected element and to offset any further business disruption. Many of the operational elements do not fully understand what other operational elements actually do. This will often impede the planning and preparedness efforts of the organization with respect to identifying cross-functional dependencies, input-process-output assessments, and external touch points.

There is generally a "distance" between operational elements within the enterprise brought on by the persistent and pervasive use of communications and information technologies to bring together the work being done. This virtual separation is exacerbated many times by the actual geographic separation of widespread enterprises.

There are three factors that are primary contributors to this. The first is physical distance. Many enterprises have a large geographic footprint operating in multiple locations or geographic regions. Physical distance can also be created by distinct operational silos within an enterprise, with various organizational-level elements operating as if they were stand-alone entities. In a pandemic, which can have a broad-based impact, the enterprise could experience significant degrees of disruption as a result of the physical distance.

Operational distance, the second factor, is a result of size as well as the extended value chain that many organizations operate within today. Employees, consultants, contractors, and vendors, working on full-time, part-time, temporary, or some other type of extended capacity, form many arms of the extended enterprise. Customers, the supply chain, and strategic alliances form other arms of the extended enterprise. In a pandemic, the availability of people, their ability to meet face to face, the degree of multitasking on projects for other teams, and how skilled personnel are at using technological tools at their disposal (infrastructure may not be as responsive because of demand loads) will have a significant impact on the enterprise's ability to sustain its operations. Some operational elements may be restricted in their ability to function beyond certain geographic boundaries because of licensing requirements (for example, lawyers, engineers, and medical professionals).

Other operational elements are separated by product/service offerings. Modifying these alone will not necessarily have a significant long-term influence on pandemic preparedness. Facilitating management decision making by developing decision aids that are incorporated into the business continuity plans at all levels within the extended enterprise could facilitate decision making regarding business issues, day-to-day operational decisions, and overall responsibility for managing assets (e.g., human, technology, and facilities) during a pandemic.

The third factor involves similarity distance. Similarity distance is the degree to which team members share enterprise cultural values, similarities in communication style, and attitudes toward work. Because of distinct operational boundaries, there may be internal limitations with regard to cross-functional support between and among elements. The negative consequences of a pandemic, loss of human capital, can wreak havoc on the unprepared organization. Some examples for overcoming these three factors are as follows:

- Breakdown of silos and silo mentality
- Use of common terminology
- Use of decision aids
- Ensuring the depth of skill sets and human capital capacity

If the above appear similar to the points made about seamless communications, there is a reason. These points are critical to your pandemic planning efforts.

DO NOT FORGET SUCCESSION PLANNING AND GOVERNANCE ISSUES

Succession planning is currently not a formal element of the contingency planning process. From a management perspective, this will be a critical element during a pandemic. Succession plans should be considered to ensure that decision rights (authority for decision making), decision boundaries (limitations on scope of commitment on behalf of the enterprise), and decision "triggers" are integrated into the planning framework. Having consistent succession plans either as stand-alone components or incorporated into existing contingency plans can facilitate transition during a pandemic and ensure consistency of decision making.

Decision making regarding governance issues can only be addressed by senior executives. Senior executives will establish and manage voluntary compliance mandates as well as ensure compliance with regulatory-driven requirements.

Strategy requires management engagement to achieve 360-degree coverage. Again, this coverage consists of (1) forward-looking capabilities of active analysis and situational awareness, (2) awareness of challenges, (3) executable goals and objectives, and (4) ability to capitalize on experience and past successes. Operating in a pandemic will require that your organization have a flexible and responsive strategy. Incorporating business strategy elements into the management decision-making process at all levels of contingency planning can facilitate greater flexibility.

PARADIGM SHIFTS

Although we may be aware of the problem, we do not see it as a problem; we therefore do not see the need for urgency in getting prepared to deal with the problem. The fundamental issue is that we are dealing with incomplete information. This leads to our not being able to develop and make meaningful decisions because of the uncertainty of the situation. A classic example of incomplete information is the weekly report from WHO, entitled "Cumulative Number of Confirmed Human Cases of Avian Influenza A/(H5N1) Reported to WHO," that I referred to in Chapter 1. Go to the WHO website (www.who.int) and read the footnote "WHO reports only laboratory-confirmed cases." That means that cases the WHO cannot confirm are not getting reported. One may start to be concerned. What are the actual numbers? The simple fact is that we do not know. This also speaks to the mutation of the virus and the mortality of the virus. If we assign a high mortality based on incomplete information, we may be overshooting the mark, or, if we underreport because we have not confirmed the death as related to H5N1, then we may be undershooting the mark. In either case, incomplete information skews our knowledge, making any prediction suspect.

Now take another example that also comes from the WHO website (www.who.int), one that is probably not as frequently reviewed by those who are looking at cumulative statistics. The example is from the situation update section and is dated May 16, 2007. There were fifteen cases listed. There is a line in the report that reads as follows: "Seven of these cases had exposure to sick or dead poultry; the source of infection is unknown for eight cases." The WHO had no idea what the source of infection was for more than half of the cases? Could it be from human-to-human transmission? Could it be from caring for a sick person and getting it from contaminated surfaces? They do not know. This does not seem to correspond to the footnote from the cumulative information very well. Or perhaps the WHO did not include the eight cases with an unknown source of infection in the cumulative table?

For business planners, the above examples may present a difficult stretch. What do these tables and figures mean to my business, to my markets? How am I to make use of this information? Sometimes the forest is not seen because we are too absorbed with the composition of a leaf. A tactical focus on processes rather than a strategic focus that is broader, based on business goals, objectives, and response to the market demand, can equal less than effective business continuity. What the two tables mean in terms of a paradigm shift is that we actually do not know as much as we think that we know.

Now you are thinking, okay, but how do I apply this to my situation? When we start to project forward in our planning to the post-pandemic period and contemplate the recovery and restoration of the socioeconomic status quo, we need to recognize that, unlike a traditional recovery and restoration from a disruptive event that affects our business, recovery restoration of the socioeconomic status quo in the aftermath of a pandemic may take decades. Being prepared beforehand to realign your business to provide services and/or products that should be in demand in the post-pandemic period is a prudent exercise. One of the current planning assumptions that government and the private sector widely accept is that health services are going to experience chaos during the pandemic period. What about the potential for persistent secondary effects in the health services that will reverberate through the sector for an indeterminate time? This impact will be felt by primary health services and all the affiliated touch points that draw some form of revenue from or render some service to the health sector. This extends as far as the commodity markets that provide the raw materials that the health sector eventually transforms into goods such as medication.

In his book, *In the Wake of the Plague* (2002), Norman Cantor[7] describes how the feudal system in England was forever changed. Landowners were suddenly faced with a new economic paradigm: peasants were able to bargain more effectively for higher wages (as a result of a limited pool of workers), and they were not locked to the land and could, and did, move to where they could get higher wages. Landowners were faced with asset liability: in this sense, they had to pay taxes on land that had crops that were now worth less in the market because of less demand (resulting from fewer people surviving the plague). Furthermore, they had to pay higher wages to a smaller available pool of labor. Other sectors and services are likely to face similar problems and may also experience difficulties associated with income loss, changes in competitive position, loss of customer base, lack of raw materials, and a labor pool that is limited.

In his book *Risk Intelligence: Learning to Manage What We Don't Know*, David Apgar provides us with a list of characteristics for what he considers a risk-intelligent organization and for a risk-reactive organization.[8] Figure 6.1 summarizes Apgar's key characteristics. How does your organization measure up? Is your enterprise one that anticipates, has a strategy, operates with clear guidelines, and is objective focused? In the post-pandemic period, this will be one of the key determinants for survival of private-sector enterprises and for government at all levels.

Taking a proactive approach to risk assessment in the pre-pandemic period can facilitate the ability to execute a strategy in the post-pandemic period. In the previous section, I asked how long can you survive? Being able to develop a strategy for realignment of the socioeconomic landscape in the post-pandemic period can afford the opportunity to capitalize on situations present during the pandemic period and in the aftermath. Finding a new way of using assets could provide you, your enterprise, and your community with buffers that will lessen the impact of a pandemic event.

Risk-Intelligent Organization	Risk-Reactive Organization
Anticipates, has a strategy, operates with clear guidelines, objective focused	Often caught off guard, lacks strategy, process driven, rigid structure
Guidelines—address the situation as it unfolds, maximize flexibility	Procedures—rigid structures based on process steps, lack flexibility to adapt to the situation
Strategy and guidelines provide operational basis to actionize custom solutions based on situational awareness	Risk analysis is often limited in scope, does not take into account variables, organization does not identify learnable risks

Figure 6.1. Risk Intelligent or Risk Reactive?

CONCLUDING THOUGHTS

The World Health Organization, in its annual report, stresses the need for a more coordinated international approach to managing infectious diseases. As noted in the report, WHO cites that these diseases are spreading throughout the world faster than ever before. When we prepare our plans to address a pandemic, we have to remember that it may not be an influenza pandemic with which we are faced. The WHO Epidemic and Pandemic Alert and Response current coverage is of sixteen potential epidemic and/or pandemic producers. We have seen diseases that we thought had been wiped out, such as tuberculosis, reemerge as drug-resistant varieties.

It is certain that there will be, sooner or later, a pandemic; if it is not influenza, it will be some disease that mutates, becomes transmissible from human to human, and to which we have little or no immune system defense.

The main focus of this chapter has been to direct your attention to the possibility of a vastly changed socioeconomic landscape that will emerge during and after a pandemic.

Although the worst-case scenario evokes a vision of great pain and suffering, a far worse case could be the aftermath of a pandemic from a socioeconomic standpoint, especially if you, your enterprise, and your government are not focused on the appropriate planning models.

In the next chapter, I will look further at economic impacts and will also touch on possible geopolitical ramifications that could result from a pandemic.

Paradigm Shifts: Socioeconomic and Market Ramifications

> We evaluate an organisation's resilience on three dimensions: its situation awareness of both its own operations and the environment within which it operates, how well it understands and manages its keystone vulnerabilities, and the organisation's adaptive capacity, its attitude and ability to cope with change.
> —Dr. Erica Seville, University of Canterbury, New Zealand

In a post-pandemic world, what will the socioeconomic landscape look like? How long will it take to get things back to normal pre-pandemic levels of activity? Recently, I had the opportunity to speculate with two informed speculators, my friends and colleagues, Robert J. Pierce (Jay) and his wife Cathy. Jay and Cathy both traded commodities at the Chicago Board of Trade and in the postmerger era at the newly formed CME Group (Chicago Mercantile Exchange and Chicago Board of Trade). Jay also is a principal with M1 Energy Risk Management. M1 Energy Risk Management consults with renewable energy firms to reduce their commodity-related risks by creating and managing customized hedging programs. In effect, they are in the disaster insurance business, providing insurance against the financial dangers that can visit firms with commodity exposure. Because virtually all firms have a risk exposure related to commodity exposure, whether direct or indirect, I feel that the insights provided by Jay and Cathy provide a value added component to all business continuity planning programs. We have had an ongoing discussion on the potential effect of pandemics and other types of disasters on various markets and firms.

We recently discussed the commodities markets and how they would react to a pandemic. At the end of our discussion, I came to the conclusion that markets would, for the most part, be in turmoil. Trading in commodities may not reflect the actual price that we would pay for goods at point of possession. For example, soybean meal (a feedstock for poultry) could go down because of a drop in demand, yet fats and soybean oil could see a rise in price because of a need to offset deficiencies and a greater demand for nonpoultry products (fats and soybean oil are feedstock for hogs and steers). Corn could see demand increase, although cattle prices may drop because of curtailed personal consumption (steak is a luxury) in favor of pork (hogs), a mainstay. So, hog prices should go up, as well as pork bellies (currently only traded electronically), because we will be dining in versus going to restaurants during a pandemic. Cotton will most likely drop because of reduced demand for consumer goods. The same is true with coffee, except we may see point-of-sale prices rise because of transportation disruptions.

On the metals side of our discussion, Jay speculated that gold will go up because of international insecurity and concerns about the stability of governments. Other metals (copper, aluminum, and silver) face extraction issues; specialized skill sets are needed to extract metal from the ground (gone are the days of striking it rich with a pan in a stream). Platinum could see a drop because of lack of consumer demand (catalytic converters) for automobiles.

In the energy sector, Jay and Cathy set out a particularly interesting scenario. Coal from open-pit mines (anthracite) could be little affected, whereas coal from mining (bituminous) could see price fluctuation attributable to the impact of worker shortages (skill sets for mining). Crude oil could drop because demand for gasoline, diesel, and jet fuel will drop (less driving and flying); heating oil and natural gas demand could rise (staying home) but see the effects of degradation of the workforce (skill sets) affecting the price. This could be offset by less industrial demand because factories are going to be operating less in many industries. This, of course, does not mean that factories will shut down entirely. Even with drops in demand, some industrial facilities, such as office buildings, will have to run at minimal levels of energy consumption.

There will be a spike in demand for bulk wood (e.g., plywood) during a pandemic. This should drive prices for wood-related products higher. The reason is simple: current estimates indicate that, in the United States, we will run out of caskets in about a week. If the death toll is within the range of the Spanish Influenza, we can expect to see funerals and burials at the same rate they experienced in 1918–1919; that is very short in duration for the funeral and using available materials to inter the bodies. Although I do not think that we will experience the mass burials that occurred during the plague, I do think that we will see people being buried in makeshift coffins.

Real estate markets should be heavily affected. This will be true for both commercial and residential. Commercial real estate could get a double whammy from, first, loss of occupancy leading to broken leases and drop in rental income, and second, from a drop in real value as more real estate becomes available on the market, driving down prices. Additionally, building owners will still have to service their mortgages and pay taxes, and may have to decontaminate their property as well.

Residential real estate could fare no better. Yes, people will be staying at home, but, much the same as commercial real estate, mortgages, real estate taxes, and utility bills will not go away. Also, you could be staying at home because you are unemployed, not just sick.

A drop in the value of real estate and in demand for real estate has another impact, this time on government. Government generates its money in two ways. The first is through taxation; the second is through the creation of fiat currency (they print it). With a potentially significant drop in tax revenue and huge demand for government to do something, we could see the system begin to fray and potentially collapse, leading to draconian measures to ensure that national security is maintained. Do not think that just because there is a pandemic going on that we will see the end of war or terrorism. As a matter of fact, we may see a surge in terrorist acts. That is because governments worldwide might not be able to marshal enough resources to deal with the pandemic, creating opportunities for terrorists to attempt to destabilize governments.

I will have more to say regarding the markets later in this chapter. Right now I want to turn our attention to the geopolitical issues that we could encounter in the pandemic and post-pandemic periods.

GLOBAL INSECURITY OR GLOBAL INSTABILITY?

Whether you are staying at home, expanding overseas, outsourcing, or just dependent on trade and infrastructure—this means all of you!—this chapter may give you some insights that you had not considered previously.

Keep in mind that an influenza pandemic is just one of the many potential disruptive situations that could create global instability. As in our previous discussions on conflation and confluence, we have to keep in mind that disruptive events, such as earthquakes, fires, explosions, war, and terrorism, do not stop just because there is a pandemic. In the same vein, we have to realize that, even in a pandemic, the socioeconomic activities of the world will not come to a screeching halt either. Life will go on; people will work, eat, and do the things that need to be done. The real question is how much the socioeconomic system will degrade. It has taken six years since the events of September 11, 2001, to see markets recover to near their levels before September 11. Although September 11 was a devastating day in history, it was still a relatively isolated event. Hurricane Katrina, although affecting a much greater geographic region, was still a relatively localized event. The tsunami that occurred on December 26, 2004, was still a localized event. A pandemic is capable of creating an effect that we have never experienced, much greater than that of two world wars and the cumulative effects of all of the above catastrophes.

To understand the magnitude of a pandemic and its potential to take life, consider that the combined death toll of the ten deadliest natural disasters, approximately 7.8 million, would only rank ahead of the 5 million estimated dead during the Antonine Plague of 165–180 A.D. that the Roman Empire experienced. The Antonine Plague only ranks fifth on the list of all-time pandemics.

The Asian Flu of 1957 took an estimated 4 million lives. Smallpox killed more than 300 million (the population of the United States of America) in the twentieth century alone. Bubonic Plague in three recurrences has accounted for more than 300 million. The Spanish Flu pales in comparison, with an estimated 20–100 million dead. AIDS, which emerged in 1981, has killed an estimated 25.3 million.

For a comparison of the ten deadliest natural disasters, the 1931 Yellow River flood in China has a death toll estimated between 1 and 2 million. World War I gives a range of between 9 and 119 million, with the higher figure taking into account the Spanish Influenza. World War II saw an estimated 40–70 million lose their lives. Political repression (the Great Leap Forward) accounted for between 27 and 72 million dead under Mao Tse-tung. One could go on and on. The fact is, none of these events comes close to the death tolls that occur during a pandemic. To top that, most pandemics have a relatively short-duration timeframe, lasting between 500 and 800 days, as I have noted previously.

DEFINING A GLOBAL RISK

To develop a robust list of global risks, the World Economic Forum[1] applied six selection criteria to a broader list of risks. A time horizon of ten years was selected to ensure rigor in considering each risk against the others. The six criteria are grouped into four classes.

Scale and scope of impact: A global risk has global scope, with the potential (including both primary and secondary impacts) to affect at least three world regions on at least two continents. A global risk has cross-industry impact, potentially affecting three or more industries. Each global risk must satisfy both of these criteria.

Nature of impact—economic, social, or both: A global risk has an economic impact exceeding $10 billion and/or a major social impact in terms of human suffering and loss of life, triggering public pressure to respond. Each global risk must satisfy one of these two criteria.

Uncertainty: To warrant inclusion in the list of global risks, there must be uncertainty as to how the risk will manifest itself over ten years or at least as to the severity of its impact. A trend whose path is already clear and has been discounted or otherwise fully accommodated in forward planning does not constitute a global risk in the context of the program.

Need for multistakeholder response: A global risk is defined as one demanding a multistakeholder approach to respond to it. This might be because cooperation between the public and private sectors is required to understand the drivers of the risk, to assess its interlinkages with other risks, or to assess its impacts on different industries or countries, or because concerted endeavors by governments, multilateral organizations, businesses, and civil society institutions are needed to address the causes or mitigate the effects.

A pandemic is defined as a "global epidemic." Does it meet the criteria for inclusion in the World Economic Forum list of risks?

Scale and scope of impact: A pandemic, by definition, has global scope. A pandemic will have a primary impact (large-scale loss of life) and secondary impacts in that it will affect socioeconomic activity the world over. A pandemic will create cascading effects throughout the global economy, primarily affecting healthcare services, transportation, and consumer goods industries. Based on this assessment, a pandemic meets the criteria of scale and scope of impact. A study by Harvard University professor Christopher Murray, based on death registration data from 27 countries to estimate deaths from the Spanish Influenza, found that a global pandemic of a novel, contagious, and lethal form of influenza could kill as many people in a year as died in World War II. Researchers believe at least 62 million people could die in the space of twelve months if a similar pathogen emerged today.[2]

Nature of impact—economic, social, or both: The Congressional Budget Office and World Bank originally published studies that estimate the economic impact of a pandemic ranging between $670 billion and $800 billion U.S. Since the initial studies, the World Bank has raised its estimate to more than $1 trillion U.S. Human suffering and loss of life have already been addressed above. What the studies did not reflect is the long-term effect in terms of the impact to the worldwide socioeconomic system that could take decades from which to recover.

Uncertainty: How much more uncertainty can an event contain? Viruses mutate to survive. The current virus of concern, H5N1, is showing signs that it has mutated to a point at which antiviral medication is less effective. While researchers are studying the H5N1 virus, all appear to agree that there is great uncertainty as to how the virus may manifest itself over time. Currently, the H5N1 virus is lethal in more than 50 percent of the human cases that have been confirmed by the WHO. The Spanish Influenza virus was only 2–3 percent lethal, and the death estimates are more than 50 million. Many have discounted the occurrence of a pandemic. Worldwide, government and industry have, according to most studies, not prepared and planned for a pandemic. Furthermore, who is to say that it will be the H5N1 virus that causes a pandemic? There is Ebola, Marburg, and a host of other potential pandemic creators that lurk out there, not to mention things we have yet to encounter.

Need for multistakeholder response: The public sector and private sector will have to cooperate to survive a pandemic. Currently, there is very little cooperation. A recent trilateral agreement between Canada, Mexico, and the United States has begun to address the issue from a governmental perspective. However, are we too late in the process to make much use of the effort? And is the effort well focused? Remember that a pandemic is not just a medical event. A pandemic will have the potential to create great economic devastation. Too little cooperation between the public and private sectors exists today to understand risk.

THE FACTS

The following facts must be considered when developing an overview of global insecurity issues as they relate to a pandemic:

- The emergence of new and deadly viruses, such as SARS, AIDS, Ebola, and others, combined with expanding terrorism and civil unrest, presents the potential for a change in the balance of power. North America, Europe, Africa, the Middle East, and Asia are susceptible because of the growing gap between haves and have nots.

- America is not immune from the effects of a pandemic. Quite the contrary, we are less prepared than many nations, and we are not used to having to do without. According to the American Medical Association, there is a physician shortage in many areas within the United States. This presents a serious healthcare issue during a pandemic. Today, more than 20 million people are affected by an inability to access quality medical services in the United States. The situation in other parts of the world is even worse. The stakes for the global community are high, and the issues are indeed, life, death, and economic survival.

- The last two pandemic events, the Hong Kong Flu and Asian Flu, were mild compared with previous pandemics. A pandemic, even if it were mild, could destabilize the world.

- In a pandemic, all people are at risk. In an insecure world, all people and all facilities/operations and, therefore, all governments and businesses are at risk.

- Planning priorities should be placed on long-term management of the consequences of a pandemic. A pandemic will most likely affect population centers because of the density of people in them. In many parts of the world, the concentration of people in mega-cities is such that government services cannot keep up with demand. In the United States, we have been very fortunate to have created a robust infrastructure. However, that robustness is being constantly threatened by age, increased demand, and less profitability. Maintaining the aging infrastructure system costs companies more that just brokering the products delivered through the system, specifically utilities, including gas, electric, and water; energy-related products; and transportation of good and services. For example, it costs more to maintain a gas line than to broker gas through the line. Therefore, maintenance is seen as a profit drain and less is scheduled and accomplished. The longer I can keep costs for maintenance down, the higher my profits potentially will be and, hence, my bonus. A strained infrastructure system in many parts of the world could readily collapse in a pandemic, creating a cascade effect throughout a global infrastructure that, although not hard-wired, is inexorably linked.

- Governments and corporations present targets of opportunity to individuals and organizations that seek change or want to do damage. When looking at terrorism, this is obvious. During a pandemic, one has to assess the ability of the government to care for its citizens. For corporations, many of which today have maximized just-in-time systems and niche marketing, a pandemic presents a quandary in many ways. A corporation has an obligation to provide a safe workplace and to offer products and services that people want to purchase. The intelligent corporation is today beginning to assess the ability to stay in business during a pandemic. Its CEOs are questioning whether their products and/or services will be in demand, and, if not, what they can do to shift out of one market into others to offer products/services that are needed. They are also taking steps to address employee safety and security through programs that are forward thinking.

- Government cannot be the end-all to everyone. Individuals and corporations must take personal responsibility for their survival. Individuals must plan for the long term, not just the 500–800 days of the pandemic but also for the recovery and restoration period (which could last decades).

- Governments must concentrate their efforts on ensuring the protection and preservation of critical infrastructures essential to their respective nation's continued well-being. These infrastructures include the following:

  - Electric power supplies
  - Gas and oil
  - Telecommunications
  - Banking and finance
  - Transportation
  - Water supply systems
  - Emergency services
  - Continuity of government

Interestingly enough, in the United States, most of what is considered critical infrastructure by the government is owned by private enterprise. This presents a quandary in a pandemic situation when, perhaps, government will be forced to step in and nationalize companies to stabilize.

- Government and business must act now to make key assets (human resources, information resources, equipment, and facilities) available for dispersal during a pandemic. Personal preparation for ourselves and families is going to be critical to surviving a pandemic. This means learning how to survive in a chaotic environment. It means that one must take to heart the CDC's advice on social distancing, cough etiquette, and use of hand sanitizers. Failure to do so is to be vulnerable.

- An integrated approach to continuity of operations, whether government, business, or personal, will provide the most effective use of resources. It will facilitate risk reduction and minimize the potential disruption to the complex network structure of modern government, business, and our global socioeconomic system.

WHAT TO EXPECT

Let us look into my crystal ball and see what is in store for us in the future with a particular focus on a pandemic and its impact. Friends have often called me a pessimist because they say I always see the downside to everything. I prefer to consider myself a realist. I look at the future with great expectations and a healthy dose of reality. We live in a world that has seen significant change in the last century. We are early in the twenty-first century and already we are seeing technologies that were only dreamed of late in the last century. Can we sustain this steep ascent at such dizzying speeds? Or will the world be less and less capable of managing the acceleration? Fewer and fewer people understand technology. More and more of the world is feeling disenfranchised and unable to keep up. Throw in the threat of a pandemic, whether influenza, plague, Ebola, or some other exotic, yet to be discovered virus, and you have a recipe for a significant paradigm shift.

Should a pandemic occur, we can expect more uncertainty, rapid change, new threats, and in general a potentially rough ride for those who are not prepared. During and after a pandemic, the resilient organizations will survive. Ask yourself this question: "Can our organization adjust rapidly to the changes that a pandemic will bring?" If the answer is no or you are uncertain, then you should hasten to develop an integrated business continuity plan for your organization and its value chain.

Because of the random nature of the occurrence of pandemic influenza and the inability on our part to predict where it will strike, what sector of the population will be affected, or how long it will last, much of our planning efforts should be directed forward instead of attempting, as many are, to develop essentially tactical-level response plans for triage. We need these plans and are currently woefully unprepared for any mass casualty situation that could befall us. However, the great damage to our socioeconomic system will be the long-term shock to the global economy. We could see decades pass before we restore the current socioeconomic balance, if ever. McKibbin and Sidorenko in their study use four shocks to define each scenario:[3]

- Shocks to the labor force (mortality and morbidity)
- Supply shocks (increase in costs by sector)
- Demand shocks (by sector)
- Risk premium shocks (three components: quality of government response, health policy index, and financial risks index)

The study assumes an attack rate among the labor force in each country of 30 percent. Under this assumption, an employee is sick for ten working days on average and either dies or recovers within that timeframe. The second component of their sickness index is attributable to absenteeism as a result of workers staying home to care for sick family members. The numbers that they produce are insightful. Focusing the four scenarios on the United States, we come up with the following numbers from the study:

- Mild scenario: 20,200 U.S. deaths (mortality rate of 0.007 percent) and 1.4 million deaths worldwide (mortality rate of 0.022 percent)
- Moderate scenario: 202,000 U.S. deaths (mortality rate of 0.07 percent) and 14.2 million deaths worldwide (mortality rate of 0.22 percent)
- Severe scenario: 1 million U.S. deaths (mortality rate of 0.35 percent) and 71 million deaths worldwide (mortality rate of 1.1 percent)
- Ultra scenario: 2 million U.S. deaths (mortality rate of 0.7 percent) and 142.2 million deaths worldwide (mortality rate of 2.21 percent).

The severe scenario is modeled after the mortality of the Spanish Influenza outbreak of 1918–1919, which seems to be the most common planning default for most organizations doing any planning. But how prepared are we for dealing with the consequences of the ultra scenario? If, in fact, we are not prepared to deal with mild and moderate scenarios, how can anyone expect that we could deal with anything worse?

The post-pandemic implications are significant. How long would it take to recover and restore the socioeconomic status to pre-pandemic levels? The authors estimate the economic impacts at between $330 billion in lost economic output for a mild scenario and $4.4 trillion in lost economic output for an ultra scenario. These figures reflect what the pandemic will take away directly from economic output; they do not reflect what the long-term loss of economic output will be during the post-pandemic period as we restart the stalled world economic engine.

Consider the impact of the loss of foreign direct investment (FDI) for the duration of the pandemic and hesitancy on the part of investors (e.g., companies and countries) or an inability on the part of the recipient nations to attract FDI in the post-pandemic timeframe. Currently, China has vast amounts of capital flooding into the country (an estimated $60 billion in 2006). What would happen if the source of investment dried up? India, Russia, Brazil, and Africa all depend on FDI for their economic existence. The United States and Europe are major investors at present. If any one of the scenarios in McKibbin and Sidorenko's study materialize, the United States and Europe may not have the means to invest in these areas. We may be too preoccupied with our own recovery and restoration efforts. Demand could be such that the United States and Europe would not require the same degree of products/services that these countries currently provide. Furthermore, if the mortality figures play out, could these countries export the same talent that they are currently capable of doing? Indians obtain more than 2 million college degrees annually, approximately 300,000 of them in engineering. How long would it take to recover to these levels?

A worldwide depression could be the end result of the pandemic. A depression occurs when distortions and misallocations of capital are liquidated. Over the period of the pandemic, distortions and misallocations of capital will occur as governments are forced to infuse capital into failing companies to keep them from collapse (airlines, hospitality, and health care). However, when governments are forced to liquidate these distortions and misallocations of capital, we are likely to see a depression or an extremely prolonged period of economic stagnation. Most people's standard of living will go down significantly. In the long run, recovery will occur; there is no question about it, but that does not mean that we are not going to have many false starts and setbacks during the course of recovery and restoration. If history is any indication, the last recovery from a global depression was brought on by a world war. The socioeconomic picture does not look to be good right away in the post-pandemic timeframe.

I have prepared a broad overview of key areas that should be assessed, impacts that could occur, and what you need to plan for, as follows:

- Human factors
- Infrastructure
- Capital assets (facilities and equipment)
- Intangible assets (knowledge)
- Technology value chain (domestic and foreign)

Human factors: As I see it, human factors is the wild card category. Human factors present one of the most unpredictable areas. Why? No one knows with any certainty who will fall victim to disease. The odds are greater that you will succumb to illness in a pandemic because of the widespread nature of illness, lack of medical aid, and loss of normal socioeconomic activities. How will humans react as a pandemic unfolds? Companies that appeared to be viable suddenly collapse because of the lack of demand for their products/services, taking with them the retirement plans of many. Pressures to survive in the workplace, at home, socially, nationally, and internationally will be greater in a pandemic than anything we ever will experience. With technological innovation came the acceleration of everything. A pandemic could bring technology to its knees, not because technology will fail but as a result of the human factor. Because of illness, we may not have enough people with the right skills sets to run things.

People are less patient, are more stressed, and have a greater tendency to act out their frustrations than ever before. In a pandemic, the stress level will be even greater because of the uncertainty of whether or not one will become infected. Set aside for a moment family, friends, and coworkers, and you can imagine what it may be like when we start to see the pandemic unfold. There will be panic as people rush to stockpile essential items, such as food and water. More panic will emerge as people find that medicines that are now more regulated are unavailable or require that you produce identification to get them. Drug stores can expect to see their shelves emptied rapidly. Prescription medication supplies will be in short supply. Companies that produce pharmaceuticals are already querying health insurance providers to ascertain whether insurance companies are going to let people fill prescriptions early or double up on supplies. This is a great example of how just-in-time can become an albatross for companies.

People will exit the workplace, taking essential skills with them. This will initially be attributable to fear, actually getting sick, having to take care of someone who is sick, staying at home with children who are there because schools are closed, or any of a myriad of reasons. The people who will enter the workplace to replace those who are ill or do not show may not have the skills to replace those that are being lost. In many instances, the people entering the workplace will also have different ethics, morals, and codes of conduct. This will affect how organizations do business. If we look at the complexity assumption, human factors is one of the key components that must be assessed before a pandemic.

Human capital issues will not resolve themselves in the post-pandemic timeframe either. As a matter of fact, they may actually be exacerbated because of the loss of life that could be suffered and a degradation to the healthcare system that results in fewer healthcare services available for a potentially less healthy world population. The long-term effects on health could be staggering. Life expectancy may drop significantly. Worker productivity could be affected as a result of collateral health issues with which the survivors have to contend. Replenishing the workforce could be as great a challenge as the English faced after the plague and could result in the same social upheaval that was experienced.

Infrastructure: Infrastructure worldwide is going to be put to the test in a pandemic. In the United States, our infrastructure systems are already beginning to be stretched to the maximum. As corporate America downsized, right-sized, and reorganized and continues the process, we saw and continue to see a greater dependency created on ensuring our standard of living through external sources. In a pandemic, external sources will be severely restricted because of the fact that they are also experiencing high levels of illness. A heavy dependence on imported oil and other raw materials creates significant infrastructure issues. As Michael Morris, Chairman, President, and CEO of American Electric Power said, "If someone wanted to really dent the U.S. economy, a handful of pointed attacks on critical substations could leave you with a seriously affected economy. It's conceivable that energy wouldn't be available in pockets of the country for months, if not years."[4] Well, it may not be a terrorist attack that interdicts the infrastructure. It could be that many of those responsible for operating the infrastructure are too sick to attend to their duties. The net effect could be similar in that we could see outages attributable to lack of maintenance or operators being on hand to run the Supervisory Control and Data Acquisition systems. The world at large is also faced with infrastructure concerns. Most of Europe (including the former Soviet Union) is facing the same, if not worse, aging infrastructure issues. In the developing nations, infrastructure is a major concern on a daily basis. An estimate developed by Booz Allen Hamilton suggests the magnitude of the problem. Over the next twenty-five years, modernizing and expanding the water, electricity, and transportation systems of the cities of the world will require approximately $40 trillion, a figure roughly equivalent to the 2006 market capitalization of all shares held in all stock markets in the world. Add to that timeframe the possible occurrence of a pandemic and you can see that figure skyrocket, whereas at the same time, there will be fewer of the skill sets needed to build, operate, and maintain the infrastructure worldwide.

Capital assets (facilities and equipment): Since the massive efforts to address the Y2K transition, many industries have let their attention slip in this area. Capital assets are often looked at as liabilities instead of assets. In a pandemic, capital assets may prove to be a liability. Mortgages will still have to be paid even if your offices are vacant and real estate prices plummet. Corporations worldwide will have to assess whether or not they can continue to maintain capital assets while the pandemic runs its course. Capital assets will remain under scrutiny even as the pandemic dies down. How long the recovery period lasts will be anyone's guess. Fixed assets will remain vulnerable to being worth less than what is owed on them or even what can be salvaged from selling them. If the subprime mortgage meltdown is any indication, we could also be in for a rough ride on the personal side of the ledger. Many mortgages will go unpaid because of the death of the mortgage holder, and many more will see the survivors walk away because of an inability to pay resulting from the loss of jobs based on demand or lack thereof for products/services.

There is also the U.S. deficit, which would swell during a pandemic, because the government would have to infuse capital into the system to attempt to maintain stability. In the post-pandemic period, that deficit will have to be addressed. What could be the possible impact on asset prices? The International Monetary Fund has produced several studies on financial globalization and its effects. According to an International Monetary Fund study, globalization means that world trade and financial markets are becoming more and more integrated. With the United States being the number one contributor to the World Bank and China and India two of the bank's biggest recipients, with Africa running a close third, what will happen to integrated capital markets (financial and trade) in the wake of a pandemic? Developing countries generally have the least amount of healthcare services, they have younger populations, and they are more dependent on trade than developed nations. Capital assets, financial markets, and worldwide trading could be in for a rough ride. Trade represents almost 30 percent of gross world product today. Direct investment in foreign nations has risen significantly. People cross borders for business and leisure in greater numbers today than twenty years ago.

A positive twist is that there could also be a boom in the post-pandemic period as companies realign and people return and/or reenter the workforce. There will be an infusion of capital from the governments of the world as they realize that they cannot have certain industries fail for national security reasons.

Intangible assets (knowledge and skill sets): Recognize that intangible assets are not replaceable; once gone, they are gone forever. If people with knowledge (skill sets) that cannot be easily replaced are lost in a pandemic, it may take decades to gain back that knowledge, if ever. Knowledge management will be a prime area of focus for business continuity planning in the future. When we link strategic planning, competitive intelligence, and event management into a comprehensive business continuity planning process, we see that these traditionally distinct areas are interdependent, and each depends on knowledgeable individuals to prepare, implement, and manage them. For example, an aging workforce driving knowledge retention and hiring demands have been identified by UtiliPoint International, Inc. as one of the utility industry's most pressing issues. Not only is institutional knowledge transfer at risk, but an understanding of the business and the role of the utility as a consumer service-based enterprise is challenged.[5] One can imagine the chaos that would result with the loss of, or impairment of, the workforce as a result of a pandemic, but this example is indicative of the issues faced by most industry sectors.

It is common practice for organizations to default to work-at-home as an option for continuing business during a pandemic. The reality is that the Internet could not handle the load of work-at-home employees during a pandemic because the current infrastructure in most communities could not support the mass shift from offices to home. This becomes significant if we consider that knowledge can be lost if it cannot be accessed. So, you may be very alive, but I cannot access your knowledge because we cannot communicate. Very few companies capture the intellectual capital of their employees and institutionalize it. Take a look at the training and education budgets of most companies and you will find that they are woefully low. A pandemic will affect the world's knowledge base in ways that cannot be determined because of the randomness of infection and death. This is an area that government and business worldwide should seriously consider as they address pandemic preparedness.

Technology: Infrastructure worldwide is going to be put to the test in the near future. In the United States, our infrastructure systems are already beginning to be stretched to the maximum. As corporate America downsized, right-sized, and reorganized and continues the process, we are seeing a greater dependency created on ensuring our standard of living through external sources. The world at large is also faced with infrastructure concerns. Most of Europe (including the former Soviet Union) is facing aging infrastructure issues. In the developing nations, infrastructure is a major concern on a daily basis. Technology is present in almost all of the infrastructures on which we depend. Technology is integral to the operation of infrastructure, and therefore, although it is a standalone topic, much of the previous discussion on infrastructure ties to technology. For example, since the 1990s, international telephone traffic has grown by more than 300 percent; cell phones have become the norm as at least one-third of the world population is connected via wireless telecommunications. Although we would not normally think of our cell phone as part of infrastructure, this technology is becoming the backbone of communications systems for much of the world. This is an excellent example of the complexity we face when planning for a pandemic.

PRESERVING THE VALUE CHAIN

This area is so important that we will spend most of the rest of the chapter on it. Why? Your organization, whether private or public sector, depends on its value chain for its very existence. This is also one of the most overlooked areas of business continuity planning. In a pandemic, the value chain may become one of the most critical aspects of your organization's survival. As you read the following paragraphs, remember that the value chain is composed of suppliers, those who provide you goods and services and customers and those to whom you provide goods and services.

Most of the value added in business today is created by knowledge-based service activities, such as research and development, marketing research, and customer information, to cite a few. The value chain, for the purposes of this book, is defined as all of the touch points that your organization encounters as it conducts its primary business functions. As such, your business continuity initiatives should assess all of these touch points as they relate to strategy, competitive intelligence, and event management. All too often, the analysis stops at the boundary of the organization. We can no longer make the assumption that the value chain (upstream is suppliers, partners, and vendors, and downstream is customers, resellers, distributors, and wholesalers) is consistent with our mission, vision, and value proposition.

Cargo security is already a major problem for industry. Annual losses attributable to cargo theft run between $10 billion and $15 billion. According to the National Cargo Security Council, motor carriers are the victims in 85 percent of all cargo theft, the majority taking place at terminals, transfer facilities, and cargo consolidation areas. However, these statistics may not reflect the actual situation. The Federal Bureau of Investigation reports that only 40 percent of businesses or individuals actually report theft. If indirect costs are factored in, total losses are estimated to be between $20 billion and $60 billion a year. In a pandemic, the numbers could go off scale, especially for essential goods such as pharmaceuticals and food.[6]

Most organizations have a supply chain that is a mix of competencies, from manufacturing to professional advisory services. Developing a pandemic preparedness strategy for the supply chain can enhance the organization's ability to actively assess vendor capabilities. By creating a flexible framework for augmenting, retaining, or shedding vendor competencies to ensure supply chain integrity, the organization can meet customer demand and customer expectations and generate consistent performance.

No one company can deliver end-to-end products and/or services in today's complex business environment. Your company, like other companies, is most likely dependent on vendors of various types (manufacturing, profession services, software, and transportation) to meet customer expectations.

Supply chains are generally composed of a mix of competencies, from manufacturing to professional advisory services. As such, the supply chain is critical to the success of a company in meeting its customer obligations. In the area of procurement and supply chain management, accountability and innovation are critical success factors. According to Canadian Manufacturers and Exporters, a lack of preparedness not only threatens the viability of a large sector of the Canadian economy but also jeopardizes the delivery of critical goods that depend on complex supply chain systems. This is a particular concern for companies with fewer than one hundred employees, which make up 97 percent of goods-producing businesses and 98 percent of all service-producing businesses in Canada.[7]

An examination of eight key risk areas within supply chain operations was conducted by Ernst & Young.[8] Three of the areas studied revealed the following:

- Business continuity planning: Almost all indicated that they do data backup, but less than 25 percent test for recovery preparedness.
- Collaborative relationships: About 20 percent of vendors overall are not monitored for cost, quality, or delivery. Just 47 percent of companies have documented competitive bidding processes in place.
- Workforce training: 24 percent of consumer goods companies and 18 percent of retailers say workers are not adequately trained in the use of supply chain management tools.

If these three areas reflect the current state of supply chain management, imagine what will happen during a pandemic, when much of the workforce is unavailable. If the statistics from the Canadian Manufacturers and Exporters are indicative of worldwide manufacturing and exporting, then one can anticipate significant disruption in the movement of goods.

One of the first steps toward pandemic preparedness for the value chain is identifying procurement touch points (internally and externally). Developing a custom-fitted questionnaire for vendors as well as internal stakeholders can provide a basis for moving forward. Applicable policies, procedures, recognized "best practices," and regulatory requirements set the benchmarks from which metrics for assessing vendor capabilities can be developed. Pandemic preparedness criteria should be contained in the vendor's contract and spelled out in specific terms. Developing the vendor pandemic preparedness questionnaire needs to be carefully thought through. You are, in essence, creating a legal document that could contain sensitive information and must be protected. You are also creating a potential liability document for yourself.

With the type of information that you will need to collect to assess vendor pandemic preparedness, your organization could be held liable, under the concepts of negligence (foreseeability), constructive notice, and/or constructive knowledge, for *not* taking action to mitigate potential losses. For example, if you find that your vendor has inadequate data backup or lacks a continuity plan, this constitutes constructive knowledge (if one by the exercise of reasonable care would have known a fact, he is deemed to have constructive knowledge of such fact, e.g. matters of public record) and could be construed as negligence if you do nothing to correct the situation (foreseeability). *Black's Law Dictionary*[9] provides definitions for these and other legal constructs that may be helpful as you work your way through the pandemic planning process. I also highly recommend getting the legal staff or outside counsel involved in the planning process to ensure that your organization is properly addressing the legal issues that could lead to liability exposure.

The questionnaire that Logical Management Systems has most often used consists of eight parts that address criteria for assessing vendor capabilities and for vendor certification of answers on the questionnaire. The structure of the questionnaire is summarized below.

- Part 1: Governance Provisions and Management Commitment. Purpose: to establish that the vendor has a formal business continuity program in place that has management commitment. You also want to ascertain whether the vendor's program is integrated into the way it does business or whether it is an adjunct to the business that they are in.

- Part 2: Business Continuity Plans. Purpose: to gain an understanding of the vendor's continuity capabilities in terms of their strategy for continuity and how they implement their business continuity plan.

- Part 3: Business Impact Analysis, Risk Evaluation, and Control Mechanisms. Purpose: to gain an understanding of the extent of the vendor's business impact analysis, frequency of analysis, identification and evaluation of risks, and what control mechanisms the vendor has in place to address risk, threat, hazard, and vulnerability mitigation.

- Part 4: Maintaining Continuity. Purpose: to gain an understanding of the extent and adequacy of training and maintenance program for business continuity.

- Part 5: Incident Response Operations. Purpose: to look at the tactical level of business continuity, seeking to gain understanding of how the vendor identifies, responds to, and communicates information on disruptive events.

- Part 6: Crisis Communications. Purpose: to focus on internal and external communications of the vendor as they relate to policies, information flow, and how crisis communications are managed.

- Part 7: Coordination (External Entities). Purpose: to assess vendor coordination with external parties, be they government, customers, the vendors' vendors, and key components of the coordination process.

- Part 8: Vendor Certification. Purpose: to gain vendor certification of the answers they provided on the questionnaire.

The length of the vendor questionnaires will vary with the industry group represented and the depth of initial analysis that your organization chooses to perform. Generally, the questionnaires that have been developed for clients have contained approximately fifty questions. The questions are designed to require the vendor to provide quantifiable answers. Should the procurement group assessing the adequacy of the answers determine that there is a need for additional analysis, a formal audit team is assembled to determine how to resolve the concern over vendor continuity capability.

Procurement planning considerations will generally consist of the normal day-to-day functioning of the procurement process. In general, these considerations consist of embedding pandemic preparedness criteria and periodic assessment processes into the procurement process.

Pandemic preparedness criteria for your supply chain should consist of a tiered evaluation structure focused on four aspects as presented in Figure 7.1. The pandemic taskforce should be responsible for managing this area and should make it part of the pandemic planning process for the organization. These elements consist of the following:

- Comprehending and describing supply chain continuity requirements
- Conducting business continuity capability assessments
- Evaluating business continuity capabilities
- Identifying actions to be taken.

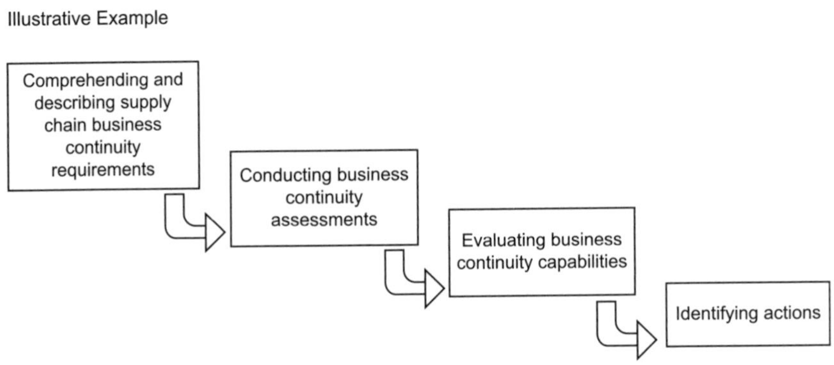

Illustrative Example

Figure 7.1. Supply Chain Business Continuity Elements

During a pandemic, your company will face a variety of risks that have a potential impact on supply chain assurance. These can be articulated as either internal or external, as depicted in Figure 7.2.

These drivers and the ability to manage them (put into place contingency measures) often are interconnected. Understanding this potential interconnectedness is a key factor in assessing vendor business continuity capabilities. Internal and external vulnerability drivers can materialize in a variety of ways. Making vertical, horizontal, and diagonal connections between drivers can provide a conceptual understanding and potentially reduce unexpected outcomes as you identify how risk is uniquely embedded in your company's supply chain.

Risk can be context sensitive, because risk elements interact in different ways depending on the situation. Understanding the potential interaction of risk factors facilitates the ability to measure business continuity capabilities and plan for offsets that can be implemented should a disruptive event occur.

Figure 7.3 is an example of a roadmap for the process of assessing vendor capabilities. The recommended assessment process has been designed to provide a phased approach with progressively more detail accumulated at each phase of the procurement process. This assessment process can be easily embedded into your company's procurement scorecard system, enabling you to incorporate vendor business

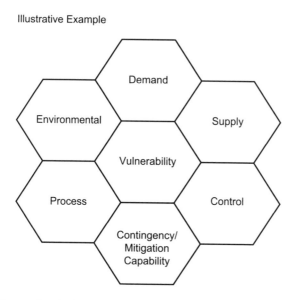

Figure 7.2. Internal and External Vulnerability Drivers

A simple test for organizational maturity might be determining whether the organization has a blueprint outlining the necessary business continuity, operational support processes, and transition plans that need to be developed.

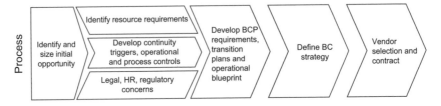

Figure 7.3. Sample Roadmap for Assessing Vendor Capabilites

continuity evaluation as an integral component of the procurement process.

As depicted in Figure 7.4, the integration of recommended business continuity metrics in the procurement process should be related to the key elements of the procurement process. Incorporating the recommended business continuity capability assessment at each phase of the procurement process can help identify vulnerabilities, develop consequence management strategies and plans, and implement mitigation strategies.

On conclusion of assessment at each phase of the procurement process, you can evaluate vendor business continuity capabilities, allowing a "go/no go" decision based on measurable criteria. Before proceeding to the next stage in the procurement process, the vendor will have been vetted, and the next stage of evaluation can allow you to continue to refine the vetting requirements and gather more detail on vendor

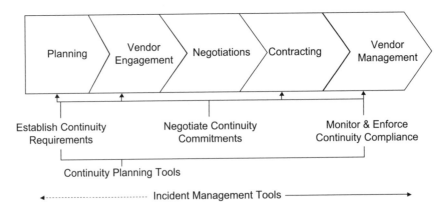

Figure 7.4. Typical Procurement Process

continuity capabilities. Having an in-depth understanding of vendor capabilities at each phase of the procurement process can allow critical decision making at earlier stages of procurement and can thus can enhance communications between you and your vendors regarding business continuity issues.

Embedding into the procurement process specific business continuity objectives, guidelines, and assessment metrics can enhance decision making, communications (vertical/horizontal), and resource management. In addition to the Vendor Continuity Questionnaire, you can develop worksheets that can be incorporated into each phase of the procurement process to further facilitate the assessment of vendor business continuity capabilities. I recommend designing your worksheets to be stand-alone evaluation tools. Consolidating the results from each worksheet to gain a comprehensive perspective can be extremely valuable as an overall risk-ranking statement can be developed.

The benefit of having vendor continuity capabilities catalogued and indexed is threefold. First, the company can assess and quantify the risk impact of an event. Second, you can determine how long the risk exposure will last before the event is mitigated and/or the exposure is rectified. Third, you can estimate potential recovery costs in terms of emergency actions. Put in question form, these three considerations are as follows:

- What is the exposure of the company? How will this risk impact the company, and what is the financial scale?
- How long would the exposure last before it could be fixed?
- What is the cost of recovery in terms of emergency actions?

Early assessment and quantification of vendor and supplier business continuity capabilities are essential. It is recommended that your company and its vendors negotiate periodic assessments of subtier vendors (vendor's suppliers) to further ensure business continuity capabilities. This can be accomplished through contractual requirements executed at the initial stages of vendor engagement. Your company can use the Vendor Continuity Questionnaire and Risk Analysis Worksheets to facilitate consistency of the vendor's depth analysis.

PROCUREMENT INCIDENT MANAGEMENT CONSIDERATIONS

The second part of the procurement process relating to vendor continuity should address incident-management considerations. A vendor can complete the vetting process (Vendor Continuity Questionnaire, Risk Analysis Worksheets, and Scorecard) and still experience a disruption that could affect your company's ability to meet customer requirements. Having an incident-management system as a component of the procurement process can allow your company to respond, recover, and restore supply chain operations with less potential for massive disruption. Incident management can range from assessing and classifying a vendor incident to implementing response actions, such as sending your personnel to vendor facilities to help resolve the problem.

Contingency alternatives can range from having backup response plans to alternative sources of supply. Once the risk themes (natural disasters to manmade crises) are identified and evaluated, actions to address consistent themes throughout the procurement process can be taken. Identifying consistent risk themes across a number of risk dimensions can help to determine where your company should place significant effort to mitigate the risk exposure. For example, if your organization has a high level of exposure to financial market disruption because your organization is in the financial sector, your risk themes would naturally take into account fraud, inflation, and currency fluctuations.

Disruptive events (Figure 7.5) as they occur need to be classified by their level of severity in order to determine the potential impact they may have. A classification system can provide a consistent framework for evaluation. It can also enhance the communication process, allowing ease of communication between internal and external groups and facilitate response, management, recovery, and restoration efforts.

In addition to the event classification system, you could incorporate an event-assessment form that would be used in conjunction with the Event Classification System. This will help you determine the event

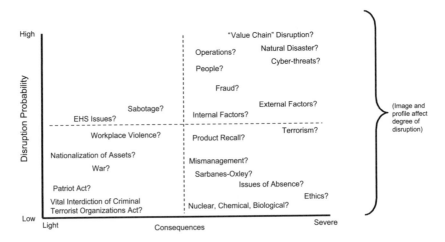

Figure 7.5. Disruptive Events

classification level and facilitate discussion within your company and with the affected vendor(s). As depicted in Figure 7.6, the degree of degradation of service minus the level of preparedness equals the time for recovery. The less prepared an organization is for service disruption, the longer it takes the organization to recover its operations and restore service levels. Having a classification system can enhance the ability to identify potentially disruptive situations early and determine how to respond effectively to minimize the level of service impacts.

The procurement process represents the first line of direct contact with vendors and suppliers. Detection by procurement personnel at any stage of the procurement cycle of potential disruption and classification of severity can allow your company to implement its continuity plan and coordinate with the affected vendor to ensure continuity of operations and to mitigate the disruptive event.

Early detection, classification, and response can lead to less of a drop in service, a potential reduction in the chaos associated with a disruptive event, and shorter recovery and restoration timeframes. Figure 7.7 depicts the typical functions performed at various levels within an organization as it moves from response to restoration. This figure also depicts the focus for an organization at the tactical, grand tactical, and

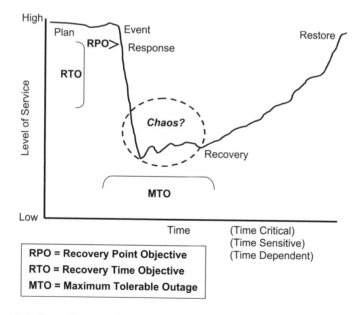

Figure 7.6. Degradation of Service – Degree of Preparedness = Time for Recovery

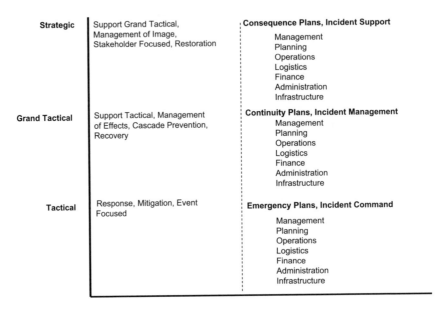

Figure 7.7. Typical Functions Performed at Various Levels within an Organization as It Moves from Response to Restoration

strategic levels. At the tactical level, the focus is generally on event response and mitigation. The focus at the tactical level should be on response and mitigation, although the need at the tactical level is for support from the next level (grand tactical). At the grand tactical level, the focus should be on support for the tactical response.

Additionally, at the grand tactical level, the focus should be on the prevention of cascade and containment of cascade effects on the organization. At the strategic level, the focus should be on management oversight, coordination, and facilitation of restoration of services. It is important to note that a key element in this vertical and horizontal process of detection, classification, response, management, recovery, and restoration is seamless communications. Seamless communication is based on the adoption of common terminology and in the functions represented at each level, as shown in Figure 7.7.

Ensuring supplier continuity capabilities are of paramount concern today. Realizing that most business processes today extend beyond the boundaries of a single entity, awareness of critical supply chain interdependencies has risen sharply. Simply having profiles of potential high-risk suppliers, although extremely important, is by itself not enough. Developing capabilities to assess and monitor vendors is necessary to facilitate the active analysis process. Active analysis, recall, uses predictive metrics to identify potential problems before they occur.

CONCLUDING THOUGHTS

The World Economic Forum, led by its industry partners in financial services, convened 150 representatives from seventeen different sectors, the U.S. government, the World Bank, and a range of experts from civil society and academia to discuss strategies for reducing the risks posed by natural disasters.[10] The emphasis of the conversation was on multi-stakeholder collaboration: specifically, how the sectors represented might partner to support risk-reduction activities that no single actor has the incentives or capacities to address independently. Discussion groups tackled proposals for improving insurance, investing in infrastructure, and building economic and community resilience, among others. Some key points to consider include the following:

- Critical infrastructures: A key issue is the potential for "cascade failure," a disaster that disrupts a piece of critical infrastructure that may trigger cascading disruptions in the global supply chain and economy.

- Risk assessment: There is a need for a standard infrastructural risk assessment and reporting framework.

- Risk transfer: Cascade failures are not classically insurable, and therefore mandatory catastrophe bonds may be the most appropriate way of spreading infrastructure risk in the financial markets.

- Resilience and redundancy: There are many models for mandating spare capacity requirements in the private sector, from the Basel Capital Accords in banking to strategic petroleum reserves in oil markets.

- Retrofitting: Private-sector capabilities can be harnessed for retrofitting vulnerable critical infrastructure (both public and private). "Good Samaritan" legislation should be extended to protect corporate partners from liability, whereas incentives and penalties for maintenance of privatized assets need to be created.

- Hazard assessment and reduction: Thorough risk management should take an "all hazards" approach. Businesses can play an important part in assessing hazards, particularly through the support of monitoring, surveillance, and the development of early-warning systems. Companies undertaking holistic enterprise risk-management activities can provide governments and international organizations many ways to integrate planning and regulatory guidance into a "win-win" situation.

- Risk mitigation: Risk-mitigating activities may include everything from business continuity planning, to building retrofits, to the broader extension of insurance to information and expertise sharing.

Tick, Tick, Tick ... Geopolitical Impacts of a Pandemic

The real value of operational risk modeling lies not in the beauty of the mathematical calculations but in the practical business benefits it can bring to an organization. Data only has value if it can be turned into meaningful intelligence that facilitates decision-making.

—Geary W. Sikich

In a post-pandemic world, what will the socioeconomic landscape look like? How long will it take to get things back to normal pre-pandemic levels of socioeconomic activity? Based on the events of September 11, 2001, I see that returning to a pre-pandemic level of socioeconomic activity could take decades, if not longer. As I write this chapter, we are finally seeing the U.S. stock market getting back to pre–September 11 levels. However, based on my portfolio's performance, it appears that some sectors are still reeling from the shock of the event. We now have the subprime issue to deal with, energy and food prices escalating, political tensions within Iraq, and the Iranian quest for a nuclear something (energy or bomb?).

RANDOM PROBABILITY: RISK REALIZATION

In my discussions with colleagues and over the course of running numerous simulations from tabletops-supervised instruction periods aimed at validating, developing, and maintaining skills in a particular operation by business continuity teams (tabletops are role-playing discussions focused on a predefined crisis or disaster scenario) to participating in collaborative drills focusing on various business sectors, I have begun to develop some risk perspectives that focus on the national security consequences of a pandemic. The timeframe of restoration from a pandemic (a return to socioeconomic activity levels of today) could last three to four decades (thirty to forty years).

Random probability will play a significant role in the outcome of any pandemic. Who will contract influenza is anyone's guess. Events as they unfold will not occur in a neat, linear manner. Rather, they will be nonlinear and affected by variables that we tacitly acknowledge today. In the post-pandemic recovery period, we will not see the U-shaped bell curve that I often see in the simulations that are run by organizations. Figure 8.1 depicts this bell curve. We will, in fact, see tremendous swings that have great potential for chaotic repercussions, the reality being that we cannot accurately predict future events, especially in the case of pandemics in which there will be no adequate reasoning when it comes to mortality.

Today's virtual world measures its ability to answer questions that are never tested in real life. Successful exercises that claim to simulate the events of a pandemic often lack proper focus, rewarding the participants without sufficiently discerning the issues that will be faced and their cascading effects. Solving the apparent problem alone is deemed the necessary condition for success. As such, many of the hidden issues, not readily apparent when you practice the "identify–shoot–solved"–type activities that most exercises reflect, lay simmering in the background ready to come forth in a game of "gotcha."

Too many exercises are considered successful although actual results remain hidden because we focus on the "low-hanging fruit"

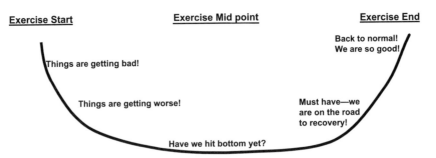

Most exercises reflect a happy smiley face as we go through confirmation that what we think we can accomplish is accomplished because we say that it has been accomplished. Instead we should raise issues, acknowledging that the issues identified lead us to a better understanding of what our organization is capable of accomplishing and where we have dependencies beyond our span of control.

Figure 8.1. Typical Exercise "U"-Shaped Bell Curve

that ensure successful outcomes. Exercises often fail to establish links between cause and effect and ignore the effect of variables that can produce extraordinary results. The linear method of seeking a solution to a problem in an exercise fails to confront the nonlinearity of issues that problems bring. What is often overlooked is information that seemingly is unimportant but is, in effect, extremely valuable and can potentially turn a solution into a bigger crisis as a result of overlooking the information. Correct and effective assessments permit decision makers the opportunity to effectively prioritize activities, allocate scarce resources, and adjust to events quickly. Before real problems can be solved, they must first be characterized in terms recognizable to all stakeholders. Critical thinking is the ability to see problems from multiple perspectives, expose critical underlying assumptions, challenge and reverse one's assumptions, and reformulate basic arguments.[1]

An excellent example of practicing critical thinking and not practicing critical thinking is the case of Nokia and Ericsson. On March 17, 2000, a lightning bolt struck a Philips Electronics semiconductor plant in Albuquerque, New Mexico, causing a fire. The fire lasted only ten minutes, but the outcome was devastating. Water and smoke damage destroyed millions of computer chips. It would take weeks for the plant to be back to full capacity. The flow of computer chips, crucial components in the mobile phones Nokia and Ericsson sell around the world, would suddenly stop. The Philips plant would run at a greatly reduced output for weeks. The fire would have a profound impact on two of the largest distributors during a time when mobile handset sales were at a record pace.[2] Nokia's response was as follows:

- Recognized immediately the reduced flow of chips.
- Purchasing manager, although not terribly alarmed, notified senior management immediately.
- Dispatched a team of experts to identify a solution.
- Sped up a project to boost production and used its leverage with other suppliers to counteract the chip shortfall.
- Pressured other suppliers to produce more chips in a hurry.
- Offered to send two engineers to the Philips plant in Albuquerque to assist.
- Placed components generated at the Philips plant on a special watch list.
- Began daily talks with the officials at the Philips plant.
- Organized an executive "hit squad" aimed at reducing the bottleneck and giving authority for on-the-ground decisions.
- Insisted that Philips reroute production to other Philips plants.
- Operated with Philips as one company to resolve the crisis.

Ericsson's response was as follows:

- Did not notice the reduced flow of chips until they were notified by Philips three days after the fire.
- Did not brief senior management after learning of the fire.
- Moved slowly in responding and were not equipped to handle a crisis situation.
- Had previously consolidated suppliers so they did not have alternate suppliers to produce the chips.
- Were unable to obtain needed production capacity from Philips.

The outcome was that Nokia stayed on target for production and saw its market share increase from 27 percent to 30 percent. Ericsson, conversely, was unable to meet production targets, saw its stock price fall 14 percent a few hours after the impact of the fire was revealed, lost $400 million U.S. in potential revenue, saw its market share drop from 12 percent to 9 percent, watched its stock price fall 50 percent, reported a total loss of $1.68 billion U.S. for the mobile phone division, and exited the mobile phone handset market completely.

Applying a military-type target acquisition methodology of identify, find, fix, track, target, and engage produces results that are little better, unless one practices active analysis and constantly assesses the situation to determine the appropriate engagement (problem resolution) methodology. The trick with a pandemic will be, of course, determining and, more critically, assessing the nature of risk going into decisions. Mistakes in the post-pandemic era could be extremely costly. Organizations will have to be vigilant and aware of the ramifications of failure to discern the real issues, especially if they affect survivability as an ongoing concern.

In the post-pandemic era, do not bet more than you can happily afford to lose. Question everything. Examine the evidence. Be humble. Accept adversity with good grace.

Answering a few simple questions can provide your organization with a broader array of solutions to unseen or unrealized problems. For example, in Table 8.1, I have taken five questions and created a matrix against very broad market sectors. One could easily segment the market sectors into their various component parts and come up with extremely detailed analysis for each sector. The purpose initially would be to assess the broad sectors against each of the questions to come up with some level of confidence and determination of what your organization can afford to lose. Secondary assessment (more detailed and in-depth) will provide fine-tuning of your initial analysis and get the active analysis process underway.

Table 8.1. How Will Market Sectors Fare in a Pandemic?

	Questions			
Market Sectors	What is the worst-case scenario?	What is the best-case scenario?	What is the most likely scenario?	How confident am I in the assessments?	What can I afford to lose?
Information Technology				
Energy				
Industrials				
Health Care				
Telecommunications				
Commodities/Materials				
Financials				
Consumer Staples				
Consumer Discretionary				
Utilities—Gas, Electric, Water				

GLOBAL INSTABILITY

In the remainder of this chapter, I will seek to highlight possible issues that could affect our national security during the years after a pandemic. I have developed some risk perspectives that focus on the national security consequences of a pandemic. Remember that we are addressing a post-pandemic timeframe that could last three to four decades.

Three specific questions need to be addressed:

- What conditions would a pandemic likely produce around the world that would represent security risks to the United States?
- What are the ways in which these conditions may affect America's national security interests?
- What actions should the United States take to address the national security consequences of a pandemic?

These three questions can be framed against the four scenarios that McKibbin and Sidorenko developed in their study.[3] The study assumes an attack rate among the labor force in each country of 30 percent. Under this assumption, an employee is sick for ten working days on average and either dies or recovers within that timeframe. The second component of the sickness index is absenteeism attributable to workers staying home to care for sick family members. The numbers the authors produce are insightful. Please refer to the previous chapter for a detailed discussion of the four scenarios. The following paragraphs present an overview of what the four scenarios could present to the United States in terms of national security issues.

Mild pandemic poses a threat to America's national security. The predicted effect of a mild pandemic, 20,200 deaths in the United States and 1.4 million deaths worldwide, could cause degradation to our national security because of the shifting of our focus from dealing with threats such as terrorism to dealing with the socioeconomic disruption created by media-driven panic. Impacts that could occur as a result of the human death toll could be long-term health side effects for those that are ill and recover from the virus. Other impacts to the population could include civil unrest and intermittent disruption of critical infrastructures attributable to resource constraints. In some industries, we may see individuals who would not be able to leave the workforce because of a lack of trained replacements, and others being recalled from retirement. This would be significant for the military, utilities (electric, water, and gas), healthcare, and heavy industry sectors. Skill sets that could be lost during a mild pandemic would eventually be replaced. However, the disruption to our society, even in the short term, could change our ability in the coming decades to maintain America's presence as a global peacekeeper. With attention diverted toward internal issues, we could see conditions develop that have the potential to alter our way of life and change the way we keep ourselves safe and secure. Internationally, a mild pandemic could lead to new threats as countries reduce aid through nongovernmental organizations, such as the World Bank. Countries whose stability often depends on external sources of aid may be faced with increased internal unrest attributable to the lack of medical capabilities and resulting economic stress. A mild pandemic has the potential to create sustained humanitarian disasters for many less developed nations. The consequences of a mild pandemic could easily foster political instability in which socioeconomic demands exceed the capacity of a government to cope with the situation. Recovery from a mild pandemic could take several years.

Moderate pandemic poses a serious threat to America's national security. The predicted effect of a moderate pandemic, 202,000 deaths in the United States and more than 14 million worldwide, would create a serious threat to national security. The impact would be all those mentioned above but worse in each case. A moderate pandemic has the potential to create sustained humanitarian disasters on a scale far beyond those we have currently experienced. For example, MSRA is a virulent strain of bacteria that resists many antibiotics. MRSA is a bacterium responsible for some difficult-to-treat infections in humans. It has evolved an ability to survive treatment with beta-lactam antibiotics, including penicillin and methicillin. MRSA is especially troublesome in hospital-acquired (nosocomial) infections. In hospitals, patients with open wounds and weakened immune systems are at greater risk for infection than the general public. MRSA is often referred to in the press as a "superbug." It could evolve into a pandemic in and of itself. MRSA definitely presents a secondary problem for those affected by the pandemic because of the decrease in immune system capability. A moderate pandemic could leave the medical systems of the world less capable of handling other health conditions, thereby creating widespread demand for change. The resultant political instability in countries in which socioeconomic demands exceed the capacity of their government to cope with the situation could lead to rampant use of force to stabilize situations. With America in a weakened state as a result of the loss of more than 200,000, not to mention the related effects of other illnesses, the worldwide situation could deteriorate swiftly. Instability could last decades. Recovery from a moderate pandemic could take up to a decade or more.

Severe pandemic poses a very serious threat to America's national security. The predicted effect of a severe pandemic, 1 million deaths in the United States, creates a substantial threat to our national security. A significantly weakened America (militarily and socioeconomically) could lead to conditions that have the potential to disrupt our way of life. America and the rest of the world would be forced to rethink the way we see national security. The threat of war could loom larger with the consequences being far greater because we could see greater potential for nuclear exchanges between nations possessing this type of weaponry. Internationally, a severe pandemic, with an estimated 71 million deaths worldwide, could have great impacts on trade, outsourcing, stability of governments, and pressure on nongovernmental organizations, such as the United Nations, International Monetary Fund, and World Bank, to maintain current levels of assistance and oversight. A greater portion of the world's population could find themselves in situations of great instability. External sources of aid could be greatly reduced or even suspended, thereby creating new hostile and economic stress factors. A severe pandemic could create sustained humanitarian and economic disasters many times greater than have been predicted. The consequences of a severe pandemic most likely would be greater political instability throughout the world, the United States of America included. Socioeconomic systems could be so severely affected that the capacity of governments to cope with the situation could create a rise of paramilitary forces, and we could see a redefining of some countries' borders. Recovery from a severe pandemic could take several decades.

Ultra pandemic poses an extremely serious threat to America's national security. The predicted effect of the ultra pandemic, 2 million deaths in the United States and more than 142 million deaths worldwide, would create the greatest threat to our national security in the history of the United States. Impacts to the population could include significant loss of the generation that is destined to replace older Americans in the workforce, if a Spanish Influenza scenario occurs. This would put a tremendous burden on government (e.g., tax revenue, Social Security, and military recruitment). An ultra pandemic could have devastating repercussions for world trade and affect economies everywhere. Virulence of the virus is a significant factor. The strain of influenza virus that caused the Spanish Flu was exceptionally aggressive. It showed a high capacity to cause severe disease and a propensity to kill fit young adults rather than the elderly. The mortality rate among the infected was more than 2.5 percent compared with less than 0.1 percent in other influenza epidemics. This high mortality rate, especially amongst the younger population, lowered the average life expectancy in the United States by almost ten years. The mortality rate (virulence) of the virus will play a major factor in determining the overall economic impact of the pandemic on trade, production, and consumption patterns. However, other factors, such as fear, overreaction, the role of the media, national and local levels of preparedness, and government policies, can influence the extent that world trade will contract. A complete shift in the socioeconomic structure of the world could occur because the effect of the deaths worldwide could alter the structure of the workforce as a result of a lack of trained replacements or having to rethink child labor laws. For many western nations, this would be extremely significant for the military forces, potentially creating greater reliance on the deployment and use of nuclear deterrents. The capacity of utility systems (electric, water, and gas) and healthcare providers could be significantly eroded for substantially longer than people expect. Service industries could see their workforce shrink because of demands for basic services and potentially a conscripted workforce in some areas of the world. Skill sets that could be lost during the ultra pandemic could permanently change our ability, in the decades that it will take to recover, to ensure the security of America, let alone ensure its ability to continue as a global peacekeeper. A significantly weakened America (militarily and socioeconomically) could lead to conditions that disrupt our current way of life. Reliable utilities (e.g., power and clean water) heavily dependent on information technology could be a thing of the past for decades after an ultra pandemic scenario as a result of missing or inadequate knowledge. Security of the American homeland could be significantly impaired from a variety of external factors over which we have no control and that we no longer can influence. Internationally, an ultra pandemic could lead to collapse for several nations. New threats of war in less developed areas could become common because the United States and other developed nations could be unable to provide peacekeepers and aid through nongovernmental organizations, such as the United Nations, International Monetary Fund, Asia Development Bank, North Atlantic Treaty Organization, and World Bank. Nations whose stability often depends on external sources of aid may be faced with new hostile and economic stress factors. An ultra pandemic has the potential to create sustained socioeconomic and humanitarian disasters that could last for decades. The consequences of the ultra pandemic scenario could easily foster long-term political instability in much of the world. Nations in which socioeconomic demands exceed the capacity of their government to cope with the situation could seek to rectify their situation by war against nations that are faring better. Recovery from an ultra pandemic could take more than three decades.

Pandemic: a threat multiplier for instability. Projected deaths from the four pandemic scenarios range from very low (1.4 million deaths worldwide) in the mild pandemic scenario to somewhat beyond comprehension (142.2 million deaths worldwide) in the ultra scenario. A pandemic in any form will seriously exacerbate already marginal living standards in many Asian, African, and Middle Eastern nations, potentially increasing widespread political instability and the likelihood of failed states. A pandemic has the potential to result in widespread multiple chronic conditions, occurring worldwide within the same time-frame. Economic and environmental conditions in already fragile areas could erode on an accelerated basis as a result of declines in food pro-duction, increased susceptibility to diseases, and breakdowns in infra-structure occurring more frequently, exacerbated by large-scale movements of populations in search of aid. Weakened and failing gov-ernments, unable to provide medical aid, food, clean water, and a sem-blance of infrastructure, could foster the conditions for internal conflicts, extremism, and government crackdowns that are fueled by reaction to radical ideologies. The United States may not be able to react to these situations as it has in the past, and our allies may also be ren-dered impotent because of the pandemic situation in their homelands. Instability conditions could significantly worsen as the masses are exploited by extremists. The United States may not be able to undertake reconstruction and stability efforts once the pandemic has run its course. Conflicts begun may expand, creating further disaster and lead-ing to more instability.

Pandemic effects will strain the socioeconomic fabric in stable regions of the world. The United States and Europe may experience mounting pressure to accept large numbers of refugee populations as pandemic conditions cause medical systems to collapse, economic chaos increases, and food production is interrupted in Asia, Latin America, Africa, and Eastern Europe. One should also note that, during a pan-demic, we will not be exempt from extreme weather events and natural and manmade disasters. This could lead to the inability of a number of U.S. agencies, including state and local governments, the Department of Homeland Security, the Department of Health and Human Services, the Centers for Disease Control, and already weakened military forces, to accomplish their primary missions.

Pandemic confluence and/or conflation: an overlaid set of challenges. A pandemic would overlay already identified issues such as global warming, dependence on foreign oil, growing instability in many areas, and threats from extremists leaving the United States and Western Europe and other regions more vulnerable to the emergence of hostile regimes, terrorists, and other socioeconomic challenges. A pandemic could exacerbate energy dependence attributable to curtailment or dis-ruption of supply as a result of medical situations in exporting countries and/or restrictions emplaced by importing countries in attempts to reduce exposure to illness. These and other issues are linked; therefore, solutions to one can cascade positively or negatively to other areas. A key will be to leverage active analysis, assessing the potential impacts of actions and sharing information to reduce the effect of negative impacts. Technology alone cannot remedy the situations that will arise from a pandemic; we must be able to recognize the interconnectedness of the issues and to act in a manner that ensures stability.

THE UNITED STATES NO LONGER THE WORLD'S POLICEMAN?

A pandemic could lead to a degradation of U.S. power and the rise of regional power centers with interests opposed to the United States. A pandemic could create difficulties far greater than the ones encountered in the occupation of Iraq. Competing power centers may attempt to challenge the United States in the belief that the United States, weakened by a pandemic, could be opposed effectively without incurring unacceptable costs. Regional powers that have population density far greater than the United States would have more human capital available, even with high mortality.

This could lead to extreme global geopolitical instability because unpredictability and equally unpredictable effects could result from a pandemic. This could produce a torrent of foreign capital flight from instead of into the United States. A weakened United States could see historical trends (geopolitical instability usually prompts a flight to the safe haven of the U.S. dollar) reversed. The current level of geopolitical instability has not been of such global proportion since World War II.

The development of post-pandemic geopolitical scenarios is categorized into three timeframes:

- Short term (up to five years)
- Medium term (ten to fifteen years)
- Long term (twenty or more years)

Confidence in any projection diminishes rapidly when it moves beyond a short-term horizon attributable to randomness of events that could occur and the probability that the impact of possible events could compound geometrically. Even the post-pandemic short-term prediction of relative instability could be disturbed by current and possible developments, including viral mutation, vaccine development, nuclear proliferation, actions by Islamic revolutionaries, and local wars in the Balkans, Africa, parts of Asia, and perhaps the Middle East. South America could suffer significantly from loss of its economic base. A pandemic could produce increased tensions between India and Pakistan, mainland China and Taiwan, or India and China. Russia could revert to more central authority. This is to name just a few.

The combination of panic, economic decline, and reduced government capacity to maintain order could lead to civil unrest and instability. U.S. officials and nongovernmental experts agree that two of the greatest challenges to mounting an effective response in the event of a pandemic include the following:

- Maintaining commerce and financial infrastructure to prevent the disruption of economic activity and the delivery of critical goods and services:

Such disruptions have the potential to lead to panic and civil unrest, an increase in criminal activity, including human trafficking and black market activities, drastic movements of people seeking employment and resources, and an overwhelming strain on the rule of law.

- Maintaining effective and efficient communications: Consistent and factual messaging and reliable communications systems are essential to prevent panic among the population and ensure that assistance is delivered where and when it is needed.

Actions by Iran, North Korea, or another state with hostile intent could have profound effects. Even friendly states could create significant threats to U.S. security. India and China represent major trading partners with significant outsourced and production activities. China, for example, makes a substantial portion of the needles (syringes) that are used by U.S. medical practitioners. Should the United States take military action or impose further economic sanctions against Iran or North Korea, the negative consequences could lead to a nuclear confrontation, the result of the inability to exert influence over worldwide political events.

In the pandemic and post-pandemic timeframes, we should expect and plan for a drift toward the rise of regional powers and a polarity as the balance of power remains uncertain. The configuration of regional powers would not show signs of settling into any sort of stable alignment in the near-term (first five years) post-pandemic period. There may be no great power capable of taking major military initiatives outside of their internal borders because of degradation of capabilities to support an expeditionary force at a great distance. This could lead to an era of sporadic upheaval in some regions, somewhat similar to what we see in the former Soviet Union and in the Middle East.

The short-term likelihood in the post-pandemic period could be global instability in a time period from one decade to several decades in which all the major regional power centers would be forced to turn inward to cope with domestic socioeconomic and political strains, a highly likely scenario.

Short-term instability could be exacerbated by economic downturns and inability or limited ability to exert military force. The United States, the European Union, and Russia could be most affected because of population degradation, whereas China, India, and Brazil could exert more influence because of large population bases and dependence by Western states for economic goods and services from these countries.

The United States would still remain a genuine world power, but its global reach could be limited with regard to conventional forces. Western states could see a breakdown of multilateral diplomacy capabilities attributable to the effects of a pandemic. The ability of the world's powers to exert decisive pressure against aggression may be crippled for some time in the post-pandemic timeframe.

Based on the way each of the major regional power centers perceives its interests and assesses its relative power after a pandemic, the world could experience instability in global politics with the potential of coming into more intense conflict in areas that feel greater and greater disenfranchisement.

RESOURCE CONSUMPTION SHIFTS

Another important consideration that we could face in the post-pandemic period will be access to natural resources such as oil, gas, and various metals and minerals. Additionally, access to and management of agricultural products internally or on the international market could likely experience shifts as a result of the need to feed their populations.

Nations such as Indonesia, the world's most populous Muslim country and currently the fourth most populous state in the world, could experience significant downturns in its economy. This could lead to Indonesia's overall stability suffering. Indonesia's limited natural resources could potentially force it to look to other countries to supplement its diminishing supplies in the post-pandemic period. Given that Indonesia appears to be at the epicenter of the avian flu outbreaks, it is likely that a pandemic could emerge from this country. With a powerful military establishment, assuming it could hold together in the face of a pandemic, it could exert significant influence over its neighbors in the post-pandemic timeframe. If Indonesia cannot maintain stability, it could generate instability in the entire region.

Africa could see the emergence of more unrest and strife because the impact of a pandemic could generate frictions along economic and social fault lines. Nigeria could be joined by several states that see populations decimated by a pandemic. This could lead to actions by nations with strong military forces to become aggressive in an attempt to secure natural and agricultural resources for their populations. Military conflicts in Africa are common, and, in a post-pandemic period, we could see increased low-level fighting over vast natural and agricultural resources. The United States and other international powers, weakened by a pandemic, might not be able to put a stop to armed struggle as a means to achieve necessary economic and social gains.

SOCIAL WELFARE SYSTEMS: WHAT DEGREE OF DEGRADATION?

According to Marshall's Generalized Iceberg Theorem, "Seven-eighths of everything can't be seen." If that is a reality, then what is in store for our worldwide social welfare systems during and in the aftermath of a pandemic? A quote from Richard Neustadt and Graham Allison seems appropriate: "There is an awesome crack between unlikelihood and impossibility." We need to keep in mind that the possibility of a pandemic is not an impossibility and that the reactions of governments and individuals will not be necessarily predictable.

Take the example of remittances. Remittances are the transfer of funds between individuals. Remittances represent an increasingly significant flow of capital to the developing world. The World Bank has reported that migrant remittances to developing countries totaled more than $160 billion U.S. in 2004. This is an increase of more than 65 percent since 2001, when remittances stood at an estimated $96.5 billion U.S. If informal and underreported flows are included, estimates of migrant remittances are two to three times higher. Compared with other forms of capital transfers and investments, the volume of remittances surpassed that of official development assistance in the mid-1990s and is currently second only to the volume of foreign direct investment.

Along with savings and credit services, remittance services are among the most important financial services for low-income people. Many people who receive remittances live in rural areas that lack or have limited access to financial services, including efficient and reliable remittance services. Traveling to the nearest payout point is often time consuming and costly, thus reducing the remittances received. Because each withdrawal has a high personal overhead cost, saving some amount of the remittance is not attractive. Remittances could suffer greatly in a pandemic. This could occur in several ways. First, there would be the general slowdown of services from mail services to wire transfer services. Second, there would be the impact of a dislocated workforce; most low-income jobs relate to service sector (food, beverage, and hotel) operations that could be closed because of a lack of demand. Third, there is the impact of degradation of the workforce attributable to illness and death. Remember, these are the workers who generally do not have or cannot afford any medical insurance and are least likely to seek medical aid. Fourth, compound this by adding in other forms of illness that could create additional problems and you can easily create a catastrophic scenario that could make even Australia's Lowy Institute's ultra scenario pale. Last, we must realize that the economy will not bounce back quickly. This would further exacerbate the problem for developing nations and for the low-income groups worldwide. Welfare and international aid could operate in a degraded manner for many years, if not decades, after a pandemic runs its course.

Another example is the crop cycle. If agricultural inspectors cannot inspect and certify crops, deliveries may be delayed because receiving organizations may not want to take the risk of tainted produce that could be passed on to consumers. This begets a simple yet potentially overlooked fact. Crops have a shelf life. The time to replace them is long, a growing season. The ability to manage the crop cycle in many parts of the world is still dependent on manual labor and is heavily dependent on transportation. The labor force in most instances falls into the low-income category, again, the most likely to suffer in a pandemic because of the inability to get medical aid. This could create a situation in which crops are not able to be harvested because of a lack of manual labor. Complicate this by not having the transportation network working as it does now as a result of travel restrictions, port and border closures, or fear of risking exposure, and we see that there will be a potential for significant interdiction of the economy at the base level.

This was dramatically brought out in a news article:

> An avian influenza pandemic could kill millions of people, cripple economies, bring international trade and travel to a standstill and even jeopardize political stability. ... Avian influenza is not merely a health issue, it has economic ramifications, social ramifications, security ramifications.[4]

An area that seems to be overlooked in most discussions is the disposal of trash. This is one area that large cities are already having difficulty addressing. New York City has a well-known rat problem as a result of the tremendous amount of garbage generated and inconsistent containment, bagging, and disposal issues. In a pandemic situation, this could compound the health effects should regular services be disrupted or degraded in some manner. Imagine a week's worth of garbage sitting on streets awaiting disposal; aside from the stench, the health issues create a nightmare scenario. In many areas of the world, this is already a problem that is getting out of control.

Turn your attention to the courts and justice system, and you have another area on which a pandemic will have a tremendous effect. In the aftermath of September 11, 2001, I was asked to speak at a conference for the New York State Bar Association. The perspective of a panel of three judges caught my interest. They discussed the aftermath of September 11 and acknowledged that crime did drop initially but returned to normal patterns quickly. The panel said that, if the New York City courts had been closed longer than they were, a cascading collapse of the court system could have transpired. This could have led to the releasing of many from jail as a result of the court system not being able to meet the requirements for a speedy trial, as an example. A pandemic could disrupt the justice system in ways that we have yet to conceive of.

Economic and political tensions combined with fear and panic as a result of a pandemic could lead to a worldwide recession, resulting in social upheaval attributable to the inability of governments to provide the social services, welfare, and security that people have grown to expect.

SUMMARY: WHAT CAN WE DO NOW?

The potential for a pandemic is high, even overdue, according to medical science. The level of preparedness worldwide is low as governments, businesses, and people wrestle with other, readily apparent and immediately pressing issues.

One of the things that we can do right now is to rethink how we are preparing for a pandemic. Although it is of utmost importance that we have the medical capability and capacity available to deal with the massive disruption caused by illness and death, we must also focus our efforts on key elements of economic activity that will sustain us during and after a pandemic.

Following is a list of strategic initiatives that society can take to minimize the impact of a pandemic. These are broad based and are in no particular order of priority. To ensure availability of the infrastructure, we need to set specific objectives within four strategic areas:

- Improve current urban services (health, safety, infrastructure maintenance, and sanitation) planning to optimize available resource use to ensure that we minimize the cascade effects of a pandemic. This involves comprehensive planning to ensure that public services and facilities can provide these services in a pandemic.

- Meet and secure infrastructure (energy, electricity, telecommunications, and water) needs. This involves securing long-term supplies and studying options for managing demand. If work-at-home is going to be feasible, then we must have the infrastructure in place to meet the demand for access to the Internet.

- Provide a plan for transporting goods and moving commodities during a pandemic that ensures safety levels for all system users. This involves addressing public transportation, identifying demand, and developing management systems that include emergency management as an integral component.

- Ensure adequate medical capabilities. This involves upgrading and aligning current healthcare initiatives for stockpiling antiviral medications with increasing surge capacity and capability. It also involves international cooperation to set standards, develop the required enforcement mechanisms, integrate healthcare-related issues into development policies and programs, and raise the level of awareness regarding communicable diseases.

- To address the impact to various economic sectors, we must have an integrated plan that is designed to ensure that we can maintain the security and safety of communities so that economic impacts are minimized as much as possible. This means that companies must plan for realigning their services and/or products to meet the new demands that a pandemic will place on the worldwide business community. Government must ensure that businesses are protected as much as possible to facilitate recovery in the post-pandemic timeframe.

There is a huge hidden cost to any pandemic. As a result of actions that will need to be taken (e.g., restrictions and quarantines), all very necessary to ensure the preservation of health, all sorts of problems will be created for those caught up in their implementation. Enforcement by public-sector services has not been met well by any population that has experienced a widespread health issue, from the plagues of the ancient world to the modern-day situations that we have faced, most recently with SARS. Industry will suffer because of economic downturn and chaotic markets.

Impacts can be immediate and expensive. It is therefore prudent that your pandemic planning efforts consider the dynamic nature of the world's markets as part of your overall strategy. This makes good sense. It can be readily applied to situations other than a pandemic. With this broader perspective in mind, your pandemic preparations can be leveraged into greater management awareness and perhaps more of a competitive edge for your enterprise. This is true for public-sector entities, too. Government can be more competitive and forward thinking and can gain leverage with the constituents (taxpayers) whether they are individuals or businesses.

One key issue that we face with a pandemic that is different from other disasters is that multiple locations could be affected simultaneously. This is complicated by loss of personnel that could occur for several reasons: sickness, caring for sick individuals, school closures, and fear of contamination at the workplace. Most of the current business continuity models are based on the recovery of technology and facilities (brick-and-mortar type structures). Few are addressing the human component, and, if they do, they are not doing it very well. First and foremost, a basis for ensuring that communication and information flow seamlessly vertically and horizontally throughout the enterprise is essential. This means that you must have common terminology within and with all the external touch points (customers to vendors) that is clearly understood by all. Most organizations come up short when an analysis of the communication and information flow is undertaken. The general finding is that fragmentation and a lack of seamlessness exist.

Decision making regarding governance issues can only be addressed by senior executives. Senior executives will establish and manage voluntary compliance mandates as well as ensure compliance with regulatory-driven requirements.

Strategy requires management engagement to achieve 360-degree coverage. This coverage consists of (1) forward-looking capabilities of active analysis and situational awareness, (2) awareness of challenges, (3) executable goals and objectives, and (4) ability to capitalize on experience and past successes. Operating in a pandemic will require that your organization have a flexible and responsive strategy. Incorporating business strategy elements into the management decision-making process at all levels of contingency planning can facilitate greater flexibility.

A tactical focus on processes rather than a strategic focus that is broader based (business goals, objectives, and response to market demands) can equal less than effective business continuity.

The ability to effectively respond to and manage the consequences of an event in a timely manner is essential to ensure an organization's survivability in today's fast-paced business environment. With the emergence of new threats, such as cyberterrorism and bioterrorism, and the increasing exposure of companies to traditional threats, such as fraud, systems failure, fire, explosions, spills, and natural disasters, an integrated approach to business continuity planning is essential. The integrated approach, as presented in this chapter, is based on the concept of graceful degradation and agile restoration, covered in Chapter 2. Recall that graceful degradation refers to the ability of an organization to identify the event, classify it into a level of severity, determine its consequences, establish minimal stable functionality, devolve to the most robust less functional configuration available, and direct initial efforts for rapid restoration of services in a timely manner.[5]

In the United States, revitalizing the economy after the Spanish Flu in 1919 and the Great Depression meant getting the domestic economy restarted. Today, we no longer have the luxury of restarting just one economy; economic recovery after a pandemic will be an international undertaking. For this reason, the economic implications of a pandemic will last substantially longer than the medical and social implications. The pandemic will most likely subside within eighteen to twenty-four months. However, economic implications will last for years after the pandemic. The only way to shorten this recovery cycle will be to rethink how we do business. This may require that we establish new processes and procedures to take advantage of the intermittent recovery opportunities that will arise during the span of the pandemic. With the passage of time, there will be lulls in the intensity of the pandemic that may allow sectors of the global economy to partially recover. To wait for a full economic recovery (all sectors returning to pre-pandemic state) will be a very risky strategy. Intermittent recovery will provide some measure of financial relief and at the same time establish market share for those companies able to effect recovery, whereas other companies are absent as a result of not planning or as a result of plans that have focused on the wrong recovery strategy. This will require a whole new operational response strategy. Thinking and reacting to a new planning paradigm must become commonplace if economic recovery is to materialize.

Although H5N1 may never materialize in pandemic form, there is little doubt that the world is having to deal with pandemics such as AIDS and will, sooner or later, have to deal with a pandemic that, because of its transmission capability, will expose more of society to its effects. There is also little doubt that the international business community is inadequately prepared for the unique problems that will arise from such a widespread illness. By examining the implications associated with the avian flu as a pandemic, we have established the needed orientation to deal with the immediate medical impact of a pandemic and at the same time prepare a company to survive the long recovery period associated with an international economic collapse.

Government and business leaders have a responsibility to protect their organizations by facilitating continuity planning and preparedness efforts. Using their status as leaders, senior officials, senior management, and board members can and must deliver the message that survivability depends on being able to find the opportunity within the crisis.

Humans by their very nature are resilient. We have managed to evolve through the ages and have survived ice ages, volcanic eruptions, wars, pandemics, and other maladies. We will survive this challenge, too. We may not, however, return to the status quo. Will it be a better world? Will it be a more difficult world? Only time will tell.

The mortality rate of the pandemic will only be the tip of the iceberg; the speed with which it achieves global contamination and economic impact over time will be the major issues to be addressed. Preparing yourself and your organization now is one of the key steps to effectively dealing with the disruption that may run rampant. We cannot afford to abdicate personal responsibility for our well-being to entities that may not have the capability to ensure our well-being. Being personally responsible engenders personal accountability, something that we need to instill now, not when the pandemic is on us.

Terms and Definitions

To better digest the information contained in this book, certain terms and words used herein need to be defined. These definitions may or may not reflect the standard and normally acceptable meaning of the words or terms; however, for the purposes of this assessment, it is necessary to define them thus.

- **Antiviral**: A substance or process that destroys or weakens a virus or interferes with its ability to replicate.
- **Avian influenza (AI)**: The bird flu—This is a virus that infects wild birds (such as ducks, gulls, and shorebirds) and domestic poultry (such as chickens, turkeys, ducks, and geese). There is flu for birds just as there is for humans, and as with people, some forms of the flu in birds are worse than others. AI viruses are classified by a combination of two groups of proteins: the hemagglutinin or H proteins, of which there are sixteen (H1-H16), and neuraminidase or N proteins, of which there are nine (N1-N9).
- **Business Continuity**: All initiatives taken to assure the survival, growth, and resilience of the enterprise.
- **Consequence**: Something that logically or naturally follows from an action or condition.
- **Crisis**: A disruptive event that is amplified, elevated, and magnified.
- **Hazard**: A source of danger; a possibility of incurring loss or misfortune.
- **Hemaggluttinin (HA)**: A substance, such as an antibody, that causes agglutination of red blood cells.

- **Highly Pathogenic or "high path" avian influenza (HPAI)**: HPAI is often fatal in chickens and turkeys. HPAI spreads rapidly and has a higher death rate in birds than LPAI. HPAI has been detected and eradicated three times in U.S. domestic poultry. HPAI H5N1 is the subtype rapidly spreading in some parts of the world.

- **Influenza**: An acute contagious viral infection.

- **Low Pathogenic or "low path" avian influenza (LPAI)**: LPAI occurs naturally in wild birds and can spread to domestic birds. In most cases it causes no signs of infection or only minor symptoms in birds. These strains of the disease pose little significant threat to human health. These strains are common in the U.S. and around the world.

- **Mutation**: Process of adaptation for viruses. A virus reproduces by infecting a cell. Viruses change their surface proteins so they can attach to cell surface receptors. "The influenza virus genome has remarkable plasticity because of a high mutation rate and its segmentation into eight separate RNA molecules. This segmentation allows frequent genetic exchange by segment reassortment in hosts co-infected with two different influenza viruses." Source: http://www.avianinfluenza.org.

- **Neuraminidase (NA)**: An enzyme that forms a mushroom-shaped projection on the surface of an influenza virus particle. The enzyme assists in the release of newly formed virus particles from the surface of an infected cell.

- **Pandemic**: An epidemic occurring over a very wide area, crossing international boundaries, and usually affecting a large number of people; a global epidemic.

- **Pathogenicity**: The ability of the virus to produce disease. AI strains are divided into two groups based upon the ability of the virus to produce disease: low pathogenic (LP) and highly pathogenic (HP).

- **Plague**: A serious (sometimes fatal) infection of rodents caused by *Yersinia pestis* and accidentally transmitted to humans by the bite of a flea that has bitten an infected animal.

- **Reassortment**: The genetic material (RNA) of the influenza virus is in eight separate segments. If a cell is co-infected by two viruses of different genetic make-up (either different strains or different sub-types), the eight segments can "mix and match" so that a virus with a new combination of the eight segments is produced. In theory, two viruses, each with eight segments, can produce 256 different combinations.

- **Risk**: A quantifiable likelihood of something materializing.

- **Threat**: An expression of an intention to act.

- **Vector**: A "vehicle," such as a modified virus or DNA molecule, used to deliver genetic material into the body.

- **Virus**: Ultramicroscopic infectious agent that replicates itself only within cells of living hosts; many are pathogenic; a piece of nucleic acid (DNA or RNA) wrapped in a thin coat of protein.

Notes

CHAPTER 1

1. McNeil Jr., Donald G. "Scientists Hope Vigilance Stymies Avian Flu Mutations," *New York Times*, March 27, 2006.

2. Zuckerman, Mortimer B. "A Nightmare Scenario—H5N1 Pandemic," *New York Daily News*, June 20, 2005.

3. Tsang, Kenneth W. T., Eng, Philip, Liam C. K., Shim, Young-soo, and Lam, Wah K. "H5N1 influenza pandemic: contingency plans." *Lancet* (2005) 366:533–4.

4. Harris, Gardner. "Economic Shock Waves from Avian Influenza Spreading Faster than the Disease," *New York Times*, October 7, 2005.

5. Branswell, Helen. "Flu Pandemic Could Trigger a Second Great Depression, Brokerage Warns Clients: An Investor's Guide to Avian Flu," BMO Nesbitt Burns, Special Report, 2005.

6. Google alert. "Fears that the first line of defence against a bird flu pandemic ..."

CHAPTER 2

1. Bloomberg. "Pandemic could cost insurers $47 billion," March 28, 2006.

2. Cooper, Sherry. "Don't Fear Fear or Panic Panic," BMO Nesbitt Burns, Special Report, October 11, 2005.

3. Woodcock, Chris. "The Rise and Rise of Horizon Scanning in Risk Management Programmes." *Continuity Central*, 2007, www.continuitycentral.com.

4. Immelt, Jeffrey. Interview with Charlie Rose. *The Charlie Rose Show*, September 3, 2002.

5. Mitroff, Ian, I. "Avoid 'E3' Thinking," *Management General Webzine* (publication suspended in 2000), 1998.

6. Darryll Hendricks, Kambhu, John, and Mosser, Patricia. "Systemic Risk and the Financial System Background Paper," NAS-FRBNY Conference on New Directions in Understanding Systemic Risk, Federal Reserve Bank of New York, May 2006.

7. Sikich, Geary W. "Futureproofing"—The Process of Active Analysis, Industry IDS Online Conference, June 2004.

8. Sikich, Geary W. *Integrated Business Continuity: Maintaining Resilience in Times of Uncertainty*. Tulsa, OK: PennWell Publishing, 2003.

9. Mitroff, Ian, I. *Smart Thinking for Crazy Times: The Art of Solving the Right Problems*. San Francisco: Berrett-Koehler Publishers, 1998; and Mitroff, Ian, I. "Solving the Right Problems," *Innovative Leader* (1998) vol 7, #328.

10. Sikich, Geary W. "Global Vulnerabilities—Local Impacts: Redefining Business Continuity Planning." *Business Continuity e-Journal*, May 2003; and Sikich, Geary W. Turning Information into Intelligence, National Cargo Security Council Annual Conference, June 2003.

CHAPTER 3

1. Eisenam, Elaine. "Why Didn't They See It Coming? How CEOs Can Avoid Being Blindsided in Business," *Chief Executive*, June 6, 2007.

2. Sikich, Geary W. *Integrated Business Continuity: Maintaining Resilience in Times of Uncertainty*. Tulsa, OK: PennWell Publishing, 2003; and Sikich, Geary W. "Futureproofing"—The Process of Active Analysis, Industry IDS Online Conference, June 2004.

CHAPTER 4

1. Department of Health and Human Services (www.dhhs.gov) and Department of Homeland Security (www.dhs.gov). "Number of Episodes of Illness, Healthcare Utilization and Death Associated with Moderate and Severe Pandemic Influenza Scenarios."

2. Taleb, Nicholas Nasim. *The Black Swan: The Impact of the Highly Improbable*. New York: Random House, 2007.

3. Minsky, Steven. "Looking for Risks in All the Wrong Places?" June 1, 2006, http://www.ebizq.net/.

4. Surmacz, Jon. "Disaster Preparedness," *CSO Magazine*, 14 August 2003.

5. Odiorne, George S. *Management and the Activity Trap*. New York: Harper and Row Publishers, 1974.

6. Sikich, Geary W., Auditrak, 1994; Sikich, Geary W. *Integrated Business Continuity: Maintaining Resilience in Times of Uncertainty*. Tulsa, OK: PennWell Publishing, 2003; and Sikich, Geary W. "'Global Vulnerabilities'—Local Impacts: Redefining Business Continuity Planning," *Business Continuity e-Journal*, May 2003.

CHAPTER 5

1. Luke Catherine J., and Subbarao, Kanta. *Vaccines for Pandemic Influenza*, paragraph "Developing Vaccines for Pandemic Influenza," Emerging Infectious Diseases, January 2006, http://www.cdc.gov/ncidod/EID/vol12no01/05-1147.htm; and Centers for Disease Control. *Preparing for Pandemic Influenza*, November 28, 2005, http://www.cdc.gov/flu/pandemic/pdf/preparingforpandemicflu.pdf.Influenza.

2. Department of Psychology, University of Utah Human Factors Certificate Program. http://www.utah.edu and http://www.psych.utah.edu.

3. Taleb, Nicholas Nasim. *The Black Swan: The Impact of the Highly Improbable*. New York: Random House, 2007.

4. Masch, Vladimir A. "Return to the 'natural' process of decision-making leads to good strategies." *Journal of Evolutionary Economics* (2004) 14:431–62.

5. Gladwell, Malcolm. *Blink: The Power of Thinking without Thinking*. New York: Back Bay Books, 2007.

6. Davis, Stanley M., and Meyer, Christopher. *Blur: The Speed of Change in the Connected Economy*, New York: Perseus Books Group, 1998.

7. Wohlstetter, Roberta. *Pearl Harbor: Warning and Decision*, in the foreword by Thomas C. Schelling. Palo Alto, CA: Stanford University Press, 1962.

8. Herodotus, *The Histories*, written in 450 B.C.

9. Tainter, Joseph A. *The Collapse of Complex Societies*, Reprint 11. Cambridge, UK: Cambridge University Press, 2004.

10. Frist, William. "Safeguard economy against pandemic's devastation." Special to the *Des Moines Register*, December 9, 2005.

11. Congressional Budget Office. "A Potential Influenza Pandemic: Possible Macroeconomic Effects and Policy Issues," assessment, December 8, 2005, revised July 27, 2006.

CHAPTER 6

1. Taleb, Nicholas Nasim. *The Black Swan: The Impact of the Highly Improbable*. New York: Random House, 2007.

2. Maplecroft Index. "Fast Facts," August 2007.

3. Taleb, Nicholas Nasim. *The Black Swan: The Impact of the Highly Improbable*. New York: Random House, 2007.

4. Sikich Geary W., and Stagl, John M. "The Economic Consequences of a Pandemic," Discover Financial Services Business Continuity Summit, 2005; and Sikich Geary W. "A New Planning Paradigm: Economic Consequences of a Pandemic," *Continuity Central*, 2005 (also published in Disaster Resource Guide and Continuity Forum, 2005).

5. Cooper, Sherry. "Don't Fear Fear or Panic Panic," BMO Nesbitt Burns, Special Report, October 11, 2005.

6. "Just Plane Gross," *Wall Street Journal*, August 14, 2007. See also http://www.redeye.chicagotribune.com/.../controversy/red-081407-plane-main.o.7693249.story?coll=red-coverstory-hed.

7. Cantor, Norman F. *In the Wake of the Plague*. New York: Harper Perennial, 2002.

8. Apgar, David. *Risk Intelligence—Learning to Manage What We Don't Know*. Boston: Harvard Business School Press, 2006.

CHAPTER 7

1. *Global Risks 2006 and 2007*, published by the World Economic Forum, in collaboration with Marsh & McLennan Companies, Merrill Lynch, and Swiss Re and in association with the Risk Management and Decision Processes Center at the Wharton School of the University of Pennsylvania.

2. Murray, Christopher J. L., Lopez, Alan D., Chin, Brian, Feehan, Dennis, and Hill, Kenneth H. "Estimation of potential global pandemic influenza mortality on the basis of vital registry data from the 1918–20 pandemic: a quantitative analysis." *Lancet* (2006) 368:2211–8.

3. McKibbin, Warwick J., and Sidorenko, Alexandra. *Global Macroeconomic Consequences of Pandemic Influenza*. Sydney: Lowy Institute for International Policy, 2006.

4. Parrett, William G. *The Sentinel CEO: Perspectives on Security, Risk, and Leadership in a Post-9/11 World*. New York: Wiley, 2007.

5. Cohen, Ethan. "Energy Risk—The Future Is Hard to Predict, but Here It Goes," *Today's Risk eNews*, December 26, 2007. http:www.garp.com or http://www.SourceRiskCenter.com.

6. Sikich, Geary W. "Turning Information into Intelligence," Presented at the National Cargo Security Council Annual Conference, June 2003; Sikich, Geary W. "Cargo Security—Supply Chain Continuity," 2007; Sikich, Geary W. "Supply Chain Continuity," *Supply & Demand Chain Executive*, Cygnus Media, February 2006.

7. Business Development Bank of Canada, "Continuity Planning: Is Your Company Prepared for the Worst?" and "Influenza Pandemic:

Continuity Planning Guide for Canadian Business," Canadian Manufacturers and Exporters (CME), March 2006.

8. Ericson, Jim. *Supply Chain Risk Categorized: Eight Key Areas Identified by Ernst & Young; Measurement Important, Think Operational as Well as Technological*, Ernst and Young, December 9, 2003; and "Understanding Supply Chain Risk," prepared by LCP Consulting in conjunction with the Centre for Logistics and Supply Chain Management, Cranfield School of Management, Cranfield University, Cranfield, UK, 2003.

9. Black, Henry Campbell. *Black's Law Dictionary*, 5th ed. St. Paul, MN: West Publishing Company, 1979.

10. *Global Risks 2006 and 2007*, published by the World Economic Forum, in collaboration with Marsh & McLennan Companies, Merrill Lynch, and Swiss Re and in association with the Risk Management and Decision Processes Center at the Wharton School of the University of Pennsylvania; and National Security and the Threat of Climate Change, published by the CNA Corporation, prepared by a military advisory board comprising retired generals and admirals from the U.S. military branches; and Doshi, Viren, Schulman, Gary, and Gabaldon, Daniel. "Lights! Water! Motion!" *Strategy+Business*, April 17, 2007.

CHAPTER 8

1. Mitroff, Ian I. "Avoid 'E3' Thinking," Management General, 1998; Mitroff, Ian I. *Smart Thinking for Crazy Times: The Art of Solving the Right Problems*. San Francisco: Berrett-Koehler Publishers, 1998; and Mitroff, Ian I. "Solving the Right Problems." *Innovative Leader* (1998) vol. 7, 328.

2. Latour, A. "Trial by Fire: A Blaze in Albuquerque Sets off Major Crisis for Cell-Phone Giants," *Wall Street Journal*, January 29, 2001, p. A1.

3. McKibbin, Warwick J., and Sidorenko, Alexandra. *Global Macroeconomic Consequences of Pandemic Influenza*. Sydney: Lowy Institute for International Policy, 2006.

4. O'Connell, Meghan A. "Effects of Avian Flu Pandemic Disasterous (Disastrous)." Washington, DC: UPI, June 30, 2006.

5. Sikich, Geary W. "Graceful Degradation and Agile Restoration Synopsis." *Disaster Resource Guide*, 2002; and Sikich, Geary W. *Integrated Business Continuity: Maintaining Resilience in Times of Uncertainty*. Tulsa, OK: PennWell Publishing, 2003.

Index

About the Author

GEARY W. SIKICH is the author of *It Can't Happen Here: All Hazards Crisis Management Planning, Emergency Management Planning Handbook,* and *Integrated Business Continuity: Maintaining Resilience in Uncertain Times.* The author of more than 175 published articles, in journals such as *Continuity Insights* and *Supply & Demand Chain Executive,* Sikich is the founder and a principal of Logical Management Systems. An internationally recognized speaker and symposium leader, he consults on a regular basis with companies worldwide on continuity, crisis management, and issues of operational resilience.